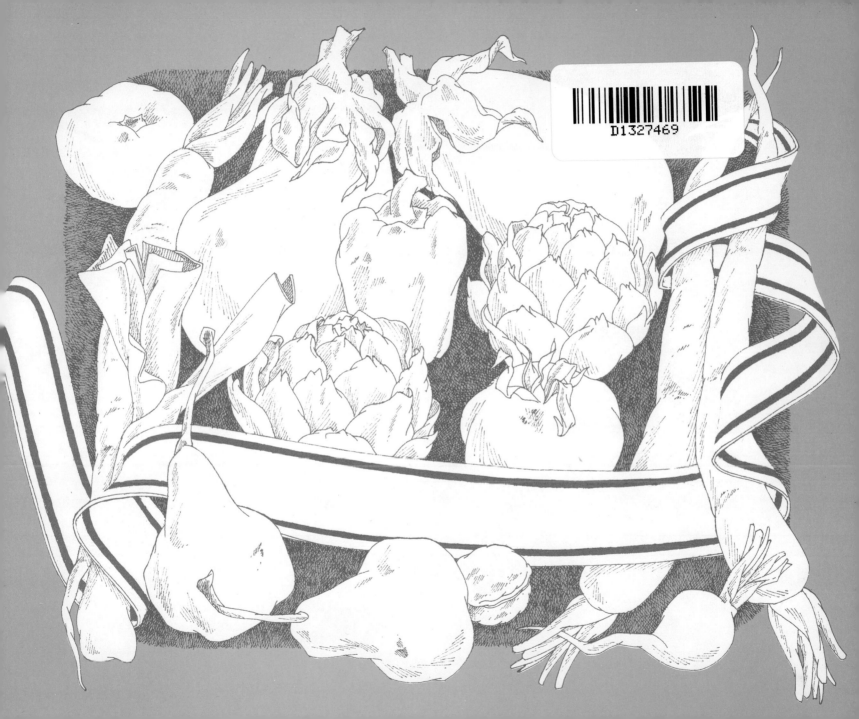

COLD FOODS

for Summer and Winter

COLD FOODS

for Summer and Winter

LILLIAN LANGSETH-CHRISTENSEN

ILLUSTRATED BY BILL GOLDSMITH

1974

DOUBLEDAY & COMPANY, INC., GARDEN CITY, NEW YORK

ISBN: 0-385-08282-7
Library of Congress Catalog Card Number 73–11713
Copyright © 1974 by Lillian Langseth-Christensen
Printed in the United States of America
First Edition

Contents

Introduction, The Advantages of Cold Cookery   vi

Part I   *For Summer and Warm Climates*

CHAPTER 1   A   Menus, with Explanations, for Luncheons, Dinners, Suppers, and Buffets. Suggestions for Brunches, Teas, Cocktails, Picnics, and Box Lunches   3
B   A New Meal-Planning Schedule, Cooking Ahead, and Hot Weather Short Cuts
C   New Combinations

CHAPTER 2   Appetizers, First Courses, and Luncheon Courses, Cooked and Uncooked   29

CHAPTER 3   Soups, Clear, Creamed, and Canned Soups Enhanced   55

CHAPTER 4   Eggs, Poached, Hard-Cooked, Six-Minute Eggs   77

CHAPTER 5   Main Courses, Aspics, Seafood, Meat, and Poultry   95

CHAPTER 6   Salad Dressings, Sauces, Relishes, and Salads   119

CHAPTER 7   Desserts, Fruits, and Dessert Sauces   163

Part II   *For Winter and Cool Climates*

CHAPTER 8   Menus, with Explanations, for All Meals. Introducing New Cold Dishes to Serve with One Hot Course for Year-Round Cookery in Any Climate   177

CHAPTER 9   Appetizers for Cold Weather   185

CHAPTER 10   Main Courses, Cold Meats, Poultry, Game, and Seafood Suitable for Winter Service   199

CHAPTER 11   Desserts and Dessert Sauces, Including Heavier Chocolate, Chestnut, and Other Cold Desserts That Are Not Light Enough for Summer Service   227

Index   251

Introduction

IT TAKES just one hot day or one overheated kitchen to wipe out all desire for warm food and make the thought of cold cookery extremely attractive.

My search for recipes for cold meals began during a sweltering August in New York and has gone on ever since. Considering that hot summer comes to forty-nine of our states and remains year round weather south of the fortieth degree, we have an extremely limited cold food repertoire. Housewives add an iced melon, iced tea, and possibly a sherbet, but the winter-meal pattern remains the same although the thermometer rises by more than sixty degrees.

Restaurants do make a change-over in June. The hot soups turn into jellied madrilène and cold vichyssoise, meats decline, and cold salmon appears on every menu. Hot desserts change into cold fruits. But no one takes real advantage of the infinite variety, the unusual possibilities, and the charms of cold cookery.

This book approaches cold food, not as an isolated dish served cold and out of context because the thermometer has risen, but as a whole new way of making menus and preparing meals. Cold food should be surrounded by dishes that influence and enhance it. Our whole attitude toward cold cookery should be changed. Many dishes that have never been served cold under any circumstances are the very ones that lend themselves beautifully to cold service. I have come to think that refrigerators are more often raided because the hot dishes are better cold than because one is hungry.

When cooked food is chilled it changes character, it combines with different ingredients, and it calls for an entirely new pattern of menu making.

There are hundreds of examples of changes that take place in a dish when the temperature is lowered. A hot cream of spinach soup calls for toasted croutons or sliced hard-cooked egg. The same soup, served cold in summer, is enormously enhanced by a dash of sherry and a slice of orange. We could not possibly start off a winter dinner party with a warm poached egg, but in summer, when all values change, a cold poached egg under tarragon aspic becomes gala. This is especially true when it is followed by a trout that took six minutes to poach, a few more minutes to cool, and an instant to stuff with chilled horseradish cream.

Summer, or hot climate, menus have to take into account that any weather that is hot enough to call for cold food is also hot enough to call for less work in the kitchen. While it is very pleasant to eat cold roast beef with sauce rémoulade on a shady terrace in July, it still has to be roasted in a hot oven before it can be chilled. Hot weather and hot climate food has to be cool in its preparation as well as its taste.

As long as we plan our summer menus along the same general lines as our winter meals, we will not derive any benefits from cold cookery. The work will remain exactly the same in summer as in winter. When the menus are organized to make cold cookery into leisure cookery, the full pleasures and comforts will be realized.

Part One of this book brings menus and recipes for cold cookery in summer, in warm climates and for all occasions when time and effort must be saved. Part Two brings menus and recipes that are for heavier cold foods, more suitable for winter cookery and for menus that contain one hot dish or one hot course. The recipes in Part One and Part Two are interchangeable, the only difference would be that cold cucumber soup is more refreshing and cooling in summer, while a cold lobster bisque, laced with sherry would seem to be winter food. A cold chocolate mousse would be a winter dessert, while a lime sherbet calls for a hot summer evening.

In our efficiently heated, or overheated, homes and our servantless state, cold cookery in summer and easily prepared cold dishes woven through our winter menus are inevitably the cookery of the future.

THE ADVANTAGES OF COLD COOKERY

1. All cold dishes can be prepared ahead. There is no cold dish that has to be served immediately upon completion, as a hot soufflé.

2. Cold cookery is economical, since eggs, vegetables, or fruits can be made into an important part of the meal. The main course does not need to be an expensive roast. A warm poached egg is a breakfast course—a cold poached egg can start a gala dinner. Hot soups are no longer popular, but gazpacho and vichyssoise start off the smartest meals. There are at least twenty cold soups that are equally *with it* and equally good.

3. Cold food is thinning. It is never pan-fried, deep-fat-fried, or saturated with butter, gravy, grated cheeses, and cream sauce.

4. Cold food is healthy. It includes a large variety of foods, more fruits and vegetables, and lighter combinations. As mentioned before, it does not include fried foods.

5. Cold food is patient. It can be prepared when you have time and it will wait without deteriorating.

6. Cold cookery is versatile. It allows more variations, more interesting menus, and less monotony.

7. Finally, cold food is pretty. There is time to garnish and take care in arranging it. It is prepared at leisure and does not depend upon a last minute sprig of parsley for its sole adornment.

for Summer and Warm Climates

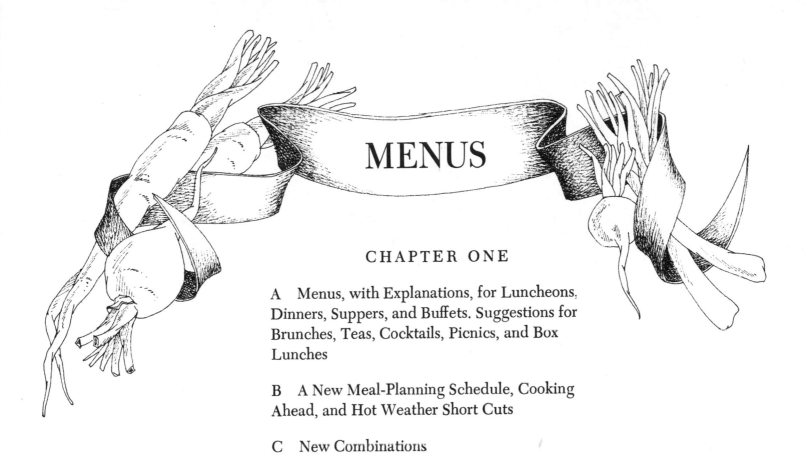

MENUS

CHAPTER ONE

A   Menus, with Explanations, for Luncheons, Dinners, Suppers, and Buffets. Suggestions for Brunches, Teas, Cocktails, Picnics, and Box Lunches

B   A New Meal-Planning Schedule, Cooking Ahead, and Hot Weather Short Cuts

C   New Combinations

THE dinner menu, whether hot or cold, is almost always predictable and low on new ideas and surprises. There is a great monotony, and when anyone tries for a startling combination, it is often farfetched. We are told that surprise is the great essential in recreation, and the same thing can be said for cookery. Dinner only then becomes an enjoyable recreation when it isn't more or less the same dinner we have eaten over and over again.

Serving a cold meal, when it is not a blisteringly hot midsummer day, is in itself a mild and pleasant surprise, but it should not be the *same old dinner in cold*. The cold foods lend themselves to different treatments and different rotations, and it would be a waste of opportunities to shift over to a cold way of dining without including some changes and some of those essential surprises.

This is not a matter of turning from the old familiar standbys, but rather a matter of including them in new surroundings or eating them cold. Many of us have enjoyed the turkey or ham or roast beef more because of the cold meat that couldn't be far behind, and now we are reversing the procedure. Serve a beautifully decorated rare roast beef cold when there are guests and obligations and a great to-do, then serve the leftover roast beef, when you are alone and at leisure, in a hot concoction.

Serving more imaginative menus has the advantage that they turn the old favorites into surprises, and we are astounded at how much better they seem to taste in their new environments. Shifting a hot dinner over into a cold dinner calls for a little more work in garnishing and presentation, but it saves time when there isn't any, namely in the last moment, and it uses time when there is no pressure. We can choose that time and fit it into our schedule when it is most convenient.

When a hostess invites a few guests and plans a perfectly simple hot dinner of soup, roast leg of lamb, gravy, a proper vegetable, potatoes, hot rolls, and a warm deep-dish apple pie, she either has to have two ovens or she has to be on her toes. She will have contented guests, but she will see very little of them until dinner, and then she will only be with them in snatches until dinner is over. It is small wonder that so many people take each other out to country clubs and restaurants.

With a cold meal they can all be together all the time except when plates are removed and food is served, and the two most important guests are not left for long periods with an empty chair between them. Many hostesses have worked the whole thing out, with double boilers to keep food hot and casseroled main dishes, but they are still harassed and, beautiful as casseroles can be, a cold roast or an encompassing salad are a welcome change.

HOW TO USE THE MENUS

Read the menus in this chapter or in Part II, Chapter 8, page 180, and select one that appeals to you for the season, for your purpose, and for your budget. The dishes are either well known or they are shortly described so that it is not necessary to search the Index for the recipe and then check the recipe ingredients. The short descriptions serve to give you a picture of the menu and in some cases the short description takes the place of a recipe. As an example there are recipes for Salmon Ring and Glazed Peach Tart, Salade Niçoise, and Gazpacho, but none for Iced Melon Wedges or thin-sliced Italian ham.

The menus for cooking ahead serve only as examples; schedules can and should be made for all menus so that work can be organized and a marketing list made. These suggested menus do not take a deep freeze into account, which would enable the hostess to freeze breads, desserts, and other items for longer periods.

Menus for cold cookery are as patient and versatile as the cold dishes. Switch them around and adapt them to your tastes and prepare the food in such a way that the hours before dinner are free.

Menus for Cold Dinners

CEBOLLA ESPAÑOLA

SESAME SEED BREAD STICKS

COLD SPENCER ROAST

chilled Spanish onion soup
rare eye of the roast beef sliced diagonally

SAUCE ALEXIS

thin mayonnaise with caviar and minced onion
stirred into it before serving

POTATO SALAD STEPHAN

made with white wine French dressing and freshly
ground black pepper

RASPBERRIES OR STRAWBERRIES

in iced Sabayon Sauce

COFFEE

serve an iced sangría

❀

KOLODNIK

Polish herb soup served over ice, garnished with
sliced shrimp, cucumbers, and chives

SLICED BREADS, CRACKERS, AND FLAT BREADS

BUFFET PLATTER OF SPRING ROAST BEEF

partially carved roast of beef, cut from ribs, remaining roast decorated with vegetable flowers,
plum tomatoes, and parsley. Sliced beef arranged
down center of platter. Green asparagus spears and
tomatoes filled with cold Béarnaise Sauce arranged
on both sides

PICKLED FIGS

MINCEMEAT RELISH

ENDIVE SALAD WITH FRENCH DRESSING

BUTTER APPLES

cored apples filled with brandy hard sauce, baked,
chilled and served with heavy cream

COFFEE

serve a vin rosé

❀

POACHED EGGS MARGOT

soft eggs on artichoke bottoms, covered with Lemon
Mayonnaise Collée and garnished with chopped
chives

OVEN DRIED GARLIC BREAD

GALANTINE OF LAMB

boned shoulder of lamb flattened and filled with
onions, parsley, diced tongue, pickles, and liver.
Rolled up, poached, cooled, and served sliced

CURRY SAUCE AND TRIANON SAUCE
curry-flavored mayonnaise and onion-flavored mayonnaise with chopped tomatoes and pimento added

GERMAN COLESLAW

STRAWBERRIES MADRID
macerated in Framboise and kirsch and brandy, poured over vanilla ice cream and garnished with chopped hazelnuts

COFFEE
serve a Moselle wine

⚙

GREEK MUSHROOMS
marinated in white wine, lemon juice, and herbs. Serve in the marinade, sprinkled with shreds of lemon rind

TOAST MELBA

POLLO AL RISO
cold roast or rotisseried broilers on a bed of saffron rice lightly mixed with herb dressing, pimento dice, and olives

GREEN SPINACH SALAD WITH TOASTED BREAD CROUTONS

BACON DRESSING

SLICED ORANGES WITH CURAÇAO

COFFEE
serve a dry white wine

⚙

ICED CREAM OF TOMATO SOUP WITH ORANGE SLICES AND CHOPPED MINT

OVEN-TOASTED BRIOCHE SLICES

CRAB RING
filled with cucumber salad

WATER CRESS AND CHIVE MAYONNAISE

SMALL PECAN TARTS

ICED TEA

or GESPRITZTER
dry white wine in tall glasses with soda

⚙

PIPERADE
chilled Basque vegetable dish sprinkled with chopped parsley

HOME-BAKED WHOLE-WHEAT BREAD
with soft churned butter (whip heavy cream to butter, drain, and half chill)

INDIVIDUAL MOLDS OF CHICKEN LIVER MOUSSE

GREEN SALAD MIMOSA
crisp salad greens with French Dressing, riced hard-cooked eggs, and chopped chives or parsley

APPLES GLAZED WITH RUM BUTTERSCOTCH

ICED COFFEE
or a light vin rosé

⚙

ASPARAGUS VINAIGRETTE

HOMEMADE TOAST MELBA

COLD SCRAMBLED EGGS WITH SMOKED SALMON AND CHIVES
a specialty in Norway, use mild smoked salmon and, if preferred, garnish with cut dill instead of chives

STRAWBERRIES
serve splits of iced champagne for anyone who wants to pour it over strawberries in tall glasses

COFFEE

⚙

SCALLOP SOUP

chilled cream of scallops, laced with sherry and garnished with cooked scallops, cut chives, and a little caviar if possible

RATATOUILLE

vegetables baked in a casserole and chilled

FLAT BREADS

WAIDHOFEN HAM

smoked pork hocks cooked in burgundy and glazed with brown sugar. 1 hock serves 2 to 3

MUSTARD MAYONNAISE

PICKLED PEACHES

fresh peaches poached with cinnamon and cloves and chilled

NORWEGIAN GJTOST CHEESE

serve a dry light red wine
serve coffee later with crisp SPRITZ TONGUES

❀

FILLETS OF SMOKED TROUT

HORSERADISH-FLAVORED WHIPPED CREAM

BUTTERED PUMPERNICKEL

AUSTRIAN CHEF'S SALAD

a mixed green salad with diced ham and cheese, cooked lentils, just enough diced pickle to give it a crisp and interesting flavor. Garnish with sliced hard-cooked egg

RASPBERRIES VILLA D'ESTE

large raspberries with whipped vanilla ice cream sauce

COFFEE

serve a light white wine

❀

PEACHES IN PORT WINE

fresh peaches, lightly poached, skinned, and sliced into tall glasses with port wine poured over

FINGERS OF CINNAMON TOAST

use brown instead of white sugar

SMOKED TONGUE

with a garnish of aspic and halved small tomatoes filled with horseradish mayonnaise

WATER CRESS SALAD

VIENNESE EIS KAFFEE

dessert and coffee in one, vanilla ice cream in cold coffee

serve a light red wine

❀

POLISH BEET SOUP

garnished with whipped sour cream and snipped dill and may be served in half cantaloupes

BUTTERED BLACK BREAD

BUFFET PLATTER OF DANISH HAM

partially sliced Danish ham arranged on a large platter. Slices glazed with aspic, unsliced ham decorated with a small bunch of green grapes and grape leaves. Platter garnished with small peeled apples, filled with lingonberries and lightly baked

RELISH TRAY AND SPICED CURRANT SAUCE

DANISH COLESLAW SALAD

DANISH CHEESE PLATTER

sliced cheeses, butter curls, crackers, sliced dill pickles, and radish roses

COFFEE

serve beer or an iced vin rosé

❀

CEVICHE OF SOLE

paper-thin onion slices and strips of sole marinated in lemon juice. Diced tomatoes, avocados, chopped parsley, add just before serving, see Shrimp Ceviche

COLD MEAT PIE

Cornish pastry filled with meat or game and well-seasoned aspic chilled and sliced

CUMBERLAND SAUCE

GREEN BEAN SALAD

with hard-cooked eggs, chopped onions and parsley

RUM MOUSSE

COFFEE

serve a red wine

Menus for Cold Sunday Luncheons or Suppers

THIN-SLICED WESTPHALIAN HAM OR PROSCIUTTO

WITH RIPE FIGS (or melon wedges)

SALMON RING

mousse of salmon filled with green pea salad, garnished with halved tomatoes filled with horseradish cream

CUCUMBER SALAD

LEMON MAYONNAISE

GLAZED PEACH TART

sprinkled with shaved almonds

ICED COFFEE

or serve a dry white wine and soda

❖

SALADE NIÇOISE

haricot beans, tomatoes, potato dice, and olives garnished with anchovies and capers, a French appetizer salad

TOASTED BREAD STICKS

COLD TURKEY

boned raw turkey breast, stuffed and baked, chilled and sliced across

CUMBERLAND SAUCE

CRISP WATER CRESS

BAKED PLUMS

under melted apricot jam and apricot brandy sauce

COFFEE

serve a light white wine

❖

SPANISH MELON WITH MINCED CHUTNEY

VERY LIGHTLY CHEESED MELBA TOAST

BUFFET PLATTER OF COLD MEATS

sliced ham, beef, veal, and sausages rolled and arranged around a cooked cauliflower covered with curried mayonnaise. A circle of scooped-out cucumbers filled with vegetable salad arranged around the meat rolls and sprinkled with chopped dill

RELISH TRAY

MINTED SHERBET

PETITS FOURS

COFFEE

serve decanters of red and white wine

❖

GAZPACHO ANDALUZ

ASSORTED BREADS AND CRACKERS

German packaged breads, salty rye bread, pumpernickel, and various crackers

BOWL OF RADISHES AND OLIVES

GARNISHED LIPTAUER CHEESE

caraway seeds, chopped pickles, capers, paprika, and
other variations stirred into a combination of three
soft cheeses, Camembert, cream, and Liederkranz

COLD BEER

❀

NORWEGIAN THIN BREAD

buttered and sprinkled with grated cheese, then
browned in a slow oven and served crisp and cold

CURRIED EGGS BARODA

six-minute eggs in tomatoes (see recipe)

MELON WEDGES

ICED TEA

or

a light white wine

❀

DANISH OPEN SANDWICHES

an assortment of ham, egg, anchovy, cheese, meat,
and shrimp sandwiches. Garnished with onions, pickles, nuts, and tomatoes

GERMAN COLESLAW

scalded cabbage and grapes (see recipe)

DANISH DESSERT

raspberries and currants cooked with sugar, blended,
chilled and served with thick cream

LEMONADE

❀

THIN-SLICED AND BUTTERED RYE BREAD AND PUMPER-
NICKEL

PAPER-THIN SLICES OF RARE COLD STEAK

MUSTARDS AND RELISHES

A BOWL OF CRISP WATER CRESS AND CUCUMBER SLICES
ON CHOPPED ICE

SLICED ORANGES WITH CRYSTAL SUGAR

SANGRÍA

Menus for Cold Luncheons

MAIN DISH SÉNÉGALAISE

curried chicken soup with side dishes of salted
whipped cream, toasted coconut, cooked chicken,
diced chutney, and chopped peanuts and raisins

PURI, IF OBTAINABLE, OTHERWISE ROLLS OF THIN MELBA
TOAST

BOWL OF CHILLED FRUIT

apples, pears, and green and purple grapes

TRAY OF SWEETS, NUTS, AND CONFECTIONS

ICED MINT TEA

❀

MAIN DISH CAESAR SALAD

salad greens, raw egg, ham dice, Roquefort and
Parmesan cheeses, toasted garlic croutons

CHUNKS OF FRENCH BREAD

COMPOTE OF DRIED FRUITS

BRANDIED CREAM

SPRITZ TONGUES

ICED COFFEE

❀

STUFFED ARTICHOKES

leaves trimmed, center removed, and stuffed with a piquant egg, caper, and herb salad

TOASTED RYE BREAD FINGERS

STEWED PEARS WITH BRANDY SAUCE

sprinkled with chocolate curls

COFFEE

MAY WINE

❈

STUFFED MELON

large cantaloupe or Spanish melon stuffed with shrimp salad. A wedge of melon served with each portion of salad

OVEN-DRIED RAISIN BREAD

ENGLISH TRIFLE

spongecake and sherry, custard sauce, and a little whipped cream

ICED TEA

❈

SIX-MINUTE EGGS FELIX

eggs on a bed of chopped spinach salad garnished with cauliflower sections and asparagus spears

LEMON DILL MAYONNAISE

TOASTED CHEESE BREAD

SLICED BABA IN APRICOT-RUM SAUCE

ICED TEA WITH ORANGE

❈

SHRIMP AND GRAPEFRUIT

cooked shrimp and sections of fresh grapefruit in equal quantities, bound with herbed mayonnaise flavored with a little grapefruit juice

TOASTED ITALIAN BREAD

MONT BLANC NOIR

chestnuts riced over whipped cream, sprinkled with grated bitter chocolate

ICED COFFEE

❈

CELERY BOUILLON

iced celery bouillon poured over diced tomatoes and celery

SHRIMP VINAIGRETTE

cooked shrimp buried under chopped onions, minced capers, riced hard-cooked eggs, and chopped parsley

CHILI-RELISH MAYONNAISE

LEMON ICE

THIN-SLICED SPONGECAKE

ICED TEA

❈

MACEDONIA DE FRUITAS

Spanish fruit cocktail macerated in liqueured syrup

EGGS CZARINA

six-minute eggs on asparagus spears masked in pale green herbed mayonnaise

BITTER CHOCOLATE MOUSSE

ICED COFFEE

❈

MAIN DISH MULLIGATAWNY
CRISP INDIAN BREAD OR LARGE FRITOS
LIME SHERBET
CASHEW NUT FINGERS
ICED TEA

Menus for Cocktail Parties

The menu for a cocktail party depends on the number of guests and the time of day. A Sunday noon cocktail party should provide more appetizers than a Sunday afternoon party, and a large standing party should only include appetizers that can be taken and eaten with one hand. Appetizers for a large party should, if possible, include fish, meat, cheese, eggs, crisp raw vegetables, and fruit. At a small cocktail party, when all guests are seated, appetizers can include some of those which are eaten with a fork.

A LARGE COCKTAIL PARTY

CHEESE DOUBLES
filled with herbed Boursin cheese

CRISP CELERY, CARROT STICKS, AND RADISHES

SHRIMP ON WOODEN PICKS IN CHILI-RELISH MAYONNAISE

STUFFED CHERRY TOMATOES
filled with curry-flavored cream cheese

ANCHOVY-STUFFED EGGS

STRIPS OF PROSCIUTTO WRAPPED AROUND MELON CUBES

❀

A SIT-DOWN COCKTAIL PARTY

CARROT STICKS IN ONION DIP

SHRIMP AND GRAPEFRUIT
in a relish mayonnaise thinned with grapefruit juice

CHICKEN LIVER PÂTÉ WITH CRACKERS

PAPER-THIN SLICES OF SALAMI
wrapped around miniature gherkins

CURRY STUFFED EGGS

CHILLED CUCUMBER WEDGES
sprinkled with freshly ground pepper and seasoning salt, served on a bed of shaved ice

❀

A SMALL SUNDAY NOON BLOODY MARY PARTY

BIRD'S NEST

THIN BUTTERED PUMPERNICKEL AND RYE BREAD

STUFFED MUSHROOMS
filled with chicken livers

BOLOGNA WEDGES
bologna spread with cream cheese, flavored with mustard, sandwiched together in stacks of 5 slices and chilled, cut into 8 wedges before serving

❀

A SMALL SIT-DOWN COCKTAIL PARTY

CHEESE WAFERS
topped with almonds

RED CAVIAR ROUNDS

PICKLED MUSHROOMS
served with thin buttered black bread squares

A PLATTER OF CHILLED FRUIT AND VEGETABLES
center with a bowl of curried mayonnaise. Serve celery, fennel, cauliflower, melon and zucchini wedges, apple slices

Menus for Teas

The afternoon tea hour is returning in many homes, and the old custom of serving something salty and something sweet should be revived. The English have made a fine art of thin sandwiches and plain cakes, while the Viennese have always specialized in small baking.

CHEESE WAFERS
topped with poppy, caraway, or sesame seeds and salt

THIN SANDWICHES
thin white bread, trimmed and pressed thinner between pieces of waxed paper. Spread with soft butter, filled with ham, cucumbers, crushed sardines, or a finely minced egg salad

PECAN HALF-MOONS

JAM TURNOVERS

❈

HAM CRESCENTS

SMALL OPEN-FACED SANDWICHES
ham, shrimp, smoked salmon, liver pâté can all be garnished attractively with egg or lemon or pickle slices and dill or parsley

LINZER STRIP
filled with apricot jam flavored with a very little apricot brandy

❈

VERY SMALL CHEESE DOUBLES

HAM CRESCENTS
substitute liver pâté mixed with chopped pecans for the ham filling in half the crescents

SPRITZ TONGUES

BISCUIT ROLL

Menus for Brunches

The combination of breakfast and lunch is a lovely meal to eat between eleven and twelve after having had early bed tea and nothing more. This is a favorite meal in some countries where it is called a "fork breakfast." It eliminates lunch and tides over the gap between early tea and afternoon tea (or coffee).

OPEN-FACED EGG SANDWICHES
cold scrambled eggs on slices of mild smoked salmon on dark bread, garnished with dill and accompanied by a pepper mill

BOWL OF FRESH BERRIES

CINNAMON TOAST FINGERS

TEA

❈

COLD CELERY BOUILLON

THIN BUTTERED CHEESE BREAD

POACHED EGGS VALENCIA
with tomato sauce

STEWED PRUNES

TEA OR COFFEE

❀

TOMATO JUICE

MOLLET OR 6-MINUTE EGGS FRANKONIA

OVEN-DRIED BRIOCHE SLICES

HERBED BUTTER BALLS

FRESH STRAWBERRIES

THICK CREAM

TEA OR COFFEE

Menus for Picnics

Fireless picnics have always consisted of cold foods, namely stuffed eggs, cold fried chicken, bread and butter sandwiches, thermoses of hot coffee, and a lopsided cake. As thermos containers have grown in size and efficiency, the traditional picnic menu has given way to rather more elaborate combinations, and now a picnic is often just a regular meal carried out of doors along with folding furniture and a tail-gate bar.

AN OLD-FASHIONED PICNIC

SARDINE-STUFFED EGGS

WATER CRESS ROLLS

thin white bread strips spread with chopped water cress and soft salt butter, rolled up and chilled

COLD VIENNESE FRIED CHICKEN

quartered and skinned broilers are dredged with flour, dipped in beaten egg, rolled in bread crumbs, and fried in deep fat until golden. Serve with lemon wedges

CUCUMBER SALAD   POTATO SALAD STEPHAN

FAT RASPBERRIES

with a sauce of whipped soft vanilla ice cream

HORSESHOES

CHILLED WHITE WINE

COFFEE

❀

AN ELABORATE PICNIC

CHILLED CREAM OF CUCUMBER SOUP

CURRIED MELBA TOAST

ROTISSERIE PORTERHOUSE STEAK

rare, 5-inches thick

COLD BÉARNAISE SAUCE   COLD MUSTARD SAUCE

SALADE NIÇOISE

RIPE CHERRIES AND CREAM

FILBERT HALF-MOONS

ICED CHAMPAGNE

COFFEE

Menus for Box Lunches

Box lunches are what hotels or airlines press into our hands when they send us off on an outing or a short hop—and there is always a feeling of GOOD RIDDANCE about it. A box lunch is also something that a hostess can prepare for her guests for a sporting event or journey. It differs from a picnic in that nothing is spread out, each person has a box with identical contents, and everything has to be small and light and delightful—no one wants to carry a *heavy* box lunch. The box is usually a paper box, and there are no chilling facilities or cutlery included. At best there is one wax paper container, a disposable plastic spoon, and a paper napkin.

1 WHOLE MUSTARD-STUFFED EGG

2 EXTREMELY THIN SANDWICHES OF BUTTERED NUT BREAD

HALF COLD ROAST GAME HEN

1 SMALL PAPER CONTAINER OF SPICED CHERRIES

1 LINZER TART

BEVERAGE AND COFFEE BY OTHERS

❋

1 SMALL CONTAINER OF EGG, CELERY, AND CUCUMBER

SALAD

bound with mayonnaise and chives

2 SMALL, RARE, JUICY RIB LAMB CHOPS

2 EXTREMELY THIN SANDWICHES OF BUTTERED

PUMPERNICKEL

1 SMALL WEDGE WELL-WRAPPED ROQUEFORT CHEESE

1 SWEET YELLOW APPLE

BEVERAGE AND COFFEE BY OTHERS

Midsummer Dinner and Luncheon Menus

All the hot weather menus are planned so that the various dishes, with the exception of some of the fruits and the freshly grated horseradish, may be prepared one day, or several days, before they are served.

Salad greens can be prepared and stored in the refrigerator in plastic bags. Celery and raw vegetables will become crisp in water in the refrigerator. The few things that have to be simmered or slowly toasted can be done early or late in the day, before or after the worst heat. Simmering and toasting do not require your presence in the kitchen.

While we are all for the homemade stocks, summer is the time for canned bouillons and jellied soups. It is also the time for the bought delicacies, smoked trout, Bar le Duc conserves; it is the time for uncooked foods and raw fruits and vegetables. The following menus are literally "cooked" in the blender and the refrigerator. Eggs have to be hard-cooked, but that is only a short 14 minutes of turning on the heat.

LUNCHEON

HAM CORNUCOPIAS FILLED WITH ASPARAGUS

SAUCE GRIBICHE

APPLE SALAD

CHEESE WAFERS

TEA

❋

SUNDAY SUPPER

HERRING IN SOUR CREAM

BAKED HAM

APPLE HORSERADISH SAUCE

POTATO SALAD STEPHAN

CHEESE PLATTER

BUTTERED PUMPERNICKEL

COLD BEER

❧

GALA BUFFET

SÉNÉGALAISE WITH TOASTED COCONUT

PARCHED BREAD

GARNISHED HAM ON ASPIC

TOMATOES FILLED WITH HERBED MAYONNAISE

CAULIFLOWER VINAIGRETTE

FRUIT WITH KIRSCH

LINZER TARTS

DEMITASSE

❧

THREE MENUS USING HAM
DINNER

CHILLED CREAM OF PEA SOUP

with sliced tomato and parsley

COLD BAKED HAM

MUSTARD MAYONNAISE   HORSERADISH MAYONNAISE

STEWED PEACHES IN CUMBERLAND SAUCE

SALADE TOURANGELLE

green beans, wax beans, and potatoes bound with
Orégano Dressing and mayonnaise

MACAROON COFFEE BISCUIT

PECAN HALF-MOONS

DEMITASSE

❧

SUPPER

POLISH CHERRY AND BEET SOUP

sour cherries, spiced borsch, and sour cream

SALT STICK TOAST

sliced across diagonally, buttered, and dried in a
slow oven

HAM VICTOR HUGO

garnished with tomato halves filled with Sauce
Béarnaise

TOSSED GREEN SALAD

with Mustard French Dressing

ROQUEFORT CHEESE

with unsalted biscuits and diced red grapes
serve a red wine

❧

LUNCHEON

SOUP CHATELAINE

jellied chicken consommé

HAM MOUSSE WITH ASPARAGUS

MUSTARD MAYONNAISE   CREAM MAYONNAISE

SMALL POPOVERS

whipped butter

RIPE RASPBERRIES

on soft vanilla ice cream, whipped with liqueur, and
sprinkled with crushed macaroons

ICED TEA

❧

A COLD FISH BUFFET

CHEESE WAFERS

SHRIMP ON ARTICHOKE BOTTOMS

LOBSTER IN MUSTARD SAUCE

CURRIED MELBA TOAST

SALMON STEAKS

WITH

LEMON DILL MAYONNAISE

CUCUMBER SALAD

POTATO SALAD STEPHAN

LEMON ICE

garnished with mint leaves and accompanied with 2 small decanters of crème de menthe and apricot brandy

ALMOND CRESCENTS

COFFEE

serve a dry white wine

❋

TWO COLD SUMMER SUPPERS

PROVINCIAL SALAD

a mixed salad of tomatoes, mushrooms, black olives, and water cress prepared with Provincial French Dressing

SLICED TONGUE IN ASPIC

the cooked tongue is arranged around steamed apples and glazed with aspic

HORSERADISH MAYONNAISE

homemade mayonnaise into which freshly grated or well-drained horseradish is folded before serving

BUTTERED THIN BLACK BREAD

use coarse Waerland Brot or packaged pumpernickel

TORLONE BISCUIT TORTONI

frozen biscuit flavored with maraschino and containing toasted filberts, chopped glacéed cherries, orange peel and citron

MACAROONS

COFFEE

SANGRÍA OR COLD ROSÉ

❋

ASPARAGUS VINAIGRETTE

HAM MOUSSE

mousse mixed with diced gherkins, poured into a soufflé dish, and chilled. The top is covered with an overlapping spiral of scored and very thinly sliced cucumbers

HERBED MAYONNAISE

OVEN-PARCHED GARLIC BREAD

thin bread, spread with garlic butter and parched in a 200° F. oven until golden and crisp (store in a covered container until needed)

CHILLED FRUIT WITH GRAND MARNIER

orange and grapefruit sections with berries in season, marinated in liqueur

FILBERT BISCUITS

COFFEE

A COLD MOSELLE WINE

Cooking Ahead

Cooking ahead is just another way of saying *Cold Cookery*. With the difference that the food that is *COOKED AHEAD* usually has to be reheated, while *COLD COOKERY* stays just as it is—ready and waiting. In order to be ready, it too has to be cooked beforehand, but the very nature of cold cookery is such that it includes a great deal of raw food, and cooking ahead for cold meals is a combination of cooking part of the menu and preparing the rest of it without having to resort to the stove or any of the cooking processes.

Most of the cold foods fall into three categories: 1. Those which can be prepared *WAY AHEAD* of time, as frozen desserts, dressings, baking, and the salads that are improved by marinating, 2. Those which can be prepared *WELL AHEAD* of time, as soups, meats, and most cold dishes, and 3. Those few which have to be prepared shortly before serving, as raw apples and peaches, avocados, grated horseradish, and freshly scraped beef.

Most cold foods do not suffer from being kept waiting, and if we are careful in planning our menus we can avoid the few cold ingredients that are perishable or change color. A hot meal deteriorates rapidly, the moment it cools off it loses a great many of its advantages, and by the time it is cold or reheated it is past its prime. Cold food has no moment of optimum, it is at its best for a long time and—unless you put an aspic or a frozen dessert in the hot sun—it will look and taste good after long periods of waiting.

If you have a freezing compartment, then cooking *WAY AHEAD* can mean a week or weeks. Cooking

WELL AHEAD can mean several days and certainly means that nothing is cooked on the day of the buffet or dinner. The following suggested menus include many of those foods which can either be cooked *WAY AHEAD* or *WELL AHEAD*, and, if all goes well, the hostess should be able to sit awaiting her guests with her hands folded in her lap.

COOKED AHEAD DINNER I

WITH COCKTAILS

CHEESE WAFERS   PARCHED NUTS

HORS D'OEUVRE TRAY

KIDNEY BEAN SALAD   HERRING IN RED WINE

PICKLED MUSHROOMS   SARDINES

MUSTARD STUFFED EGGS   OLIVES

MELBA BRIOCHE TOAST

ALSATIAN HALF HAM

CUMBERLAND SAUCE   WHITE WINE POTATO SALAD

RELISHES   CUCUMBER SALAD

APRICOT BAVARIAN CREAM

APRICOT BRANDY SAUCE

PECAN HALF-MOONS

COFFEE

VIN ROSÉ

❃

Schedule:
Prepare *way ahead* and store in closed jars in refrigerator:
Cumberland Sauce, Apricot Brandy Sauce, Kidney Bean Salad, Pickled Mushrooms, any homemade relishes

Prepare *well ahead* (3 to 4 days) and store in closed tins:
Melba Brioche Toast, Cheese Wafers, Pecan Half-Moons

Prepare *ahead* (on day before) and store in refrigerator:
Ham, Potato Salad, Hard-cooked eggs, store whites in water and yolk filling in a jar, Apricot Bavarian Cream, store covered in its mold, ice the wine

Prepare on day of dinner:
1. Stuff eggs.
2. Open cans and jars of herrings, sardines, olives, nuts, and relishes and arrange hors d'oeuvre and relish trays and cocktail nuts.
3. Arrange everything on serving dishes and platters.
4. Make coffee.

COOKED AHEAD DINNER II

WITH COCKTAILS

CARROT STICKS IN CHEESE DIP

CHICKEN LIVER PÂTÉ WITH CRACKERS

ICED CREAM OF WATER CRESS SOUP

COLD ROAST SADDLE OF LAMB

GREEN PEA SALAD IN RING OF HERBED RICE

MINTED APPLE JELLY

COFFEE MOUSSE

SPRITZ TONGUES

COFFEE

CHILLED WHITE WINE

❋

Schedule:
Prepare *way ahead* and store in closed jars in refrigerator:
Cheese Dip, Minted Apple Jelly, French Dressing for Green Pea Salad

Prepare *well ahead* (2 to 3 days) and store in a closed cracker can and in sealed jars in refrigerator:
Spritz Tongues, Chicken Liver Pâté, cook rice

Prepare *ahead* (on day before) and store in refrigerator:
Fill Rice Ring, Carrot Sticks, Water Cress Soup, Roast Lamb, Cook Green Peas, Coffee Mousse, Ice wine

Prepare on day of dinner:
1. Beat cheese dip and arrange carrot sticks in it, place crackers around jar of pâté.
2. Arrange everything on serving dishes or platters.
3. Make coffee.

COOKED AHEAD DINNER III

WITH COCKTAILS

CRISP SPRIGS OF WATER CRESS AND CELERY

CHILLED CANTALOUPE HALVES FILLED WITH

JELLIED MADRILÈNE GARNISHED WITH LEMON

CHICKEN PIE UNDER CHEESE CRUST

CRANBERRY SAUCE

COLD BROCCOLI WITH FRENCH DRESSING

COFFEE SABAYON

(substitute cold strong coffee for wine)

COFFEE

CHILLED WHITE WINE AND SODA

(Gespritzter)

◦

Schedule:

Prepare on day before and chill in refrigerator:
Celery, Chicken Pie, Broccoli, Coffee Sabayon, chill wine

Prepare on day of dinner:
1. Crisp water cress.
2. Empty melons and fill with canned soup.
3. Arrange everything on serving dishes and platters.

COOKED AHEAD DINNER IV

WITH COCKTAILS

CHEESE STICKS

RUSSIAN HARD-COOKED EGGS IN TOMATOES

COLD BEEF TONGUE IN ASPIC

HORSERADISH SAUCE   SALADE NIÇOISE

HERBED RICE SALAD

WINTER COMPOTE

PECAN HALF-MOONS

COFFEE

RED WINE

❋

Schedule:

Prepare *way ahead* and store in closed cracker cans and jars:
Bake Cheese Sticks and Pecan Half-Moons, Winter Compote, Salad Dressing and Mayonnaise

Prepare *well ahead* (3 to 4 days) and store in refrigerator:
Boil Beans and Potatoes for Salad

Prepare *ahead* (on day before) and store in refrigerator:
Rice Salad, Tongue and Aspic, Hard-cooked Eggs and Tomatoes

On day of dinner:
1. Arrange Russian Eggs.
2. Add eggs and tomatoes to Salade Niçoise.
3. Arrange everything on serving dishes and platters.
4. Make Coffee.
5. Grate horseradish into sauce.

❋

WITH COCKTAILS

CHEESE SQUARES

CELERY, CARROTS, AND FENNEL

MELONS WITH PORT WINE

OVEN-DRIED BRIOCHE SLICES

VITELLO TONNATO

veal cooked with tuna fish. The meat is sliced and the tuna fish and stock are blended with mayonnaise into a smooth sauce garnished with capers

SALADE SICILIENNE

tomatoes, celery, artichoke bottoms, and apples in equal quantities, bound with Lemon French Dressing and surrounded by romaine lettuce leaves

BISCUIT TORTONI

COFFEE

SERVE A CHILLED WHITE WINE

❋

Schedule:
Make anytime and store in covered jars in refrigerator:
Mayonnaise and Lemon French Dressing

Bake anytime and store in covered cracker cans:
Cheese Squares, Oven-Dried Brioche Slices

Make one or two days before dinner and store in freezer:
Biscuit Tortoni

Prepare on day before dinner and store in refrigerator:
Vitello Tonnato, Celery and Vegetable for Cocktails and Salad, crisp lettuce, chill wine, peel tomatoes

On day of dinner:
Drain and fill melons, arrange the veal platter, add apples to salad and arrange bowl

*

WITH COCKTAILS
ANCHOVY CANAPÉS
sliced hard-cooked eggs on black bread rounds, spread with anchovy paste
PARCHED NUTS
if homemade, parch lightly oiled and salted nuts in lowest oven, shaking them occasionally, until they are dry golden and crisp
COLD CURRIED FRUIT SOUP
purée of apples and apricots, flavored with curry, under whipped cream sprinkled with ginger
BROILED CHICKEN
SAUCE GRIBICHE   LINGONBERRIES

RICE SALAD LAKMÉ
cold cooked rice, combined with tomato and cucumber dice, bound with Lemon French Dressing and garnished with diced ham, chopped parsley, and lettuce leaves
RUM MOUSSE
MINIATURE LINZER
COFFEE
SERVE A DRY WHITE WINE

*

Schedule:
Make anytime and store in refrigerator:
Lemon French Dressing

Bake anytime and store in covered cracker cans:
Miniature Linzer and toast for canapés, parched nuts

Make one or two days before dinner:
Rum Mousse—store in freezer, Boiled Rice—store in refrigerator, Curried Soup—store in refrigerator, Anchovy Cream Cheese Paste—store in refrigerator, Hard-cooked Eggs—store in refrigerator

Prepare on day before dinner and store in **refrigerator:**
Crisp lettuce, peeled tomatoes, chill wine, Lingonberries, Sauce Gribiche

On day of dinner:
Assemble canapés, combine and arrange salad, whip cream for soup, broil chickens

*

CRISP CELERY WITH COCKTAILS
KOLODNIK SERVED OVER ICE CUBES
beets, shrimp, cucumbers, and hard-cooked eggs in bouillon and sour cream

COLD TONGUE IN ASPIC

HORSERADISH CREAM

FRUIT SALAD WITH FRUIT SALAD DRESSING

A LARGE BRIE WITH BISCUITS

CHILLED VIN ROSÉ OR ICED TEA

❧

Schedule:

Prepare one or two days before dinner and store in refrigerator:

Boil shrimp, beets, tongue, hard-cooked eggs, make aspic

Prepare on day before dinner:

Citrus fruits for salad, fruit salad dressing, chill wine, make tea

On day of dinner:

Add perishable fruits to salad, combine soup ingredients, whip cream, grate horseradish

❧

COLD CHERRY SOUP

CINNAMON TOAST FINGERS

HALF COLD HAM

garnished with stuffed eggs and cauliflower

MUSTARD MAYONNAISE

WATER CRESS SALAD

served with cheeses and buttered pumpernickel

SANGRÍA

Spanish burgundy with orange and lemon slices

❧

Schedule:

Prepare one or two days before dinner and store in refrigerator:

Boil ham, eggs, and cauliflower. Mayonnaise and dressing, soup, egg yolk mixture. Crisp the cress

On day of dinner:

Stuff eggs, garnish ham, toast fingers, make sangría, butter pumpernickel

❧

ASPARAGUS VINAIGRETTE

GARLIC MELBA TOAST

COLD ROAST BEEF

garnished with aspic and half tomatoes filled with Rémoulade Sauce

FRESHLY GRATED HORSERADISH

ENGLISH MUSTARD

RASPBERRIES ROMANOFF

CHILLED VIN ROSÉ

❧

Schedule:

Prepare one or two days before dinner and store in refrigerator:

Steam asparagus, Vinaigrette Dressing, Hard-cook eggs for Vinaigrette Sauce, Melba Toast—store in covered cracker can, Rémoulade Sauce, Aspic

On day of dinner:

Dress asparagus, peel and hollow out tomatoes, grate horseradish, pick over raspberries

❧

SMOKED TROUT

CAVIAR MAYONNAISE

CAESAR SALAD

a large bowl of romaine lettuce, dressed at the table with egg and cheese

CURRIED MELBA TOAST

CHILLED PEACHES

poached in rum-flavored raspberry syrup

GESPRITZTER

white wine and seltzer

❦

Schedule:
Buy:
Smoked Trout

Make at any time and store in refrigerator, store toast in covered cracker tin:
Mayonnaise, Curried Melba Toast, Poached Peaches, chill white wine

On day before dinner:
Crisp romaine, assemble salad ingredients

On day of dinner:
Garnish mayonnaise with caviar
Oven will only be needed, at its lowest, to parch melba toast, which toasts itself.

❦

MADRILÈNE IN CANTALOUPE HALVES

spoon softly jellied, not stiff, madrilène into chilled half melons and garnish with sour cream and lime wedges

CRAB MEAT RING

mousse of crab meat, molded in a ring form, filled with cucumber salad

DILL MAYONNAISE

finely cut dill folded into the mayonnaise

BLUEBERRIES ON LIME ICE

small scoops of lime ice, buried under fresh blue-berries. The charm of this dish is that there are many berries and not too much ice

ICED MOSELLE WINE

❦

Schedule:
Buy:
Madrilène, Sour Cream, Crab Meat, Lime Ice

Prepare one or two days before dinner and refrigerate:
Crab Meat Ring, Cucumber Salad, Mayonnaise, chill wine

On day of dinner:
Do nothing except to assemble and serve

❦

ANTIPASTO

individual plates arranged with sardines, anchovies, salami slices, ripe olives, hard-cooked egg, pickled beets, tuna fish, celery, and radishes

HOT GARLIC BREAD

cream butter with crushed garlic and salt to taste. Spread it in and on a loaf of French bread sliced down to the bottom crust. Wrap loaf in foil, leaving top open, and bake in a 350° F. oven until golden, about 20 minutes.

COLD ROLLED VEAL ROAST

GREEN PEAS IN ASPIC

fill muffin cups to the top with cold cooked baby green peas, pour on plain aspic, and chill until needed. Unmold around roast

ESCOFFIER MAYONNAISE

SPICED CHERRIES

cherries heated with currant jelly and spices, served over vanilla ice cream

COFFEE

DRY WHITE WINE

*

Schedule:

Buy:

Sardines, Anchovies, Salami, Olives, Tuna Fish, Vanilla Ice Cream, Black Cherries

Prepare on day before dinner and store in refrigerator:

Celery and Radishes, Garlic Butter, Roast Veal Mayonnaise, Peas and Aspic

On day of dinner:

Heat Cherries, heat Garlic Bread

NEW COMBINATIONS

Finding new combinations is impossible, everything has been there before, and when we are all carried away with thin Westphalian or proscuitto ham with figs or melons, it turns out that Nero ate them just as we do—ice and all. The only thing that we can hope to do is make combinations that have been forgotten for a time and eliminate combinations that have been done to boredom.

We can also change accents and nuances, and we can change the traditional rotation of courses (women are much more adventurous in this respect). I remember a dinner that was apparently inspired by the Russian cold table, there was a world of herrings, beets, sturgeon, sour cream, and dark breads, but an otherwise very enterprising and progressive guest kept whispering, "*I want my dinner.*" He finally almost burst into tears.

I am all for adventure at the table, within reason, but I am for contented appetites and happy combinations that enhance each other and are never *farfetched.*

COLD CHERRY SOUP

CINNAMON TOAST FINGERS

COLD RARE LEG OF LAMB

roasted with garlic and rosemary and garnished with tomatoes filled with stiff mayonnaise mixed with smallest capers

COLD COOKED RICE RING

filled with green pea salad bound with minted French Dressing

COFFEE

CHEESE DOUBLES

made a little larger than the recipe suggests and generously filled with Boursin

serve a white wine with the lamb
serve a red wine with the cheese doubles

*

SALADE NIÇOISE

beans, potatoes, eggs, tuna fish, and everything good combined in a very French way

PARCHED BREAD CHUNKS

white bread broken into chunks, dipped in melted garlic salt butter, and slowly parched until golden in lowest oven

AGNES SOREL SOUP
make a larger than ordinary quantity and fill it with more chicken, tongue, and mushrooms

A BOWL OF CHILLED FRUIT
with nuts and dried fruits

COFFEE
serve a dry white wine

❀

ICED CREAM OF SPINACH SOUP

BEEF VINAIGRETTE
boiled beef garnished as a curry is garnished with small bowls of pickled beets, horseradish shaved into curls, mustard pickles, cucumber dice, spiced mushrooms, and dill pickles

GERMAN COLESLAW

POTATO SALAD

CHEESE-STUFFED ENDIVE
with thin buttered pumpernickel

COFFEE

RED WINE

❀

ASPARAGUS
with French Dressing and Westphalian ham

OVEN-DRIED TOAST
thinly sliced bread, buttered and dried in a low oven until golden

POACHED EGGS MONTPELLIER
under a sauce with all the attributes of Montpellier butter

ORANGES IN SYRUP
a julienne of orange peel cooked in the syrup and poured over the oranges

LINZER STRIP
filled with raspberry jam

COFFEE

WHITE WINE

❀

ICED CREAM OF LEEK AND POTATO SOUP
more substantial than a vichyssoise, but much the same flavor with a garnish of garlic croutons

BEEFSTEAK TARTARE
scraped raw beef with piquant additions, bound with an egg yolk and served with buttered thin black bread

CHAMPAGNE FRUIT
individual iced splits of champagne to pour over lightly brandied fresh fruit

HORSESHOES

COFFEE

RED WINE

❀

CRISP DICED SALAD
a small salad of equal parts diced red radishes, celery, and peeled cucumber, bound with mayonnaise stirred with a little mustard and garnished with a little finely chopped fennel mixed with minced parsley

RARE COLD ROAST BEEF
thinly sliced and served with freshly grated horseradish

COLD BÉARNAISE SAUCE

GLAZED ASPARAGUS SPEARS
steamed asparagus, with pimento strips in aspic

CHEESE MOUNTAIN

combination of cheeses mounded in an emptied Camembert

COFFEE

MARRONS GLACÉS

RED WINE

❋

SPINACH-STUFFED MUSHROOMS

CHEESE WAFERS

VITELLO TONNATO

cold veal under a tuna fish and mayonnaise sauce with capers

SALAD OF SLICED TOMATOES

with Orégano Dressing and a garnish of finely chopped raw cauliflower

POACHED PEACHES

AMARETTI

crisp Italian macaroons

COFFEE

LIGHT ITALIAN WHITE WINE

❋

MELON WITH PORT WINE

small melons cut in half and seeded. The cavity filled with port wine and refrigerated

COLD SALMON STEAKS

served with thinly sliced buttered black bread, crisp water cress, and lemon wedges

EGGS BÉARNAISE

trimmed poached eggs on artichoke bottoms masked with cold Sauce Béarnaise

COFFEE

WHITE WINE

serve the ice cream about 1 hour after dinner in the living room

ICE CREAM FRANÇOISE

strong coffee ice cream with a sauce of softened vanilla ice cream, beaten with maraschino

SPRITZ TONGUES

❋

SUNDAY SALAD

a mixture of green beans, crisp white beans, and dill

CURRIED MELBA TOAST

CHAUD-FROID OF CHICKEN

HERB MAYONNAISE

OPEN STRAWBERRY TART

fresh strawberries in a short paste tart shell, glazed with melted red currant jelly

COFFEE

❋

SHRIMP CEVICHE

raw shrimp marinated in lime and lemon juice with paper-thin Spanish onion rings, garnished with diced avocado

HAM MOUSSE

MUSTARD MAYONNAISE

CUCUMBER SALAD

CHEESE PLATTER

with water biscuits and thin rye bread, butter curls, and radishes

RED WINE WITH THE HAM AND THE CHEESE

COFFEE

APPETIZERS

CHAPTER TWO

Appetizers, First Courses,
and Luncheon Courses,
Cooked and Uncooked

WE HAVE all heard about the appetizers that are supposed to stimulate the appetite without spoiling it and the light first courses that do not take away from the main course, but few of us have been able to find them. Anything we eat before dinner, from the standpoint of capacity alone—not to mention calories—is bound to take away part of our capability of enjoying dinner and part of our capacity for eating it. The small or light first course must be a harmonious part of dinner, not something put before the main course to make the menu longer and more impressive. Appetizers should, therefore, be light, and they should not interfere with, or overlap, the menu.

If the cocktail-hour appetizers are going to be elaborate, they should be considered as part of the dinner, and the first course should be omitted or limited accordingly. If there is going to be a good first course at table, then the thoughtful hostess will serve only the lightest appetizers or raw vegetables with the cocktails.

There is no point whatever in repeating anything that was served with cocktails; it is, after all, the same meal even if there was a shift from the living room to the table. If there is going to be a beef dinner, then do not serve cocktail hamburgers or shrimp appetizers before a lobster salad. If dinner rests entirely on a chicken menu, then serve cheese or fish appetizers.

We are advocating cold cookery all year round be-cause it is a way of keeping the servantless hostess out of the kitchen, especially at the very time when her guests have just arrived—and may not even know each other. All stages of a dinner party are pleasant, but the cocktail-appetizer hour is too important to the success of the entire evening for the guests to spend it without their host and hostess. I have attended many cocktail hours when the host was kept busy filling glasses and the hostess emerged from the kitchen at intervals with relays of beautiful hot appetizers that kept her busy over her hot broiler until it was time to go in to dinner.

The cold appetizers and first courses, prepared in advance, are the solution, but even they have to be of a sort that does not wilt or turn black or curl up before its time. They also should not monopolize too much refrigerator space. In other words, they are the hostess's "Opening Bars," the first steps toward pleasure and congeniality, and they should be light, attractive looking, enduring, patient, original, nonfilling, stimulating, varied, and they should taste good.

Cold appetizers, hors d'oeuvre, and first courses are for summer and winter, but in wintertime, when dinner is going to be cold and the broiler and oven are idle, a few hot appetizers are welcome. They are listed in Part II of this book where just a few hot dishes are admitted to point up the advantages of the cold ones.

BASIC STUFFED EGGS

Cut the eggs in half lengthwise, take out the yolks and rice them through a coarse sieve. The next step is optional and depends on the additional ingredients that will be used. If the eggs are going to be flavored with curry powder, garlic, anchovy paste, or similar ingredients, stir it into the soft butter until smooth, then whip the butter into the yolks with the mayonnaise, using a fork. If the mixture is not going to contain curry powder or a similar ingredient, the butter may be omitted and more mayonnaise added in its stead. The cream only serves to make the yolk mixture lighter and smoother. When a large number of eggs are being filled with a very light stuffing, then the cream can be replaced by whipped cream in about half the amount of the mayonnaise.

The most important thing is to *rice* the yolks. Two crushed or mashed egg yolks would only fill about 2 tablespoons, whereas, 2 riced yolks fill more than ⅓ cup, and even after they have been beaten with butter and mayonnaise they still retain a much greater volume than if they had been crushed. Do not season the basic yolk mixture until after the other ingredients have been added. When yolk mixture contains butter, chill the eggs at least 2 hours before serving.

8 hard-cooked eggs, page 80
1½ to 2 tablespoons soft butter, optional
4 tablespoons thick mayonnaise
1½ teaspoons heavy cream, optional

STUFFED EGGS WITH MUSTARD FLAVOR

Beat the mustards, onion, and relish into the yolk mixture, keeping it light. Season and fill loosely into the egg whites. Sprinkle tops with a little paprika, press in a little parsley tuft with the tip of a knife and garnish each egg with 1 or 2 capers.

Basic yolk mixture, using 8 egg yolks
1 to 1½ teaspoons brown mustard
¼ teaspoon dry English mustard
1 teaspoon minced onion
3 tablespoons pickle relish, all moisture pressed out
Salt to taste
Paprika
1 sprig parsley, or 16 little tufts
2 teaspoons capers

STUFFED EGGS WITH CURRY FLAVOR

In making the basic mixture, stir the curry powder into the soft butter until smooth, then add mayonnaise. Season and add the onion. Pipe the mixture into the egg whites through a wide fluted tube, into a large rosette. Press 1 shrimp down deep into each rosette and garnish with a little dill pressed down next to one side of the shrimp.

Basic yolk mixture, using 8 egg yolks
2 teaspoons curry powder, or to taste
1 teaspoon minced onion
16 small cooked shrimp
1 frond fresh dill, or parsley

STUFFED EGGS WITH ANCHOVY FLAVOR

In making the basic mixture, stir the anchovy paste into the soft butter until smooth, then add the mayonnaise and onion and fold in the whipped cream; the mixture should be very light. Pipe it into the egg whites through a wide fluted tube, into large rosettes. Sprinkle the tops with nuts.

Basic yolk mixture, using 8 egg yolks
2 to 3 inches anchovy paste out of a tube
2 teaspoons finely minced onion
3 tablespoons finely chopped salted pecans
  or cashew nuts

STUFFED EGGS WITH GARLIC FLAVOR

Stir the garlic with the butter in the basic mixture. Beat in mayonnaise, 1½ tablespoons of the herbs, lemon juice, and seasonings. Fill the mixture lightly into the egg whites and dip the tops into ½ tablespoon finely minced herbs.

Basic yolk mixture, using 8 egg yolks
½ clove garlic, or to taste, crushed
2 tablespoons finely minced herbs: parsley,
  chervil, chives, tarragon, and thyme
1 teaspoon lemon juice
Salt and freshly ground white pepper to taste

STUFFED EGGS WITH SARDINES

Stir the mashed sardines into the basic egg yolk mixture with mustard, lemon juice, and rind. Season the mixture to taste, fill it high into the egg whites, and garnish the tops with lemon rind and chives.

Basic yolk mixture, using 8 egg yolks
3 to 4 sardines, drained, skinned, and mashed
1½ teaspoons brown mustard
1 teaspoon lemon juice
1 teaspoon grated lemon rind
Salt and pepper to taste
1 curl lemon rind, cut into fine julienne
2 teaspoons finely cut chives

STUFFED EGGS WITH SALMON

Use Lemon Mayonnaise in making the basic mixture. Press the salmon dry and add it to the yolk mixture with the onion and gherkin. Season to taste, adding a little more mayonnaise if necessary, and pile the mixture high in the egg whites. Garnish with olive slices.

Basic yolk mixture, using 8 egg yolks
½ cup or ½ of a 7¾-ounce can salmon, drained and flaked
2 teaspoons minced onion
2 teaspoons minced gherkin
Salt and pepper to taste
6 stuffed olives, sliced across

EGGS BOULOGNAISE

Combine cauliflower, shrimp, crab meat, and mustard and fold in just enough mayonnaise to bind. Arrange the salad on a small serving dish, sprinkle it with the herbs, and arrange the eggs on it. Garnish with salmon and serve very cold with the remaining mayonnaise.

6 eggs mollet or 6-minute eggs, peeled
1 small cauliflower, cooked, separated
½ pound shrimp, peeled, deveined, and cooked
1 6½-ounce can crab meat, drained and picked
1 or 2 tablespoons Dijon mustard
1 recipe Mayonnaise
2 tablespoons finely chopped mixed herbs, parsley, tarragon, chervil, chives
2 slices smoked salmon cut into diagonal strips

EGGS CLEOPATRA

Simmer the scallops, shallots, and parsley in the white wine, shaking them frequently, until white and tender. Drain off the wine and cool the mixture. If frozen scallops were used, cut them into pieces. Add pickle and capers and season well. Wrap the eggs in smoked salmon, beat the drained wine into the mayonnaise, and add only enough to the scallop salad to bind it. Arrange the salad on a small serving dish, place the salmon-wrapped eggs on it, and serve very cold with the remaining mayonnaise.

6 eggs mollet or 6-minute eggs, peeled
2 cups smallest bay scallops, or 1 package frozen
3 shallots, chopped
2 tablespoons chopped parsley
1 cup dry white wine
1 dill pickle, chopped
1 tablespoon capers
Salt and white pepper to taste
6 slices smoked salmon
1 recipe Mayonnaise

OEUFS DES BONS VIVEURS

Arrange 6 little nests of overlapping potato salad slices, lay a trimmed poached egg in the center of each, and garnish the potatoes with slices of lobster. Whip the pink mayonnaise, place it in a porcelain bowl, and garnish the tops of the eggs with cold caviar just before serving.

6 cold poached eggs
1 recipe Dilled New Potato Salad
½ pound lobster meat
1 recipe Mayonnaise tinted pink with puréed tomato
1 1½-ounce jar beluga caviar

PINK MAYONNAISE

Scald 1 ripe red tomato for ½ minute, draw off the skin, cut it in half, and press out all seeds. Dice the tomato and stir it down into the finished mayonnaise in the blender. Blend, stir, and repeat until the mayonnaise is tinted pink.

EGGS CHRISTOPHER COLUMBUS

These undoubtedly derive their name from the fact that the egg is so arranged that it stands in the halved tomato.

Cut the egg lengthwise on an egg slicer that cuts either way. Hold them intact without spreading the slices. Cut tomatoes in half, scoop them out, and divide the chilled purée of *foie gras* over them. Set an egg into each purée-filled tomato half and pour the Montpellier mayonnaise over just before serving.

6 hard-cooked eggs, peeled
3 large round tomatoes, peeled
1 5-ounce can Purée of Foie Gras
1 cup Montpellier Mayonnaise (given below)

MONTPELLIER MAYONNAISE

Parboil 1 tablespoon finely cut chives, and 4 sprigs each of parsley, tarragon, and chervil with coarse stems removed. Dry the herbs and mince them fine. Fold them into 1 cup Mayonnaise with a squeeze of lemon juice and just enough heavy cream to make a flowing but thick sauce.

EGGS ROMANOFF "HARD-COOKED"

Cut eggs in half lengthwise, scoop out the yolks and rice them. Stir them with the butter, add olives, onion, and enough mayonnaise to just bind. Fill the mixture lightly into the egg halves. Drain the can of artichoke bottoms and place them into a bowl with the French dressing. Turn them several times and leave them in the dressing for 1 hour. Fill artichokes with pimento dice, set 1 egg half in each and garnish the top with caviar.

In the days of the Romanoffs these eggs were supposedly reversed. Large freshly cooked artichoke bottoms were filled with caviar. The stuffed eggs were set on them and pimento strips garnished the tops of the eggs.

6 hard-cooked eggs, peeled
1 tablespoon soft butter
3 tablespoons minced green olives
1 teaspoon minced onion
1 recipe Lemon Mayonnaise
1 10½-ounce can artichoke bottoms—12 to a can
½ cup French Dressing
2 pimentos, diced
1 smallest jar beluga caviar

FILLED CHERRY TOMATOES

Wash and stem the tomatoes and set them on their flattened stem ends. With a very sharp pointed knife cut a deep hole in their rounded tops. Beat the cream cheese, work the curry powder into the mayonnaise with the back of a spoon and stir it into the cheese. Pipe the mixture through a thin tube into the tomatoes, leaving a small rosette at the top. Chill until needed. If the curried cheese is too stiff to pipe easily, add a little more mayonnaise.

1 basket cherry tomatoes
1 small cream cheese at room temperature
2 teaspoons curry powder
1 tablespoon thick mayonnaise
Salt to taste

VEGETABLE APPETIZERS

In summer and all year round, crisp celery and carrot sticks, raw cauliflower roses, endive spears, red radishes and wedges of cucumber, zucchini and fennel are good to eat and good for us. Celery and endive leaves lend themselves beautifully to being filled with various *stuffings*, but they may also be dipped into sauces.

RAW CAULIFLOWER AND CURRIED MAYONNAISE

Crisp cauliflower roses in cold water in refrigerator. Work curry powder into the cream with the back of a spoon until smooth. Beat it into the mayonnaise and serve it very cold surrounded by the drained and dried cauliflower roses.

1 medium cauliflower, trimmed and divided into bite-sized flowers
2 to 4 teaspoons Madras curry powder, or any preferred type of curry, to taste
2 tablespoons heavy cream
⅔ cup thick mayonnaise

CARROT STICKS WITH ONION CREAM

Cut carrots into long slices on a slicer and cut the slices into sticks that are a little wider than they are thick. Cut them into fairly even lengths, about 4 inches long, and crisp them in cold water. Mash the cheeses with a fork, beat in the onion and enough mayonnaise to make a thick, light dip in which the carrot sticks can stand upright. Season the mixture to taste and chill until needed. If it becomes too thick, beat in a little more mayonnaise before transferring it to a shallow bowl and standing the dried carrot sticks upright into it.

4 long thick carrots, scraped
2 small cream cheeses at room temperature
1 small onion, minced
¼ cup thick mayonnaise, or to taste
Salt and pepper to taste

CELERY WITH ROQUEFORT SAUCE

Crisp the celery in the refrigerator. Combine the cheeses and mash them with a fork. Add sherry and sour cream, season to taste, and beat the mixture until smooth and light. Add more cream if necessary to make a very thick, smooth sauce. Serve in a bowl, sprinkled with parsley, and surrounded by the celery stalks.

1 head celery, cleaned, scraped, and divided into stalks
1 wedge Roquefort cheese at room temperature
1 small cream cheese at room temperature
1 tablespoon sherry, or to taste
1 tablespoon sour cream
Salt and pepper to taste
1 tablespoon chopped parsley

STUFFED ENDIVE TAYLOR TERRACE

Trim the endive and divide it into leaves by trimming off the bottom, loosening the leaves, and always trimming higher as the leaves come off. Stir or sieve the cheese until smooth, stir in enough sour cream and sherry to make a thick paste and pipe or fill it into the endive leaves. Serve very cold.

4 stalks Belgian endive
1 wedge Roquefort cheese at room temperature
1 to 2 tablespoons sour cream
1 tablespoon dry sherry
Salt to taste

GORGONZOLA STUFFED CELERY WITH GRAPES AND TOKAY WINE

Crush the cheese with the butter and pipe a strip of it onto each celery stalk through a fluted pastry tube. Sprinkle the cheese lightly with paprika and lay the celery stalks on a bed of shaved ice. Serve them at the end of a cold meal with grapes and a dessert wine, as Tokay.

1 wedge Gorgonzola cheese at room temperature
3 tablespoons butter at room temperature
3 young celery hearts, separated into stalks and trimmed
Sweet red paprika
1½ pounds green seedless grapes, chilled

ITALIAN STUFFED MUSHROOMS

Break the stems out of the mushrooms and simmer caps and stems in salted water with a squeeze of lemon juice for about 4 minutes, or until they are glossy and firm and have not fattened out. Drain them and trim the tough ends from the stems. Chop the remaining part of the stems and combine them with the egg yolk, onion, and spinach. Stir well, add the egg whites, and season the mixture. Fill it high into the mushroom caps and chill. Soften gelatin in sherry for 15 minutes. Bring 1 cup of the consommé to a boil, take it from heat, and stir in the gelatin until it is dissolved. Add the remaining consommé and cool until thickened but not set. Place mushrooms on a wire rack over a pan and coat them with the aspic. Return the rack to the refrigerator until it is set and repeat coating the mushrooms until they have a thick glaze. If the aspic becomes too thick, set it over warm water. Chill the mushrooms until needed and serve them with Italian dressing.

24 evenly sized mushrooms, measuring about 1½ inches across
½ lemon
2 hard-cooked eggs, yolks and whites riced separately
3 tablespoons finely chopped onion
8 spinach leaves, scalded and chopped
Salt to taste
1 envelope gelatin
¼ cup dry sherry
2 cups clear consommé
1 recipe Italian Dressing

GLAZED ASPARAGUS SPEARS

Trim asparagus down to 5-inch spears, tie them loosely into bunches, and steam them standing upright in about 1½ inches of boiling water. If an asparagus boiler or very deep small kettle is not available, place them in the lower section of a small double boiler and invert the upper section over them while they steam. Steam until bright green,

1 large bunch asparagus, or 6 thick stalks for each portion
1 envelope gelatin
2 cups strong clear consommé
2 or 3 pimentos cut into long strips
1 recipe Vinaigrette Sauce

just tender, and still firm, depending on thickness of stalks, about 12 minutes. Drain and untie bunches. When the asparagus is cold, mound it into log piles of 6 spears each. Chill them until ready to glaze. Stir gelatin into ¼ cup of the cold consommé and set it aside for 15 minutes. Bring 1 cup consommé to a boil, take it from heat, and stir in the gelatin until it is dissolved. Add the remaining consommé and cool the aspic. As soon as it thickens but is not set, brush it over the asparagus bunches and return them to the refrigerator. As soon as the first coat of aspic is set, repeat with another and lay 2 pimento strips across each little bunch to emulate the red ribbons that usually tie bunches of asparagus. Continue to coat with aspic until the bunches have a thick coat. Serve very cold with vinaigrette sauce.

FILLED CUCUMBER CUPS I

Cut the fluted cucumbers—the green skin is corrugated with long white lines—across into 1-inch slices. Take out centers with a large melon-ball cutter, leaving enough cucumber at the sides and bottom to make a thin case. Marinate the cases in French dressing for at least 1 hour, turning them often. Spread the parsley out on wax paper, drain the cucumber cups, and dip the top edge into the parsley to make a green border. Bind the minced salmon with a little of the tartar sauce and fill the cucumber cups with it. Sprinkle with a few raspings of horseradish and serve very cold with additional tartar sauce.

2 straight cucumbers, peeled with a fluted knife
1 cup French Dressing
2 tablespoons minced parsley
4 slices smoked salmon, minced
½ recipe thick Tartar Sauce or Tyrolean Sauce (given below)
Freshly grated horseradish

TARTAR SAUCE

Into the mayonnaise fold all remaining ingredients and refrigerate until needed. Increase or decrease any of the above ingredients to taste.

1¼ cups Mayonnaise, page 122
4 small sweet-sour gherkins, chopped
1 tablespoon drained capers, chopped
2 slices onion, chopped
1 shallot, minced, optional
2 tablespoons finely cut chives
1 tablespoon finely chopped parsley
2 finely chopped stuffed olives may be added

TYROLEAN SAUCE

Prepare 1 recipe Lemon Mayonnaise and add the same sweet-sour gherkins, chopped, as in Tartar Sauce above. Add capers, chives, and parsley, as above, but omit the onion, shallot, and olives. Substitute 2 tablespoons tomato catsup and stir the sauce until it has its characteristic reddish color.

FILLED CUCUMBER CUPS II

Cut the cucumbers into cases as described above and marinate them in the same manner in the French dressing. Press all moisture out of the crab meat and combine it with the onion, relish, and chili sauce. Add enough mayonnaise to bind, and chill the mixture. Mound it into the drained cucumber shells and sprinkle the tops heavily with parsley. Chill until ready to serve.

2 straight cucumbers, prepared as above
1 cup French Dressing
1 6½-ounce can crab meat, drained and picked over
1 tablespoon finely chopped onion
2 tablespoons pickle relish, all moisture pressed out
1 tablespoon chili sauce
Stiff Mayonnaise
3 tablespoons minced parsley

MIDSUMMER FRESH FRUIT APPETIZERS AND FIRST COURSES

The combinations of smoked meat and fruit go back to the days of Nero, and no one has improved on them since. Wrap thin-sliced meat around cold ripe fruit, secure with a wooden pick, and chill until needed. For a first course, peel the fruit if necessary, cut it into wedges, and serve accompanied by very thinly sliced smoked meat or fish.

CLASSICAL MELON WITH HAM

AS AN APPETIZER: Wrap thinly sliced prosciutto, Parma or Westphalian ham around cubes of cantaloupe or similar solid melon and secure with a wooden pick. Serve with a pepper mill that grinds pepper roughly.

AS A FIRST COURSE: Knife-thin slices of the same meats may be served with wedges of the softer melons—honeydew, Persian, or Spanish. With these a pepper mill and a small bowl of lemon chutney may be served.

HAM WITH OTHER FRUITS

AS AN APPETIZER: Wrap any of the above hams around cubes of apples, bananas, or pineapple. These have the disadvantage that apples and bananas must be served soon after they have been prepared.

AS A FIRST COURSE: Thin slices of the same hams make a lovely combination with ripe figs, or with apple slices filmed with cinnamon. Half peaches filmed with ground cloves and ground ginger are equally good.

FRUIT WITH OTHER MEATS

AS AN APPETIZER: Spread chicken liver pâté, game, or smoked turkey pâté on bread rounds, top them with green seedless grapes.

AS A FIRST COURSE: Serve sliced pâtés or cold sliced game with orange sections and Cumberland Sauce. Serve thick cross slices of peeled and cored ripe pear on thin slices of cold beef, fill the cavity with melted red currant jelly beaten with English mustard and chilled. Place a slice of cold roast pork on a slice of buttered brown bread. Cover it with a thick slice of peeled and cored apple. Trim bread and meat to be only a little wider circle than the apple. Fill the cavity with apple jelly and chopped mint.

FRUIT WITH SMOKED FISHES

AS AN APPETIZER: Wrap thin strips of smoked salmon around cubes of melon or apple and secure with a wooden pick.

AS A FIRST COURSE: Herring fillets with sliced apples and cover with half and half sour cream and mustard mayonnaise, garnish with dill. Combine sliced smoked sturgeon with ice-cold cantaloupe wedges, capers, freshly ground pepper, and lemon slices.

SHRIMP WITH FRUIT

Prepare and chill shrimp, drain grapefruit and retain the juice. Combine shrimp, grapefruit, melon balls and green pepper and chill. Beat grapefruit juice into jelly, chutney, mustard, and kirsch and add orange juice and rind. Season and pour the sauce over the shrimp and fruit and serve very cold.

1 pound large shrimp peeled, deveined, cooked
1 can grapefruit sections
1 small cantaloupe, scooped out into melon balls
¼ green pepper, seeded and finely diced
1 3½-ounce jar red Bar-le-Duc, or ¼ cup red currant jelly, melted
¼ cup chutney, chopped
1 to 2 teaspoons mild brown mustard, preferably Dijon
¼ cup kirsch
½ cup orange juice, grated rind of 1 orange
Salt and freshly ground pepper to taste

SHRIMP WITH GRAPEFRUIT

Prepare the shrimp. Prepare the grapefruit, or drain the canned grapefruit, retaining the juice in either case. Arrange the shrimp and grapefruit sections alternately on a serving dish. Beat the grapefruit juice (not more than ¼ cup) into the mayonnaise with the onion, dill, and eggs. Pour sauce over and sprinkle with parsley.

1 pound large shrimp, peeled, deveined, and cooked
2 large fresh grapefruit, cut into sections free of membrane, or 1 8-ounce can grapefruit sections
1 cup thick mayonnaise
½ onion, finely chopped
2 teaspoons finely cut dill, or 1 teaspoon dried dill weed, scalded
2 hard-cooked eggs, chopped
3 tablespoons finely chopped parsley

MELONS FILLED WITH FRUIT AND SHRIMP

Scoop all the meat out of 2 melon halves and discard the shells. Take about half the meat out of the remaining 6 halves and drain them well. Cut the melon meat into large dice, combine it with shrimp and grapes, and bind it with Italian dressing. Fill the drained melon halves with the salad and sprinkle with pistachio nuts. Garnish with mint sprigs and serve as a first course or as a luncheon salad.

4 small cantaloupes, chilled, cut in half, seeded, and drained
1 pound medium cooked shrimp or lobster meat
1 pound red grapes, cut in half and seeded
1 cup Italian Dressing
½ cup chopped pistachio nuts
6 sprigs mint

MELONS FILLED WITH MUSTARD FRUITS

Add the mustard pickle to the whipped cream with salt to taste. Drain melon halves well, divide the cream over them, and sprinkle with the candied ginger.

½ cup finely chopped mustard pickle
¾ cup heavy cream, whipped
Salt to taste
3 small cantaloupes, chilled and cut in half with a notched edge, seeded and drained
2 tablespoons finely cut candied ginger

MELON WITH SMOKED TONGUE

Cut the melon in half, remove the seeds, and cut it into 8 wedges. Peel the wedges and chill them until needed. Stir the Bar-le-Duc with ginger, mustard, orange juice and rind, and the kirsch. Season to taste with pepper. Arrange the melon wedges on 2 cold plates, pour over the sauce, and sprinkle with the slivers of tongue. Serve very cold.

1 very small ripe cantaloupe, iced
1 jar Bar-le-Duc, red currant preserve
2 teaspoons minced preserved or candied ginger
1 teaspoon Dijon mustard
3 tablespoons orange juice and grated rind
1 tablespoon kirsch, or to taste
Freshly ground black pepper to taste
4 slices smoked tongue, trimmed and cut into a fine julienne

RED CAVIAR ROUNDS

Separate eggs, rice the yolks through a sieve, and combine them lightly with red caviar, onion, and parsley. Lay a ring of egg white on each bread round, rice the remaining white into the mixture, and fill it high into the rings.

4 hard-cooked eggs, peeled and sliced
1 4-ounce jar red salmon caviar
¼ cup each chopped onion and parsley
18 to 24 buttered whole-wheat bread rounds
as large as a center egg slice

CHICKEN LIVER PÂTÉ

Sauté the onion in ½ cup of the butter until it is puffed and transparent. Add the chicken livers and brown them quickly so that the inside will remain pink. Take from heat, season to taste, and stir in mustard and ground spices. Put the contents of the pan through the finest blade of the meat grinder and stir in the sherry and remaining butter, or add sherry and remaining butter and put it through the blender in 2 or 3 batches. Pack the pâté into a crock and chill it until needed. Serve with toast fingers and small bunches of green seedless grapes.

1 onion, chopped
¾ cup butter at room temperature
1 pound chicken livers
Salt and pepper to taste
¼ teaspoon dry mustard
⅛ teaspoon each ground cloves and ground
cinnamon
3 tablespoons dry sherry
Green seedless grapes

VARIATIONS: Omit the mustard and add 2 tablespoons brandy.

Omit the spices and substitute 1 teaspoon minced thyme. Substitute 4 chopped shallots for the onion.

Add 2 tablespoons mayonnaise and stir ¼ cup chopped pecans into the finished pâté.

ICED AVOCADO

Select the smallest avocados available, but not those rare miniatures.

Cut very cold avocados in half. Remove the pits and pour a little light rum into the hollows. Grate the rind of 1 lime over the rum, cut the lime in half and squeeze the juice over the 6 avocado halves. Arrange them on 6 small plates and sprinkle them with a very little

3 very small avocados
Rum
4 limes
2 teaspoons confectioner's sugar

sugar just before serving. Garnish each half avocado with half a lime, which should be squeezed over the fruit before it is eaten out of the shell with a small spoon.

GRAPEFRUIT COCKTAIL

Peel a wide strip of the thinnest outside rind from each grapefruit with a potato peeler and cut it into long slivers with kitchen scissors. Slice remaining rind from the grapefruit with a sharp knife, and cut the grapefruit sections, free of all white pith, pulp, or pits, into a bowl. Work a little of the grapefruit juice with the mustard until smooth. Melt the jelly over boiling water and stir in the mustard mixture and the slivered rind and continue cooking, uncovered, until the rind is slightly softened. Add sherry to taste and chill the sauce. Divide the drained grapefruit sections over 6 cocktail glasses, pour over the sauce, and serve very cold.

3 grapefruit
½ cup Dijon mustard, or to taste
½ cup red currant jelly
1 to 2 cups dry sherry to taste

COLD LUXURIES

There is a glamour attached to some of the cold foods which few hot dishes can achieve. Most especially the first courses and small supper dishes provide such a contrast in tastes, textures, and color that they are automatically (and for financial reasons) always associated with *the great event*.

On these special occasions, when the hostess should celebrate with her guests, or when she wants to devote herself to a single guest, the cold luxuries—prepared well in advance—are unsurpassed. They are always gala, always beautiful and memorable. The following recipes for this little group of luxury dishes are planned for two. The extravagant hostess can simply multiply them when she has more guests.

At the turn of the century, lobster, caviar, and goose liver spelled luxury. We still use them but no longer by the Russian pound. Now they are combined and accompanied and some of the cold luxuries are based on trout, smoked fishes, and the lowly herring. It is the combinations and the contrasts that make them luxurious.

THE BEST TARTARE

Beefsteak tartare is usually prepared to taste and every tartare lover has a different and defended preference. The Best Tartare is the simplest . . . namely with no additions except caviar. It rests on the classical buttered toast and the classical accompaniment is champagne.

Cut crusts from the bread, cut each slice into quarters, and put them on a baking sheet. Toast them lightly in the broiler—but not too near the source of heat—and turn them to toast the other side. Let them cool. While all this is going on, start to scrape the beef with the edge of a silver spoon, directions on page 115. Butter the toast and as the pinkish-red portions of beef fall from the bowl of the spoon, put them on the prepared toast squares. Handle the beef as little as possible, but do fold it back from the edges. Top each square with a generous spoon of caviar and serve without waiting—toast can be prepared in advance.

4 thin slices of a dense white bread
1 slice top round of beef, about 1-inch thick
⅓ cup unsalted fresh butter
½ pound Beluga Malossol caviar, iced

CAVIAR IN TOMATO SLICES (For 2)

This recipe cannot be properly made until large tomatoes can be found; they should measure at least 3½ inches through the center. Dip them in boiling water and then in cold water and draw off the skins. Cut them across, just above and just below the center, to give yourself 2 *slabs* of tomatoes that must be 1¼ inches thick. Carefully empty them of seeds and chill them. Just before serving put them on a paper kitchen towel for a moment and pat them dry with a second towel. Arrange them on 2 small plates and fill 2 of the natural cavities of the fruit, where the seeds were, with riced egg yolk. Fill caviar into at least 2 of the cavities in each slice of tomato and onion and egg white into 1 each. Plan it in such a way that the cavities filled with the onion and the egg white will not be next to each other. With really thick slices of large tomatoes, the *fillings* will be used up (any remaining riced egg can go into a salad with the remaining tomato). Garnish the filled tomatoes with water cress, serve them very cold with a bowl of cream herb mayonnaise.

2 ripe, freshly picked, round tomatoes
2 hard-cooked eggs, yolks and whites riced separately
4 ounces Malossol caviar
2 tablespoons finely chopped onion
2 sprigs crisp water cress, coarse stems removed
1 recipe Cream Herb Mayonnaise (given below)

CREAM HERB MAYONNAISE

In the warmed mixing bowl of an electric beater, beat the egg yolks until very light. Add the white pepper and vinegar and beat well. Beat in the olive oil, drop by drop. Continue beating and add half the lemon juice. Add the salad oil, drop by drop, until the mayonnaise has thickened, then add it in a thin stream. When it is all incorporated, beat in the last of the lemon juice, onion juice, and herbs. Chill the mayonnaise until needed. Beat it with a fork and fold in the whipped cream just before serving.

If the oil is too cold, the mayonnaise *may* show signs of separating. Pour it into another bowl, rinse the beater and bowl in warm water, and dry them well. Beat a fresh egg yolk and gradually beat the separated mayonnaise into it.

2 egg yolks at room temperature
¼ teaspoon white pepper
1 teaspoon tarragon vinegar
¼ cup olive oil, at 70 to 75° F.
1 teaspoon lemon juice
¾ cup salad oil, at 70 to 75° F.
3 drops onion juice
2 tablespoons mixed minced fresh herbs. Use as many of these as possible: tarragon, chervil, parsley, and basil
¼ cup cream, stiffly whipped

ROAST BEEF WITH CAVIAR

Roast the beef according to directions on page 204, keeping it very rare. Cool and chill the roast until shortly before serving. Carve it into 7 thick slices, setting the first cut aside for another purpose. Trim the slices, and if they are from the first ribs, use only the eye. Arrange the 6 slices of beef on 6 chilled plates and add 2 tomato slices and sprigs of water cress to each serving. Spread the caviar on the beef, or center the beef with a rounded tablespoon of caviar and serve the White Wine Onion Sauce from a crystal or porcelain sauceboat or bowl. Pass cold butter and toast.

1 3-rib roast of beef or 6 thick slices of leftover rare cold roast beef
3 large tomatoes, peeled and thickly sliced
½ bunch crisp water cress
½ pound Beluga Malossol caviar

WHITE WINE ONION SAUCE

Place yolks and wine in the top of a large double boiler *over* (not touching) boiling water. Beat the mixture until it is thickened and smooth and doubled in bulk. Beat in the remaining ingredients except cream and cool the sauce. When it is cold, fold in the whipped cream and serve. If the sauce is prepared long in advance, refrigerate it until needed; fold in the cream and serve.

3 egg yolks
¾ cup white wine
1 small onion, finely minced
1 teaspoon mild brown mustard
Salt and freshly ground pepper to taste
1 lemon, juice and grated rind
½ teaspoon sugar, optional
1 tablespoon minced herbs: parsley, chervil, and tarragon
½ cup heavy cream, whipped

TROUT IN ASPIC (For 2)

This recipe can be increased to any quantity, allowing 1 trout for each person. It is here among the good dishes for 2, because boning a trout is a pleasant occupation, but it does not go well with dinner conversation. When trout are served at a small dinner, there can be a congenial silence while they are being boned.

Stir the gelatin into the wine and set it aside. Arrange the trout in a buttered small oval baking dish, which will ultimately be brought to the table, and pour over the boiling marinade. Cover the pan with foil and poach the trout over low heat until they are tender and done, depending on their size, about 10 minutes. Take from heat and carefully stir in the gelatin until it is dissolved. Cool the trout in their marinade and chill them until the aspic is set. Just before serving cover the trout with the paper-thin onion slices, the equally thin carrot slices, bright green parsley, and lemon slices.

NOTE: The pan in which the trout are poached and served must be small enough so that the marinade will almost cover the trout. If it is large, double the marinade and gelatin.

1 envelope gelatin
¼ cup dry white wine
2 fresh drawn or 1 box frozen trout, thawed
1 recipe White Wine Marinade (given below)
1 onion, sliced paper thin
1 carrot, sliced equally thin, scalded and cooled
2 tablespoons finely chopped parsley
1 lemon cut into thin slices

WHITE WINE MARINADE

Combine all ingredients, bring them to a boil, and boil for 10 minutes. Take out the bay leaf and pour the marinade over the trout while it is boiling.

2 cups dry white wine
½ cup tarragon vinegar
1 bay leaf
2 sprigs fresh thyme, or 1 teaspoon dried
4 shallots, chopped
½ onion, chopped
½ carrot, scraped and finely diced
3 tablespoons chopped parsley (if you have a garden, pull up a parsley root and slice it into the marinade)

LOBSTER IN MUSTARD SAUCE (For 2)

Split the cooked lobster, and crack the claws. Take out the tomalley (green) and the coral (pink) and set them aside. Cut the tail meat into slices with a sharp knife and clean the 2 half shells. Chill meat, shells, and shrimp until needed. Boil the sliced raw potatoes for a few minutes in salted water. Watch them carefully, as they should be firm and perfect (that is the whole reason for doing them in this way). Fish them out with a slotted spoon and immediately douse them with white wine. When ready to serve, bind the lobster meat very lightly with mayonnaise and arrange it at the head of the emptied shells. Place the shells on 2 plates, give each plate a cracked claw, a lemon wedge, and a little parsley or water cress. Stand 3 shrimp, back up, in the center of the shells and fill the potato slices into the tails. Sprinkle truffles on the lobster, and egg yolk on the shrimp, and grind white pepper over the potatoes. Serve with mustard-flavored cold Hollandaise Sauce.

1 small lobster, about 1 pound, boiled in Court Bouillon for 15 minutes and cooled in the bouillon
6 shrimp, shelled, deveined, and boiled for just 4 minutes
2 small potatoes, peeled and cut into thin slices
3 tablespoons dry white wine
Mayonnaise to bind
Lemon wedges
Parsley
1 small truffle, peeled and diced
1 hard-cooked egg yolk, riced
White pepper

LOBSTER COCKTAIL

Chill prepared lobster meat and plan to add avocados, cut in large cubes, and apple, diced, shortly before serving. Sprinkle immediately with lime juice. Beat mayonnaise with chili sauce, cream, and gin and serve with the cocktails, ice cold, and sprinkle with freshly minced herbs, hopefully containing tarragon and chervil, or marjoram.

1½ pounds lobster meat, cubed
1 or 2 avocados
1 tart apple, peeled and cored
2 tablespoons lime juice
1 cup Lemon Mayonnaise
¼ cup strained chili sauce
2 tablespoons sour cream
1 to 2 tablespoons gin, or to taste
1 tablespoon minced herbs

HEARTS OF PALM WITH CAVIAR (For 2)

Turn oven to 200° F. about 45 minutes before dinner. Trim crusts from the melba toast bread and butter it very lightly. Cut each slice into 4 fingers, lay them flat on a baking sheet, and toast them for 30 minutes. Drain the hearts of palm and cut them in half lengthwise. Arrange them on 2 small plates and keep them cold until the last minute. Put the mayonnaise into a small porcelain sauceboat or crystal bowl and keep it cold. Just before serving, when the toast fingers are golden, put the entire caviar on the center of the mayonnaise. Serve the hearts of palm with the toast and mayonnaise. Fold the caviar through the mayonnaise and divide it over the hearts of palm. The toast must still be faintly warm and the mayonnaise must be stiff enough so that the caviar does not sink down into it, but thin enough to make a *flowing* sauce.

3 slices melba toast bread
*2 tablespoons unsalted butter, at room
    temperature*
1 No. 2½ can hearts of palm, chilled
⅔ cup Lemon Mayonnaise, whipped smooth
4 ounces Beluga Malossol caviar, chilled

HEARTS OF PALM WITH SMOKED SALMON
(For 2)

Drain the hearts of palm well. Marinate them in the wine dressing for 1 hour in the refrigerator. Wrap each heart in a slice of smoked salmon. Arrange them on 2 small plates with the end of the salmon turned underneath. Pour the remaining marinade over them, sprinkle generously with truffle dice. Pass the filbert mayonnaise in a porcelain or crystal sauceboat or bowl.

1 No. 2½ can hearts of palm, chilled
¾ cup French Wine Dressing (given below)
*3 to 4 thin slices smoked salmon, or as many
    as there are hearts of palm*
1 large or 2 small peeled truffles, diced
1 recipe Filbert Mayonnaise (given below)

FRENCH WINE DRESSING

Put vinegar, wine, and salt into a shallow bowl and beat with a fork until the salt is dissolved. Add the onion and grind the pepper over the mixture. Beat in oil and continue to beat until the dressing is smooth and thickened. It may be beaten with a crackling-cold ice cube, but it must be taken out before it melts into the dressing.

2 tablespoons tarragon wine vinegar
1 tablespoon red wine
1 teaspoon salt
1 teaspoon finely minced onion or onion juice
½ teaspoon freshly ground white pepper
9 tablespoons olive or salad oil, cold

FILBERT MAYONNAISE

Blend hazelnuts with oil until they are coarsely chopped. Pour into a bowl, stir in the paprika, celery salt, and parsley and fold the mixture into cold mayonnaise. Lastly, fold in the riced egg.

½ cup hazelnuts
2 tablespoons olive oil
1 teaspoon paprika
1 teaspoon celery salt
2 teaspoons minced parsley
⅓ cup cold mayonnaise, whipped
1 hard-cooked egg, riced

HEARTS OF LEEK

Steam leeks in salted water until barely tender, depending on size, about 15 minutes. Drain and marinate them for 1 hour in marinade. When they are cold, cut a deep hollow down the side to make a small canoe. Fill hollow with caviar mixed with riced egg, parsley, and horseradish. Arrange the filled leeks on small plates and serve with mayonnaise.

1 bunch thick leeks trimmed to white part
    only and cut into even lengths
1 cup French Salad Marinade
1 ounce jar Beluga Malossol caviar
1 hard-cooked egg, riced
2 tablespoons finely chopped parsley
2 tablespoons finely grated fresh horseradish

HERRINGS

Lay the herrings into fresh water for at least 8 hours, changing the water frequently. If they are very salty, after 8 hours in water, lay them in seltzer water to cover for 2 hours. Cut off heads and tails and cut down the back with a very sharp knife. Draw off the skin and bone the fish carefully to keep the fillets intact. Arrange them in a shallow pan and cover them with milk and 4 ice cubes. Set them in the refrigerator for 2 hours. Drain the herring fillets, arrange them in a shallow crystal bowl, and prepare them in one of the following ways:

4 salt herrings
Milk to cover

ITALIAN Pour over ½ cup Italian Dressing, and cover the fillets first with 4 large pitted ripe olives, sliced across, and then with 2 tablespoons minced capers. Rice 2 hard-cooked egg whites over the capers and rice the yolks over the whites. End with 2 tablespoons chopped parsley and 1 teaspoon chopped tarragon. Add a fresh grinding of black pepper and chill until needed.

IN SOUR CREAM Combine 1 cup sour cream, ½ cup mayonnaise, 1 teaspoon paprika, ½ teaspoon dry mustard, and 1 pinch sugar. Pour this sauce over the prepared fillets. Steam 2 finely sliced onions in ½ cup white wine and 2 tablespoons wine vinegar for 2 or 2½ minutes and cool them in the wine. Divide them over the herrings and garnish the dish with a circle of very thin slices of 1 large peeled and cored apple and 1 large dill pickle.

FRENCH Arrange the fillets between 2 rows of overlapping cooked potato slices. Cover with a mixture of 6 chopped shallots, 1 tablespoon chopped chervil, 2 teaspoons chopped tarragon, and 3 tablespoons chopped fennel. Pour over French Dressing to taste and serve very cold.

SHRIMP ON ARTICHOKE BOTTOMS

Boil the shrimp for just 4 minutes in salted water to cover with dill and vinegar. Drain the artichoke bottoms well. Marinate them in the French salad marinade for 1 hour. Simmer the truffles in white wine for 15 minutes, drain, peel, and cut them into short matchsticks. Return the peels to the wine and cook until reduced to 3 tablespoons. Strain and add the truffle essence to the mayonnaise. Arrange artichoke bottoms on a small crystal serving platter and lay 1 cold shrimp on each. Spread or pipe the truffle-flavored mayonnaise over the shrimp and sprinkle the truffle matchsticks generously over the top. Serve very cold.

6 jumbo shrimp, peeled and deveined
1 sprig dill
2 tablespoons tarragon vinegar
6 canned fonds d'artichauts
1 cup French Salad Marinade
3 truffles, scrubbed
1 cup dry white wine
⅔ cup mayonnaise

SMOKED SALMON IN CUCUMBERS (For 2)

Peel the cucumbers, cut them in half lengthwise, and blanch them in salted water. Scoop out the seeds in the center, making the cucumber halves into little boats. Drain them well and fill them with a mixture of salmon, herring, and eggs. Moisten with French Dressing. Grate horseradish and pepper over them and serve them chilled with mayonnaise, whipped with cream and dill.

2 small, straight young cucumbers, not over
    5½ to 6 inches long
½ teaspoon salt
½ cup diced smoked salmon
½ cup herring fillets in wine, drained and
    chopped
2 hard-cooked eggs, riced
½ cup French Dressing
1 tablespoon finely grated horseradish
Freshly grated black pepper to taste
1 cup mayonnaise
¼ cup heavy cream
2 tablespoons finely cut dill

FRANKFORT ARTICHOKES
stuffed with ham and vegetable salad

Remove coarse outside leaves from artichokes and trim stems even with the base, so they will stand upright. Turn them on their sides and cut them through with a sharp knife just above the middle or thickest part. This removes the pointed end and the coarse ends of the leaves. Trim leaves evenly with a kitchen scissors. Boil the artichokes in a covered kettle with vinegar, salt, and water to cover for 20 to 25 minutes or until a center leaf pulls out easily. Pull out the center leaves and remove the chokes with a spoon while the artichokes are still warm. Turn them over to drain well, then turn them right side up and sprinkle the cavities with lemon juice. Combine tomato, ham, celery, peas, pepper, dill pickle, and half the chives. Beat the lemon rind into the mayonnaise and St. Regis dressing and stir half of it into the ham and vegetable salad. Fill the salad into the artichokes, sprinkle them with the chopped egg and remaining chives and serve with the remaining mayonnaise.

6 medium artichokes
2 tablespoons vinegar
2 teaspoons salt, or to taste
1 lemon, juice and grated rind
½ cup peeled, seeded, and diced tomatoes
½ cup diced ham
½ cup diced celery
½ cup cooked green peas
1 small red or green sweet pepper, seeded
    and diced
¼ cup diced and drained dill pickle
¼ cup chopped chives
¼ cup mayonnaise
½ cup St. Regis Dressing
2 hard-cooked eggs, chopped

ITALIAN ARTICHOKES
stuffed with rice and bacon salad

Remove coarse outside leaves from artichokes and trim stems even with the base so they will stand upright. Turn them on their sides and cut them through with a sharp knife just above the middle or thickest part. This removes the pointed end and the coarse ends of the leaves. Trim leaves evenly with a kitchen scissors. Boil the artichokes in a covered kettle with vinegar, salt, and water to cover for 20 to 25 minutes or until a center leaf pulls out easily. Pull out the center leaves and remove the chokes with a spoon while the artichokes are still warm. Turn them over to drain well, then turn them right side up and sprinkle the cavities with lemon juice. Combine rice, bacon, tomatoes, peas, pimento, and half the chives. Beat the mayonnaise and the Italian dressing and stir half of it into the rice and bacon salad. Fill the salad into the artichokes, sprinkle them with the remaining chives and serve with the remaining mayonnaise.

6 medium artichokes
2 tablespoons vinegar
2 teaspoons salt, or to taste
1 lemon, juice only
½ cup cold cooked rice
½ cup crisp bacon dice or ham (browned chicken liver dice may be substituted)
1½ cups peeled, seeded, and diced tomatoes
½ cup cooked green peas
¼ cup diced pimento
¼ cup cut chives or finely chopped onions
1 cup mayonnaise
½ cup Italian Dressing

SOUPS

CHAPTER THREE

Soups, Clear, Creamed,
and Canned Soups Enhanced

THE difference between hot and cold soups is enormous. Their character changes with the temperature and so does their popularity. No hostess would dream of having her dinner guests sit down to a hot leek and potato soup in winter, but she starts them off—unhesitatingly—with vichyssoise in summer. Cold soups are apparently considered worthy of the guest, while hot soups, more often, are reserved for the family. We consume millions of cans of soup a year—but rarely when we are entertaining each other.

We are not a nation of hot soup lovers. There are no soup pots constantly "smiling" on the backs of our stoves, nor do we start off one meal a day with steaming soup. Few of us own wide soup plates or a large soup kettle—let alone a soup tureen—but we all have cups for cold soup.

With our hearts in the right place, where cold soups are concerned, it seems a shame that we do not go far beyond jellied chicken soup, madrilène, and vichyssoise. Lately gazpacho has joined the list but there is still an unexplored world of fabulous cold soups . . . thick and thin . . . cooked and uncooked.

There is beautiful sénégalaise and cold mulligatawny—for a light touch of curry. For a day of activity, or after an invigorating swim, serve an ice cold black bean soup with lots of paper thin slices of lemon. Consider a chilled cream of green pea soup, garnished with scooped-out tomato slices filled with minced onion and mint leaves. Or the same soup laced with sherry and garnished with cooked shrimp and dill. Cold apricot or sour cherry soup has a faint taste of cinnamon or cloves. A slice of orange in the tomato soup . . . it goes on forever.

Above all, the cold soups can be prepared ahead. They sit patiently waiting in the refrigerator or freezer and only have to be thawed or blended before they are served. They are economical and healthy and they can shine where a hot version of the same soup would never do.

A Few Suggested Cold Soup Recipes

CLEAR SOUP

AVOCADO Place diced avocado, cucumber, tomatoes, and chopped parsley in bowls, pour over chilled tomato juice and garnish with lemon slices.

BORSCH Combine beef stock with beet juice and a julienne of beets and cabbage. Garnish with sour cream and cut dill.

KOLODNIK Fill soup bowls with quartered hard-cooked eggs, shrimp, lemon slices, cut chives and dill, diced cucumbers, and cooked diced beets. Add ice cubes and pour over a beef-beet soup or bottled borsch. Garnish with sour cream.

MADEIRA   Add Madeira wine to strong, clear chicken stock. Chill and garnish with finely diced melon and minced herbs.

CLEAR MULLIGATAWNY   Add chopped onions and ham to chicken stock, flavored with curry powder and garnished with cold cooked rice, cooked chicken pieces, and diced apple.

CREAM SOUP

ABJY L'AMID   Chill Cream of Potato Soup, thin it with cold milk and yogurt, and flavor it with lemon juice to taste. Serve the soup garnished with thin lemon slices and chopped mint.

BON VALET   Combine half chilled Cream of Potato and Leek Soup, with half Cream of Water Cress Soup, and garnish with cooked green peas and small sprigs of water cress.

BOTWINJA   Blend chilled Cream of Spinach Soup with a chilled dry white wine to taste and garnish with diced cucumbers, onions, and snipped dill. Pass grated horseradish separately, and on special occasions pass strips of smoked salmon.

BROCCOLI   Chill Cream of Chicken Soup and garnish it with rosettes of cooked broccoli covered with slivered lemon rind.

CHANTILLY   Combine half Cream of Lettuce, half Cream of Spinach soups. Garnish with salted whipped cream and riced hard-cooked egg.

CLERMONT   Combine in equal parts chilled Cream of Onion Soup, and Cream of Celery Soup. Beat or blend in ½ cup each unsweetened purée of chestnuts and heavy cream. Garnish with finely cut spring onions in summer and with chopped toasted almonds in winter.

CRÉCY   Combine Cream of Chicken and Celery soups. Blend with cooked carrots and with cream. Garnish with chopped chervil and minced raw carrot (very like a rich vichyssoise).

CRESSONIÈRE   Blend fresh water cress and Cream of Potato Soup with sliced onions and cream. Garnish with diced apple, toasted crumbs, and water cress.

HORTENSE   Serve chilled Cream of Chicken Soup with 1 cold artichoke bottom in each soup plate and fill the artichoke with diced cold chicken meat mixed with chopped parsley. For a richer soup, hard-cooked egg yolk may be riced over the filled artichoke bottom.

UNCOOKED SOUPS

APPLE   Combine raw applesauce and white wine, lightly sugared and spiced. Garnish with raisins puffed in brandy.

CEVICHE   Shrimp or fish marinated in lime and lemon juice with paper-thin onion slices, garnished with diced tomato, avocado, and chopped parsley. The citrus juices cook the shrimp or fish.

GAZPACHO   Tomatoes, cucumbers, onion and green pepper, blended with a slice of whole-wheat bread, French dressing, garlic, ice, and tomato juice.

CANNED SOUPS ENHANCED

AMBASSADRICE   Half fill chilled bouillon cups with diced cold cooked chicken meat, raw sliced mushrooms, and finely chopped parsley and pour over cold (but not stiff) jellied chicken consommé. Garnish top with hard-cooked egg slices.

AURORA   Half fill chilled bouillon cups with diced cold cooked chicken meat and peeled, seeded, and diced tomatoes. Pour over cold (but not stiff) jellied chicken consommé and garnish with chopped parsley.

BLACK BEAN   Add wine, serve as cold as possible with paper thin lemon slices.

CHATELAINE   Pour cold (but not stiff) jellied chicken consommé over finely chopped onions, cold cooked green peas, and raw sliced mushrooms.

CREAM OF TOMATO   1. Add sherry, serve as cold as possible, garnished with crab meat.
2. Add orange juice, serve as cold as possible, garnished with orance slices and mint.

LILLIENNE   Pour chilled but not set madrilène over thinly sliced mushrooms and a diced truffle if possible.

Sprinkle top with finely chopped tarragon and chervil and garnish with a thin lemon slice.

LOBSTER BISQUE   Add cream, sherry, and minced tarragon and garnish with pieces of lobster.

MADRILÈNE   Serve cold, but not stiffly jellied, over a bed of red caviar, chopped tomatoes, and parsley.

MURILLO   Garnish chilled Cream of Tomato Soup with paper-thin onion slices covered with minced basil and chopped pine nuts.

VICHYSSOISE   Flavor lightly with curry powder, serve as cold as possible with a garnish of whipped cream, toasted almonds, and water cress.

AVOCADO SOUP

Blend chilled consommé and cream with lime juice, onion, and lemon peel until smooth. Crush the avocado and combine it with the soup or blend it with the soup. Season with salt and freshly ground pepper and serve garnished with lime slices and a few retained avocado dice.

1½ cans jellied chicken consommé
1 cup sour cream
2 limes, 1 for juice and 1 sliced
1 slice onion
1 long curl lemon peel, cut into strips
1½ cups diced avocado
Salt and pepper to taste

KOLODNIK

Combine the bouillon or borsch with beets, tops, cucumbers, eggs, shrimp, and sturgeon. Season the mixture to taste and stir in the sour cream. If the soup is too thick, thin with more bouillon or borsch. Sprinkle the soup generously with cut dill and garnish with paper-thin lemon slices. Serve it with pieces of cracked ice in each bowl or plate.

2 cups cold beef bouillon or borsch
2 cooked beets, diced
1 cup cooked beet tops, chopped fine
2 cucumbers, peeled, seeded, and diced
3 hard-cooked eggs, chopped
1 pound cooked shrimp, quartered
3 slices smoked sturgeon, cut into strips
Salt and freshly ground pepper
3 cups sour cream
2 tablespoons finely cut dill
2 lemons, sliced very thin

MULLIGATAWNY

Place the chicken pieces in a large kettle with celery, 2 carrots, pepper and salted cold water to cover. Depending on the size of the kettle, there should be about 11 cups water. Cover and bring the water to a boil. Reduce heat and simmer until chicken is tender, about 3½ hours. Take out the chicken, take meat from the bones, and cut it into large dice. Return the bones to the kettle and boil uncovered until the stock is reduced to about 8 cups. Strain it and discard bones and vegetables. Melt the butter in a saucepan, sauté the chicken dice and onion until lightly browned. Take out the meat and onion with a slotted spoon. Crush the curry powder, flour, sugar, cloves, and mace in the butter into a smooth paste with the back of a wooden spoon. Rinse the kettle, return the strained broth to it with the chicken and vegetables, and cook the soup until they are almost tender. Working in the curry powder paste, about 15 minutes before the soup is done. Add the apples and tomatoes and cook for a few minutes longer. Cool and chill the soup. Lift off any fat and stir in the rice. Serve very cold in wide plates. The rice is always passed separately in India and the vegetables are puréed through a sieve. But real mulligatawny is a hot soup and the chef at the Taj Mahal Hotel in Bombay does it this way and serves it ice cold.

1 stewing chicken, disjointed
2 celery stalks
2 carrots, quartered
4 peppercorns
Salt to taste
½ cup, or 1 cube, butter
1 onion, finely chopped
1 tablespoon Madras curry powder, or to taste
1 tablespoon corn flour, or plain flour
1 teaspoon sugar, or to taste
¼ teaspoon ground cloves
½ teaspoon ground mace
1 heart of celery, scraped and finely diced
1 carrot, scraped and finely diced
1 green pepper, seeded and diced
2 cooking apples, peeled, cored, and diced
3 tomatoes, peeled, seeded, and diced
1½ cups cold cooked rice

All cream soups are as good when they are served cold as when they are hot. With the advantage that they require less or none of the butter-flour combination. Using jellied chicken consommé as a base and blending some of the ingredients tends to thicken the soups and less white sauce is needed. While we can serve a hot cream soup with an unadorned surface, the chilled cream soups need a garnish. It can be for looks only, but a sprinkling of something that compliments the flavor is much more interesting.

CREAM OF GREEN PEAS

Cook peas in stock with onion, lettuce, and seasonings until very soft. Blend in 2 or 3 batches until smooth. Melt butter in the top of a double boiler over boiling water. Stir in flour and gradually stir in the milk. Cook until thickened and stir with a French wire whisk until smooth. Take from heat and cool. Stir in the purée of peas and chill the soup until needed. Thin it to desired consistency with cream and serve it plain or in any of the following ways:

2 packages frozen green peas
2 cups chicken stock or water and 2 chicken bouillon cubes
1 small onion, sliced
2 lettuce leaves, torn into pieces
Salt and white pepper to taste
1 pinch sugar
4 tablespoons butter
4 tablespoons flour
2 cups milk
1 cup heavy cream

ARABELLA'S GREEN PEA SOUP

Center wide soup plates with rosettes of 1 large cooked and chilled cauliflower. Sprinkle with ½ cup cooked green peas and 1 tablespoon finely cut dill. Pour the cream of green peas around them and serve cold with Curry Melba Toast.

ITALIAN CREAM OF GREEN PEA SOUP

Prepare the green pea soup and have ready 1 can chilled cream of tomato soup, slightly thinned with milk, and 1 bottle chilled heavy cream, slightly beaten. Just before serving combine the 3 ingredients in such a way that each plate of green pea soup has a wide swirl of red and white—tomato soup and cream—in it. Serve at once.

CREAM OF GREEN PEA SOUP WITH SHRIMP

Garnish wide soup cups or plates of cream of green pea soup with boiled shrimp, peeled and deveined before being boiled for just 4 minutes. Sprinkle with freshly chopped chervil or chives or cut dill and pass a decanter of dry sherry separately.

POTAGE NAVARIN

Prepare as the above recipe but add enough shrimp that each portion contains at least 3. Thin the soup slightly with light cream, correct the seasoning, and add at least 1½ cups of cooked green peas and sprinkle with lots of freshly chopped parsley.

CREAM OF GREEN PEAS GASPÉ

Boil peas, pods, onion, and lettuce in salted water to cover in a covered kettle for 20 minutes or until very soft. Discard pods and blend the peas, onion, lettuce, and sugar until smooth with only as much as necessary of the water in which they boiled. Melt the butter in a heavy saucepan over very low heat. Stir in the flour until it is smooth and gradually stir in the milk. Continue to stir the soup until it is smooth and thickened. Reduce heat further and let it barely simmer, stirring occasionally, for 20 minutes. Beat the cream and the puréed peas into the soup and chill. Before serving, beat in a little cream if the soup is too thick. Garnish it with the salmon and sprinkle it with dill or parsley.

2 pounds fresh or frozen green peas
10 pea pods, if fresh peas are used
1 small onion, sliced
3 large lettuce leaves, shredded
2 teaspoons salt, or to taste
1 pinch sugar
4 tablespoons butter
5 tablespoons flour
4 cups scalded milk
1 cup heavy cream
1 salmon steak, poached and broken into large flakes
2 tablespoons snipped dill or minced parsley

CHILLED CREAM OF CAULIFLOWER SOUP

Divide the cauliflower into rosettes, slice the tenderest part of the stalk. Cook it in the stock until very soft, about 20 minutes. Put it through the blender in 2 batches until smooth. Melt butter in top of a large double boiler over boiling water. Stir in flour until smooth and gradually stir in the cauliflower soup. Cook until thickened; if too thick dilute with milk to taste, add seasoning. Just before serving whip the cream with a little salt, put it into a soup tureen or bowl with tomatoes and dill, and serve. At the table, pour over the chilled cauliflower soup and mix lightly before serving into cups, plates, or bowls.

1 small head cauliflower
5 cups white stock
4 tablespoons butter
4 tablespoons flour
Salt and pepper to taste
1 cup heavy cream
1 cup peeled, seeded, and diced tomatoes, drained
2 tablespoons finely cut dill

ICED CREAM OF ONION SOUP SOUBISE

Boil the onions in the stock until very soft, then blend them, with the stock, until smooth. Add the cream and season carefully. Chill the soup and add light cream to taste if it is too thick. Serve it in chilled cups, garnish each cup with a thin tomato slice sprinkled with chopped sage. For a smoother soup, beat the egg yolks into the cream. Return the blended soup to the heat, but do not let it come to a boil. Stir in the cream until thickened. Take from heat, season, cool, and chill.

2 pounds onions, sliced
3 cups clear chicken stock
1 cup light cream
Salt and white pepper to taste
2 tomatoes, peeled and sliced
2 tablespoons chopped sage
2 egg yolks, optional

CREAM OF CELERY

Clean celery well, remove all but the inside stalks and all the leaves, and chop them roughly. Reserve the tenderest inside stalks and the trimmed root. Boil the chopped celery and leaves in the stock until very soft. Strain off half the stock and put the remaining stock and celery through the blender. Press the blended soup through a sieve to remove the threads that did not blend, and set it aside. Melt the butter in the top of a double boiler over boiling water, stir in the flour until smooth. Gradually stir in the remaining strained stock and stir until thick and smooth. Add the blended celery mixture and the cream and stir well. Season to taste and cook, stirring occasionally, for 20 minutes. Take from heat, cool, and chill. Thin the soup to taste with milk and serve it very cold with a garnish of the celery heart cut in julienne strips and chopped parsley.

1 head celery
4 cups chicken or veal stock
4 tablespoons butter
6 tablespoons flour
1 cup heavy cream
Salt and white pepper to taste
Milk to taste
2 tablespoons chopped parsley

CREAM OF WATER CRESS

Wash and pick over the water cress carefully and remove all coarse stems. Retain 6 sprigs for garnish. Scald the remaining cress in 1 cup bouillon and set it aside with the bouillon. Melt butter in the top of a double boiler over boiling water. Stir in the flour and gradually add the remaining bouillon. Stir until the soup is smooth and lightly

2 bunches water cress
5 cups chicken bouillon
4 tablespoons butter
5 tablespoons flour
1 cup heavy cream
Salt and white pepper to taste
Milk to taste
1 sweet apple, peeled and diced
¾ cup croutons

thickened. Place the water cress and bouillon in blender, add enough of the thickened soup to cover, and blend until smooth. Add the blended green mixture to the remaining soup, add the cream, and season. Chill the soup, thin it with milk to taste, and serve it garnished with freshly diced apple, water cress sprigs and toasted croutons.

CREAM OF SPINACH

Cook onion and bay leaf in the bouillon for 20 minutes. Wash the spinach and discard the coarse stems and wilted leaves. Put it in a large kettle with only the water that clings to the leaves, and cook it covered, over low heat, until it is wilted and bright green. Set it aside with its broth. Melt the butter in the top of a double boiler over boiling water and stir in the flour until smooth. Stir in the strained stock slowly and stir until thickened and smooth. Thin with the light cream, add the spinach with its broth, and season. Put the soup through the blender in 2 batches and chill until needed. Before serving, beat the soup again and thin it with light cream if necessary. Pour it into 6 chilled cups, pipe a rosette of salted whipped cream on each cup, and sprinkle it lightly with riced hard-cooked egg yolk.

1 onion, sliced
1 bay leaf
3 cups bouillon
1 package washed spinach or ½ pound fresh
5 tablespoons butter
6 tablespoons flour
1 cup light cream
Salt and pepper to taste
1 cup heavy cream, whipped
1 hard-cooked egg yolk

CREAM OF CUCUMBER

Cut ends from the cucumbers and all the areas of the skin that are scarred or tough. Leave the cucumbers about half peeled. Cut them in 4 parts lengthwise and trim out all the seeds. Cut the remaining cucumber strips across into ½-inch slices. Sauté the cucumber slices with the dill weed in the butter over low heat. Do not let the butter brown, and cook until the cucumber pieces are transparent and soft. Over low heat sprinkle with the flour and stir until it has been smoothly absorbed. Gradually stir in the scalded milk and simmer for 15 minutes longer, stirring frequently. Take from heat, stir in the consommé, and season. Blend the contents of the saucepan, in 2 batches, until smooth. Chill the soup and beat in the cream. Serve it garnished with almonds and dill and pass the croutons separately.

3 firm cucumbers
1 pinch dried dill weed
¼ cup butter
2 tablespoons flour
2 cups scalded milk
2 cans jellied chicken consommé
Salt and white pepper to taste
1 cup heavy cream, whipped until thickened
¼ cup slivered scalded almonds
1 sprig fresh dill
1 cup curried bread croutons

CREAM OF SCALLOP SOUP

Pour the scallops into a saucepan with their liquor and sprinkle with salt, lemon juice, and onion. Cover and set in a cool place or in refrigerator for 1 hour. Add the shallots, wine, and mushrooms and simmer over low heat for 6 minutes. Strain the scallops and if they were large cut them into pieces. Retain the broth in which they cooked. Melt the butter in the top of a double boiler over boiling water, stir in the flour until smooth and gradually add the scallop broth and enough milk to make at least 4½ cups. Cook the soup, stirring until smooth and thickened. Add the scallops, strained mushrooms, onion, and shallots and cook for 5 minutes longer. Depending on the amount of liquor that came with the scallops, add milk; there should now be at least 6 cups of soup. Season it well and chill until ready to serve. Divide the soup over 6 wide cups or soup plates, and draw the scallops to the center of the plate. Cover them with a little cream, half whipped with salt, and sprinkle the cream with chives and the lemon rind. Garnish with a little black caviar.

¾ pound bay scallops
1 teaspoon seasoning salt
1 lemon, juice and grated rind
1 small onion, chopped fine
2 shallots, chopped fine
1 cup dry white wine
½ cup finely sliced mushrooms
4 tablespoons butter
4 tablespoons flour
Milk as needed
Salt and white pepper to taste
½ to 1 cup heavy cream, to taste, half whipped
3 tablespoons finely cut chives
1 small jar caviar, optional

CHILLED CREAM OF CHICKEN SOUP AGNÈS SOREL

This soup can be made by boiling a chicken for stock and using part of the chicken meat for the soup. If soup stock is available or a canned chicken consommé is used, buy 1 chicken breast and poach it to obtain the chicken garnish for the soup.

Select 6 evenly sized mushrooms, remove the stems, and set caps aside. Put the remaining mushrooms and all the stems in the chicken stock and cook it until it is well flavored with mushrooms. Melt butter in a heavy saucepan, stir in the flour, and cook for 3 minutes without browning. Gradually add strained stock and stir with a French wire whisk until thickened and smooth, about 5 minutes. Reduce heat and barely simmer the soup, stirring occasionally, for 15 minutes. Take from heat, cool, and chill. Add the heavy cream and correct season-

12 medium mushrooms
4 cups chicken stock
6 tablespoons butter
6 tablespoons flour
Salt and pepper to taste
1 cup heavy cream
1 cold cooked chicken breast, cut into julienne strips
4 slices smoked tongue cut into a fine julienne

ing depending on whether the stock was salted. Serve the soup in chilled soup plates with a julienne of cold chicken and tongue on each portion and the raw mushrooms, sliced paper thin, divided over the chicken and tongue julienne.

VICHYSSOISE I

In a saucepan sauté the leeks and onions in the butter until very soft but not browned. In a second saucepan, boil the potatoes until very soft. Slice them roughly over the leeks and stir once. Add consommé and simmer for 20 minutes. Blend the mixture in 2 batches, thin with cream, season carefully, and chill until needed. Beat in more light cream until the soup is as thin as liked. Serve in chilled cups with a sprinkling of cut chives.

1 bunch leeks, white part only, sliced
2 medium onions, sliced
½ cube butter
2 medium potatoes, peeled
3 cups clear chicken consommé
1 cup heavy cream
Salt and white pepper to taste
1 cup light cream to taste
3 tablespoons finely cut chives

VICHYSSOISE II

Wash leeks well to remove sand. Sauté them in a large kettle in the butter, without letting them get brown, until transparent and soft. Add the potato slices and stir once to coat them with butter. Add the consommé and cook until potatoes have fallen apart, about 40 minutes. Let the soup cool, then put it through the blender in 2 batches. Season it, add half the cream and chill until needed. Before serving, stir in the remaining cream and serve in chilled cups with a sprinkling of chives on each cup.

1 bunch leeks, white part only sliced
½ cube or 4 tablespoons butter
1 pound potatoes, or 3 medium, peeled and sliced
4 cups chicken consommé
Salt and freshly ground white pepper to taste
2 cups light cream, chilled
2 tablespoons finely cut chives

LOBSTER CEVICHE

Marinate 1 pound cooked lobster meat in lemon juice and lime juice and substitute red onions. Follow all other ingredients and directions as for Shrimp Ceviche (given above), but cover the top with tomatoes, melon dice, ripe olives, and parsley.

ECUADORIAN SHRIMP CEVICHE

Start marinating the raw shrimp in a bowl, in the lime and lemon juices, 6 hours before they will be served. Boil the thin onion slices in tomato juice and wine for just 2 minutes. Cool them in the liquid, then pour the whole thing over the shrimp. Beat oil, catsup, Worcestershire sauce, hot sauce, garlic, and parsley together and add them to the shrimp. Cover and refrigerate until ready to serve. Before serving, cover the top of the bowl with a mixture of chopped tomatoes, avocado, olives, and parsley. Serve very cold.

The ceviche can be made with any raw white fish, cut into pieces, steamed scallops, or cooked lobster meat. There need be no hesitation about the raw shrimp, they *cook* in the citrus juices.

1 pound shrimp, peeled and deveined, well washed and dried
Juice of 5 limes
Juice and grated rind of 2 lemons
1½ large Bermuda onions, sliced paper thin and divided into rings
1 cup tomato juice
¼ cup dry white wine
2 tablespoons oil
2 tablespoons tomato catsup
1 teaspoon Worcestershire sauce
1 dash hot sauce
1 clove garlic, crushed
2 tablespoons finely chopped parsley
2 tomatoes, peeled, seeded, and diced
1 ripe avocado, peeled, pitted, and diced
¼ cup sliced stuffed olives
¼ cup chopped parsley

GAZPACHO ANDALUZ

Blend tomatoes and onions and add the vinegar and wine to make at least 6 cups of soup. Crush the garlic with the salt, pepper, paprika, almonds, and sugar in a mortar, then gradually work it into a pliable paste by adding the oil, drop by drop. Stir the tomato soup slowly into the paste and add diced cucumbers, sliced olives and chopped mint or parsley. Chill the soup, stir it well, and serve it in chilled plates with an ice cube in each plate.

2 pounds ripe tomatoes, peeled
2 medium onions, sliced
1 tablespoon wine vinegar
½ cup dry white wine, or to taste
3 cloves garlic, sliced
1 to 2 teaspoons salt to taste
½ teaspoon pepper
1 teaspoon paprika
¼ cup roughly chopped blanched almonds
¼ teaspoon sugar
3 tablespoons olive oil
1 cucumber, about 6 inches long, peeled and diced
½ cup black or ripe olives, sliced
4 sprigs fresh mint, finely chopped
6 ice cubes, fresh out of the freezer

GAZPACHO II

Prepare this as you would a curry, with small dishes containing all the accompaniments, which are added to the gazpacho according to each guest's taste.

1 chopped onion, in a small bowl
1 chopped pimento, in a small bowl
1 cup diced celery, in a small bowl
1 diced green pepper, in a small bowl
1 diced cucumber, in a small bowl
1 bowl of 3 tomatoes, peeled, seeded, and diced
1 bowl of 2 cups garlic-flavored bread croutons

FOR THE SOUP

Prepare the accompaniments. Chill all the soup ingredients. Blend them in several batches and chill. Shake the soup well or blend again just before serving in wide cups or bowls with an ice cube in each. Garnish to taste with the accompanying ingredients.

6 ripe tomatoes, peeled and seeded
2 cucumbers, peeled and roughly sliced
1 clove garlic, sliced
1 onion, sliced
3 tablespoons oil
1 tablespoon vinegar
½ cup tomato juice, or to taste
Salt and pepper to taste

GAZPACHO III

Break the stale bread into the blender container with the garlic. Slice 3 of the tomatoes into the container with the oil and vinegar, half the onion and half the pepper. Add enough tomato juice to come halfway up the ingredients, cover, and blend until smooth. Pour the soup into a cold bowl and repeat with the remaining ingredients. Season and chill the soup until needed. Stir well and serve in wide cups with an ice cube in each. Pass a relish tray with the following ingredients:

1 slice stale whole-wheat bread, crusts removed
1 clove garlic, crushed
6 ripe tomatoes, peeled and seeded
2 tablespoons olive oil
1 tablespoon wine vinegar
1 medium onion, roughly sliced
½ green pepper, seeded and sliced
Salt to taste
Bottled tomato juice

---

2 tomatoes, peeled, seeded, and chopped
1 onion, chopped
2 pimentos, chopped
1½ cups toasted bread croutons

CHILLED OYSTER AND CHICKEN CONSOMMÉ

Cut out the eye of the oysters, remove the beards, and simmer them in the oyster liquor and 2 cups water for 30 minutes. Plump the soft parts of the oyster in 1 cup of the consommé for a few minutes, then blend them until smooth. Combine strained oyster liquor with the blended oysters and remaining consommé (use the consommé at room temperature so that it is not set). Chill the soup until it is thickened, beat in the cream, and serve it cold with a sprinkling of the minced parsley, pepper, and onion.

1 pint chucked oysters with their liquor
3 cups strong clear chicken stock (if canned
*   consommé is used, buy 2 cans jellied*
*   chicken consommé)*
Salt and freshly ground white pepper to taste
1 cup heavy cream
2 tablespoons minced parsley
2 tablespoons minced green pepper
2 tablespoons minced onion

UKRAINIAN BARSZCZ

(If the barszcz is to be served as a meal, use more boiling beef, boil it until tender, and serve cold sliced boiled beef and grated horseradish with the soup.)

Put the beef, onion, bay leaf and seasonings in cold water to cover in a large kettle and bring it to a boil. Skim, reduce heat, and simmer for 1 to 1½ hours. Strain the stock, add the chopped cabbage and beet tops, boil for 5 minutes longer, and take from heat. Dice the beef and return it to the soup. Add the raw beets mixed with vinegar and sugar. Cool the soup, correct the seasoning, and add the cold cooked vegetables, potatoes and apples. Stir in the tomato purée and about half the sour cream. Serve in chilled bowls with whipped and salted sour cream on each serving.

1½ pounds soup beef
1 large onion
1 bay leaf
4 black peppercorns
Salt to taste
1 cup chopped white cabbage
1 cup chopped beet tops
2 large raw beets, grated
¼ cup red wine vinegar
½ tablespoon sugar
6 cooked red beets, peeled and cut into strips
½ cup cooked carrot strips
½ cup cooked celery strips
3 potatoes, boiled, peeled, and diced
2 apples, peeled, cored, and diced
1 cup thick tomato purée
1 cup sour cream

DOLGORUKI

Chill all ingredients. Blend the soups and serve in wide soup plates, garnished with egg slices, ham, chicken, and parsley. This can be a meal in itself when there is leftover chicken.

3 cups Cream of Chicken Soup
3 cups Cream of Onion Soup
2 hard-cooked eggs, sliced
½ cup diced cooked ham
1 cup slivered leftover cooked chicken
3 tablespoons freshly chopped parsley, or chervil if available

MARYLAND CHICKEN SOUP

Cut the 2 half breasts of the chicken from the bones and set them aside. Put the remaining chicken into a large kettle with 2½ quarts cold water and salt to taste, or about ½ tablespoon. Bring it to a boil, skim, and add the onions, leek, and bouquet. Simmer until the chicken is done, then strain the broth through a fine sieve. Cut the raw chicken into strips, cutting across the meat, and cook them with the butter, onion, pepper, and curry for 10 minutes, stir until the curry is smooth. Return this mixture with the strained broth to the rinsed kettle, add the okra, corn, and lima beans, and cook until they are tender, 20 to 30 minutes longer. Season the soup with pepper and salt, if necessary, and strain it again. Set the *filling* of the soup in the refrigerator and the soup into the freezer. As soon as the fat has risen to the surface, lift it off, return the *filling* to the soup and refrigerate it until ready to serve. Sprinkle it with cut chives and parsley.

1 2½-pound fryer, quartered
Salt
2 onions
1 leek
1 herb bouquet
2 tablespoons butter
2 tablespoons finely chopped onion
2 tablespoons finely chopped green pepper
2 teaspoons curry powder, or to taste
8 okras, cut across into ½-inch slices
½ cup fresh corn kernels
½ cup fresh baby lima beans, or frozen and thawed
Freshly ground black pepper
2 tablespoons cut chives and parsley

SÉNÉGALAISE WITH CHICKEN

In the top of a large double boiler, over boiling water, melt the butter. Stir in the floor and cook for 3 minutes. Add the warmed chicken stock gradually and stir with a wooden spoon until smooth and thickened. Stir in the milk or cream with a French wire whisk until very smooth. Place curry powder in a cup and stir in 3 tablespoons of the hot soup to make a smooth paste. Add a little more soup until the paste is thin enough to pour. Stir it gradually back into the soup until the taste of curry is strong enough and the soup is a light yellow. Add more or less curry as preferred. Cool the soup and chill it until just before serving. Fry the coconut carefully in the butter. It burns easily and has to be lifted from the heat the instant it starts to brown. Stir it well and return it to the heat only long enough to start it browning again. Continue in this way until it is crisp and evenly browned. Invert it on paper kitchen towels to drain and cool. Whip the cream and salt it to taste. Ladle the cold soup into soup plates or wide cups, top it with whipped cream and slivers of chicken, and sprinkle generously with the coconut.

6 tablespoons butter
6 tablespoons flour
3 cups chicken stock or chicken consommé
2 cups chilled milk or light cream
2 tablespoons curry powder, preferably Madras
¾ cup grated coconut, unsweetened
3 tablespoons butter
1 cup heavy cream
Salt to taste
*1 cold cooked chicken breast, cut into
    julienne*

SÉNÉGALAISE WITH SHRIMP

Peel, devein, and rinse the shrimp. Bring 6 cups salted water to a boil with the vegetables and parsley. Drop in the shrimp, a few at a time so that the water does not stop boiling, and cook for 3 minutes after the last shrimp has been added. Take them out with a slotted spoon and sprinkle them with 2 tablespoons tarragon vinegar. Reduce the broth to about 3 cups by boiling uncovered. Substitute the strained shrimp broth for the chicken stock and substitute the cold cooked shrimp for the cold chicken meat as a garnish. Follow the recipe for sénégalaise with chicken in all other details. Serve very cold.

½ pound large shrimp
1 onion, quartered
1 carrot, quartered
1 stalk celery, with celery leaves
2 sprigs parsley
2 tablespoons tarragon vinegar

PURÉE MONGOLE

This is a traditional combination of Cream of Tomato and Cream of Green Pea soups. The canned tomato soup is perfect for the purpose, but homemade cream of green pea soup makes it very much nicer than canned pea soup. I usually make enough cream of green pea soup so that I can serve it with tomato slices once, with a garnish of shrimp and green peas, called Potage Navarin, and then I set aside the last 2 cups for Purée Mongole or one of its variations.

Blend the soups with the milk and add more milk if they are too thick. Chill the soup and add cream and sherry just before serving.

VARIATIONS: 1. Add 1 cup flaked and picked-over crab meat to the soup before serving and sprinkle with freshly chopped herbs or with parsley.
   2. Add the crab meat, as above, and garnish with ¾ cup each peeled, seeded, and diced tomato and cooked tiny green peas.

2 cans tomato soup
2 cups cream of green pea soup
1 cup milk
½ cup cream
¼ cup dry sherry, or to taste

POLISH CHERRY AND BEET SOUP

Chill the borsch, boil the cherries in the water with lemon juice, cloves, cinnamon and honey for 10 minutes. Take out the cherries with a slotted spoon and, as soon as they can be handled, pit them over the water in which they boiled in order to catch all the juice. Discard the pits and cut the cherry meat into small pieces. Strain out the cloves and cinnamon, return the cut cherries to the water with the lemon slivers, and boil for just 2 minutes. Cool and combine with the borsch. Serve very cold with a bowl of sour cream.

1 1-quart jar borsch
1 pound sour cherries, stemmed
2 cups water
1 lemon, juice and slivered rind
½ teaspoon whole cloves
1 small piece cinnamon stick
2 tablespoons honey, or to taste
1 cup sour cream, whipped

COLD CHERRY SOUP

Simmer the cherries in half wine and half water with the sugar until they are soft, about 15 minutes. Take out the cherries with a slotted spoon and let them cool. Thicken the liquid left in the saucepan with the cornstarch and simmer, stirring until it is clear. Set it aside to cool. Pit the cherries over a bowl in order to catch all juice and return them and their juice to the cooled liquid. Put them through the blender and add sugar if necessary. Chill the soup and serve it with 2 tablespoons sour cream on each portion and pass cinnamon toast fingers separately.

2 pounds sour cherries, stemmed
1½ cups dry white wine
½ cup sugar, or to taste
2 tablespoons cornstarch, stirred in a little
  cold water
¾ cup sour cream, whipped
1 recipe Cinnamon Toast Fingers (given
  below)

CINNAMON TOAST FINGERS

Cut 6 slices thin white bread, or melba toast bread, into fingers and fry them very slowly in butter until they are browned on both sides. Add a little butter as you go so that the bread pieces are never *deep* in butter. When they are golden, lay them on a platter on which sugar and cinnamon have been spread and cover them with a layer of sugar and cinnamon, or shake them in a bag of sugar and cinnamon, as in dredging a chicken. Use about 2 teaspoons cinnamon to 1 cup sugar and increase cinnamon to taste. Take out the pieces and shake lightly before serving.

COLD CURRIED FRUIT SOUP

Prepare the fruit. Melt the butter in a heavy kettle and work the curry powder and cloves into it to make a smooth paste. Add the chicken stock and fruit and simmer until the fruit is very soft. Put it through blender in 2 batches and make a smooth purée. Season it if necessary and stir in the fruit juices to obtain 6 cups of soup. Serve it very cold, topped with whipped cream sprinkled with ginger.

3 tart apples, peeled, cored, and diced
4 apricots, stoned and diced
3 tablespoons butter
2 to 3 teaspoons curry powder to taste
¼ teaspoon ground cloves
4 cups chicken stock
Salt and white pepper to taste
½ to 1 cup apple juice, as needed
½ cup apricot nectar
1 cup heavy cream, whipped
Powdered ginger or chopped crystallized
  ginger

CELERY BOUILLON

Clean celery carefully and chop it roughly with the tender leaves. Rinse it again and drain it well. Stir the gelatin into ¼ cup of the cold bouillon and set it aside. Boil the celery in the remaining bouillon for 50 minutes, strain, and discard the celery. Pour the bouillon through triple cheesecloth, wrung out in cold water. Reheat 1 cup to boiling, take it from heat, and stir in the gelatin until it is dissolved. Add it to the remaining bouillon and chill. Serve very cold, sprinkled with chervil or parsley.

1 head celery
1 envelope gelatin
7 cups clear beef bouillon
2 tablespoons finely chopped chervil or parsley

VARIATIONS:

Place finely chopped celery in each soup cup with equal quantities of diced apple and cucumber and pour over the celery bouillon.

Serve the bouillon in chilled cups with a lacing of sherry and rice a little Roquefort cheese over each cup. Sprinkle with chopped parsley.

OKROSCHKA

Combine cucumbers, meat, and dill pickle in a large bowl and set it aside. Work the onion with the next 6 ingredients, crushing them together with the back of a wooden spoon until everything is mashed to a paste. Stir in the sour cream, lemon juice, and vinegar, and when it is smooth stir in the consommé and wine. Add ½ cup of the ice and the meat mixture. Correct the seasoning and chill for 4 hours. Just before serving, stir in the remaining ice and soda water, and top with the eggs.

2 cucumbers, peeled, seeded, and diced
2 cups cold cooked leftover meat, diced
    (use beef, lamb, ham, chicken, or duck)
1 dill pickle, diced
¼ cup finely chopped onion
1 tablespoon finely cut dill
2 teaspoons brown mustard
1 teaspoon each minced tarragon and chives
1 teaspoon each salt and sugar
Freshly ground pepper
1 teaspoon grated horseradish
¼ cup sour cream
1 tablespoon lemon juice
2 teaspoons vinegar
2 cups chicken consommé
2 cups dry white wine
1½ cups shaved ice
1 cup plain soda water, chilled
3 hard-cooked eggs, chopped

CHILLED BLACK BEAN SOUP

Slightly thin black bean soup with bouillon to taste. Add sherry to taste but do not let the soup become too thin. Serve it very cold with slices of lemon on top. Rice the egg whites over the lemon slices and rice the yolks over the whites. Serve at once. A very pleasant variation can be made by adding a little lemon juice, to taste, to the soup and garnishing the top with thin slices of lime and diced avocado.

3 cans black bean soup, chilled
½ can clear beef bouillon, chilled and strained
¾ cup dry sherry, or to taste
3 lemons, sliced paper thin
2 hard-cooked eggs, separated and riced

CEBOLLA ESPAÑOLA

Slice the onions knife-blade thin and sauté them in a wide pan in the oils, without letting them brown, until very soft and transparent. Add spices, herbs, salt and bouillon (reduce salt if bouillon is salty) and simmer for 20 minutes longer. Add enough boiling water to have 2 inches of simmering soup in the pan, add the vinegar. Break the eggs into a cup, one by one, and drop them into the simmering soup, as for poached eggs. When they are cooked, ladle the soup, with 1 egg in each portion, over 6 thick slices of toasted bread in 6 wide soup plates. Garnish with chopped parsley.

2 large Spanish onions
¼ cup olive oil
¾ cup oil
6 black peppercorns
2 cloves
1 bay leaf
1 blade mace
2 teaspoons salt
4 cups clear bouillon
1 tablespoon red wine vinegar
6 eggs
6 slices bread
3 tablespoons finely chopped parsley

RAKOVA

Sauté vegetables with parsley in half the butter until soft but not brown. Add shrimp and stir until they are pink. Add wine and seasonings and water to cover and simmer for 10 minutes. Melt remaining butter over very low heat, stir in the flour, and add fennel to taste. When flour is smooth, stir in the sour cream and add the contents of the pan. Cool and chill the soup until needed. Before serving add more sour cream, if necessary, to make 6 cups of soup, correct seasoning, and serve very cold, sprinkled with chopped fennel and dill.

1 onion, sliced
1 carrot, scraped and sliced
1 stalk celery, sliced
3 sprigs parsley
6 tablespoons butter
1 pound large shrimp, peeled and deveined
1 cup dry white wine
½ teaspoon each peppercorns and caraway seeds
1 teaspoon salt
6 tablespoons flour
¼ fresh fennel, finely diced
1½ cups sour cream
2 tablespoons finely cut dill

TURKISH CHERBAH

In a large kettle, cook onions in the oil until they are puffed and glossy, about 7 minutes. Add the mint and stir for 2 minutes. Add tomatoes, peppers, garlic, and seasonings and cook covered over very low heat until pepper slivers are soft. Add beef stock and simmer covered for 20 minutes. Take soup from heat and, after it has stopped boiling, stir in the egg yolks beaten with the lemon juice. Correct seasoning and chill the soup until ready to serve. Serve garnished with thin lemon slices.

8 medium onions, chopped
⅓ cup oil
10 sprigs mint, chopped
4 tomatoes (1 pound), peeled and sliced
2 green or red sweet peppers, seeded and slivered
2 garlic cloves, crushed
Salt and pepper, to taste
6 cups strong beef stock, free of all fat
2 egg yolks
1 lemon, juice only
2 lemons, thinly sliced

EGGS

CHAPTER FOUR

Eggs, Poached, Hard-Cooked,
Six-Minute Eggs

Eggs, as soups, change character when they are served cold. A hot poached egg is usually associated with breakfast, but when you add some steamed spinach, it becomes a luncheon dish—a ladies' luncheon dish. When an egg is served cold, it can rise to a gala status worthy of a formal dinner party.

The comparison between hot and cold eggs reminds me of a disastrous luncheon that I tried to cook some years ago. There were five guests and the menu was a masterpiece of simplicity: eggs Benedict, a vegetable salad, a fruit dessert and coffee. Bread, meat, eggs, vegetables, and fruit . . . could anyone ask for more?

I prepared the salad and fruit in advance and arranged eggs, English muffins, ham, butter, and a whisk ready to hand. I didn't discover my problem until I tried to poach eggs, whisk hollandaise, fry ham, toast muffins and heat plates all at the same time. Except for the plates, there was not a single item that would not suffer and deteriorate for having to wait for the others. And only an artist can hold freshly poached eggs hot and soft at the same time. As for keeping hollandaise warm and at its best, it can't be done by someone with muffins burning and ham splattering.

Now I serve cold soft poached eggs on a slice of tomato with a lovely herbed mayonnaise. And I let curried toast turn golden in a slow oven. And all of it is done hours before the guests arrive. If it is a bitterly cold day, I heat a precooked soup in a double broiler, but the eggs stay cold, simple and uncomplicated, no matter what the weather.

A Few Suggested Cold Egg Recipes

HARD-COOKED EGGS

BYRON   sliced on finely diced vegetable salad, bound with mayonnaise, and sprinkled with dill. Garnished with alternate slices of peeled tomatoes and cooked shrimp.

GENOA   whites refilled with anchovy-flavored yolks, placed on a salad of chicken, dill pickle, anchovies, and capers, garnished with sliced radishes and served with mustard mayonnaise.

LUCULLUS   whites refilled with flavored and bound yolks, placed face down on bread rounds spread with chives and flavored cheese, garnished with anchovy paste and parsley, lemon mayonnaise separately.

MONACO   pointed end cut off to form a lid, yolks removed with a small spoon, mixed with caviar (red or black) and mayonnaise and refilled into the eggs, lid returned to egg, served on lettuce leaves, masked with herbed mayonnaise.

SEVILLE   slices placed on oval slices of bread spread with anchovy-flavored butter and garnished with parsley, stuffed olives, and half lemons filled with lemon-flavored mayonnaise.

POACHED EGGS

BERNADOT   on a slice of smoked salmon placed across a slice of ripe tomato, garnished with minced onion and parsley, dilled mayonnaise separately.

BUDAPEST   on a julienne of smoked tongue mixed with slivered black olives, ravigote sauce separately.

HAMBURG   on a shrimp mousse or salad, with mayonnaise mixed with whipped cream and grated horseradish, garnished with pimento strips.

NIÇOISE   on a salad of diced tomatoes, white beans, and potatoes, bound with mayonnaise and garnished with anchovies and tomatoes.

ROMANOFF   on marinated artichoke bottoms, garnished with chopped olives and green pepper, masked with caviar mayonnaise (or lightly flavored anchovy mayonnaise).

SIX-MINUTE EGGS—OEUFS MOLLETS

ARIZONA   on open ham sandwiches; masked with chive mayonnaise, garnished with mustard pickles.

BOMBAY   on slices of cold cooked salmon with curry mayonnaise.

FRENCH   on light chicken liver pâté filled into ramekins, the tops glazed with aspic, mayonnaise separately.

NORWEGIAN   on shrimp salad bound with dilled mayonnaise and garnished with fillets of anchovies.

RHODE ISLAND   on lobster salad bound with mayonnaise, garnished with diced aspic and ovals of cheese bakery.

Also the recipes for eggs suggested in the various menus and directions for cooking the basic hard-cooked, poached, and six-minute eggs.
How to soft-cook an egg (mollet or six-minute egg) and how to hard-cook an egg (hard-boiled egg)

SIX-MINUTE EGGS MOLLETS

Use flawless, uncracked eggs at room temperature. Lower them slowly and gently into rapidly boiling water to cover. Use a sieve or lower 2 eggs at a time with a slotted spoon. The purpose is to cook all the eggs at once and the same length of time. Boil for exactly 5½ minutes after the water returns to a boil. If the water did not stop boiling, boil for exactly 6 minutes by the clock. Plunge the eggs at once into very cold water, if the shells crack it does not matter, and peel them carefully when they are cold. Hold the eggs in salted water at room temperature until they are used. Six-minute eggs are interchangeable with poached eggs in any of the following recipes.

HARD-COOKED EGGS

Start exactly as above, but since every second does not count, as in eggs mollets, look at the clock and count exactly 10 minutes from the time the last egg was lowered into the water and the water returned to a boil. If preferred the eggs can boil for 12 minutes, but 10 minutes is adequate and anything over 12 minutes toughens the egg. Plunge them at once into cold water, crack the shells lightly, and peel them carefully after they are cooled. If an egg is one of those that clings to the shell, crack the entire shell by hitting it gently with the back of a spoon and peel it under cold water. If it still clings, use it for riced egg and boil another in its stead. Hold peeled eggs in cold water until needed. When I am eager to prepare everything beforehand and the eggs are going to be stuffed, I cut them in half, empty out the yolks and prepare the yolk mixture. I store the mixture in a covered bowl in the refrigerator and hold the egg whites in a second bowl, in water. They can then be filled and garnished on the day they are going to be served.

Stuffed Eggs

The individual half stuffed eggs, which can be eaten with the hand, are among the appetizers, but they can be served as a first course or accompaniment at any meal or buffet. The stuffed eggs in this chapter are either garnished or sauced, or both, in such a way that they become a luncheon or first course and have to be eaten with a fork. They can also be one of the hors d'oeuvre dishes among those given in Chapter 2.

EGGS JULIENNE

Cut eggs in half lengthwise and arrange the halves, cut side down, on a porcelain platter. Cover them with mayonnaise collée, emptying 1 wide tablespoon of the mayonnaise down the length of each half egg. Chill until the mayonnaise is set, then combine truffles, nuts, ham, and orange julienne and sprinkle it over the coated eggs. Serve plain mayonnaise separately.

8 hard-cooked eggs, peeled
1 recipe Mayonnaise Collée
2 peeled truffles, cut into matchsticks,
 optional
¼ cup chopped pistachio nuts
1 cup julienne of lean cooked ham or tongue
Thin outside rind of 1 orange cut into finest
 julienne and scalded
1 cup plain mayonnaise, whipped

TOTALLY STUFFED EGGS I, INDIAN

Cut eggs in half lengthwise, keeping each 2 halves together. Take out the yolks and mash them, while they are still hot, with the butter, seasonings, onion, capers, and pimento. Shape the paste into yolk-sized rounds and press them into half the egg whites. Close over the second half and wrap each egg tightly in wax paper. Arrange the chilled, unwrapped eggs on lettuce leaves or in half tomatoes and serve with Curry Mayonnaise.

6 large hard-cooked eggs
1 tablespoon soft butter
Salt and pepper to taste
1 teaspoon minced onion and juice
2 teaspoons minced capers
1 tablespoon minced pimento
3 large tomatoes, optional

TOTALLY STUFFED EGGS II, FRENCH

Cut eggs in half lengthwise, keeping each 2 halves together. Take out the yolks and mash them, while they are still hot, with anchovy paste and butter. Stir in a very little of the heavy cream and the paprika. Shape the paste into yolk-sized rounds and press them into half the egg whites. Close over with the second half, wrap each egg tightly in wax paper and chill. Arrange the unwrapped eggs on lettuce leaves and pour over the mayonnaise, beaten with the remaining cream and garnish with a rolled anchovy and a sprinkling of chopped olives.

6 large hard-cooked eggs
Anchovy paste to taste
1 tablespoon soft butter
3 tablespoons heavy cream
½ teaspoon paprika
1 cup mayonnaise
6 rolled anchovy fillets
6 stuffed olives, chopped

STUFFED EGGS MONTPELLIER

Cut eggs in half lengthwise, take out the yolks and set them aside. Parboil the chives and herbs and dry them well. Mince them and fold them into the creamed butter with minced capers and gherkins. Season and add lemon juice to taste. Rice the egg yolks and beat them into the butter. Check seasonings once more and fill the mixture into the 12 egg whites. Arrange them close together on lettuce leaves and pour over green mayonnaise.

6 large hard-cooked eggs
1 tablespoon finely cut chives
*3 sprigs each parsley, tarragon, chervil, all
    stems removed*
3 tablespoons soft butter, whipped
*1 tablespoon each minced capers and
    gherkins*
*Salt and pepper to taste with a squeeze of
    lemon juice*
1 recipe Green Mayonnaise

FRANKONIAN EGGS

Prepare the eggs. Pick over the crab meat carefully and combine it with the pepper and cucumber dice. Beat mayonnaise with chili sauce and drained relish and increase any of the ingredients to taste. Salt the sauce and use only enough to bind the crab meat, put the rest into a bowl to serve with the eggs. Arrange the crab meat in a shallow serving dish and arrange the eggs on top of it. Sprinkle with parsley and serve very cold.

6 eggs mollets or 6-minute eggs, peeled
1 pound frozen or canned crab meat
½ green pepper, seeded and finely diced
¼ cup diced cucumber
1 cup Lemon Mayonnaise
3 tablespoons chili sauce
2 tablespoons drained pickle relish
Salt to taste
1 tablespoon finely chopped parsley

BOMBAY EGGS

Prepare the eggs. Mix the rice with chutney, raisins and almonds and increase the chutney to taste. Arrange the rice in a small serving platter. Arrange the eggs on it and pour over the curried mayonnaise, beaten with enough heavy cream to make a flowing sauce.

8 eggs mollets, or 6-minute eggs, peeled
3 cups cold cooked rice (see page 145)
4 to 6 tablespoons diced chutney, or to taste
3 tablespoons raisins
3 tablespoons chopped or slivered blanched almonds
1 recipe Curried Mayonnaise
Heavy cream to taste

EGGS WITH ANCHOVIES

Prepare the eggs. Combine mayonnaise with anchovy paste, chives, and lemon juice to make a smooth sauce and chill it. Cut a lid from the tomatoes, hollow them out, and fill them with the anchovy mayonnaise. If very small tomatoes are not available, make correspondingly more anchovy mayonnaise. Arrange the tomatoes in the center of a porcelain or crystal platter. Slice the eggs intact, place them around the tomatoes and spread them into overlapping slices. Place a parsley tuft at the narrow slices of each egg. Chill until ready to serve.

8 hard-cooked eggs, peeled
1 cup mayonnaise, stiff and cold
2 teaspoons anchovy paste or a 6-inch strip anchovy paste from a tube
3 tablespoons finely cut chives
1 tablespoon lemon juice
6 small evenly sized tomatoes (about 1 pound), peeled
3 parsley sprigs

EGGS LIMOUSINE

The entire point of this salad is that it consists of a combination of variously sized rounds—eggs, ham, and potatoes—all of approximately the same thickness—about 3/8 of an inch. The usual egg cutter cuts 11 slices out of each egg. Eight eggs yield about 88 slices. Potatoes should be peeled and trimmed to be as tubular as possible; they are boiled and cut into round slices. Ham is sliced in the same thickness and cut into rounds of the size of the largest egg slices with a very sharp cookie cutter. There should be more egg slices and about as many ham as potato slices.

Prepare the potato and ham disks and layer them gently in a shallow, wide dish. Slice the eggs right over the dish and try to spread them in layers between the ham and potatoes without breaking them. Sprinkle with parsley between the layers and add dressing as you go. End with a layer of eggs. Serve very cold with additional dressing.

8 hard-cooked eggs, peeled
6 large potatoes, peeled and trimmed to be
roughly tubular in shape
6 thick slices ham, cut into rounds
3 tablespoons finely chopped parsley
1 recipe Mustard French Dressing

ZURICH EGGS

These are prepared in the same way with disks of ham, potatoes, and Swiss cheese, in equal quantities, combined with the sliced eggs.

How to Poach an Egg

Use very fresh eggs and prepare a wide pan with at least 4 cups of gently boiling salted water. The water should be 1¾ inches deep in the pan. Break the eggs immediately over the water. If 4 eggs are being poached, break them in rapid succession—do not answer the telephone—reduce heat immediately to a low simmer, and let the eggs cook for 3 minutes, or until the whites are set but the yolks are still soft. Take out the eggs with a slotted spoon and place them in cold water. Before using, trim them with a large round cookie cutter. One tablespoon vinegar may be added to the water to help set the whites.

COLD POACHED EGGS VALENCIA

Prepare the eggs. Beat mayonnaise with garlic and brown mustard, and increase both to taste. Chill the mayonnaise until very stiff, then fill it into the artichoke bottoms and place a poached egg on each. Arrange them on a serving platter and surround them with an overlapping circle of tomato slices sprinkled with parsley.

6 poached eggs, trimmed
1 recipe Mayonnaise
½ clove garlic, crushed
2 teaspoons brown mustard
6 artichoke bottoms
6 tomatoes, peeled and sliced across
2 tablespoons chopped parsley

COLD POACHED EGGS NORMANDY

Arrange the eggs on 2 sardines each, surround with lightly chopped water cress, and pour ravigote sauce over the eggs. Sprinkle with parsley and garnish with shrimp.

6 cold poached eggs, trimmed
12 large sardines
1 bunch water cress, coarse stems removed
1 recipe Ravigote Sauce
3 tablespoons finely chopped parsley
½ pound cold cooked shrimp

IMPERIAL SALAD

Place eggs on artichoke bottoms, surround with a narrow border of tomatoes and vegetables mixed with the tongue. Pour over sauce rémoulade.

6 poached eggs, trimmed
6 artichoke bottoms, cooked or canned
3 tomatoes, peeled, seeded, and diced
1½ cups cold cooked mixed vegetables—peas,
    beans, carrots, celery, cauliflower
3 slices cold smoked tongue, diced
1 recipe Sauce Rémoulade I

POACHED EGGS PAYSANNE

Prepare eggs. Combine potatoes, anchovies, radishes, and chives, and mix with just enough dressing to make the mixture glossy. Arrange it on a small serving dish, sprinkle with the bacon, and arrange the eggs on it. Beat paprika into the mayonnaise, fold in the whipped cream, and serve it with the eggs.

6 poached eggs, trimmed
4 cold boiled potatoes, cubed
3 anchovy fillets, cut into small pieces with
    kitchen scissors
4 to 5 red radishes, chopped
3 tablespoons finely cut chives
French dressing to bind
3 strips crisp bacon, crumbled
Paprika to taste
½ cup mayonnaise
½ cup whipped cream

POACHED EGGS LEXINGTON

Prepare the eggs. Arrange the ham on toast, cover with the tomato slices, and top the tomatoes with the eggs. Fold the whipped cream into the mayonnaise and add horseradish. Spoon the sauce over the eggs and sprinkle with paprika.

6 poached eggs, trimmed
6 thin slices Virginia ham
6 large toasted bread rounds
6 thick slices peeled tomato
½ cup whipped cream
⅔ cup mayonnaise
Freshly grated horseradish to taste
Paprika

POACHED EGGS VINAIGRETTE

Arrange eggs on asparagus on 6 individual plates. Pour over vinaigrette dressing and sprinkle with ham. Green beans, broccoli, or artichoke bottoms (not the small canned ones) may be substituted for the asparagus.

6 poached eggs, trimmed
36 steamed asparagus spears, chilled
1 recipe Vinaigrette Dressing
½ cup slivered ham

POACHED EGGS TOURANGELLE

Arrange the eggs on the salad and garnish each egg with slivers of tongue.

6 poached eggs, trimmed
1 recipe Salade Tourangelle
¼ cup julienne of cooked tongue

COLD POACHED EGGS WITH TONGUE

Prepare the eggs. Cut the beef tongue into rounds with a large cookie cutter, place them on a serving platter, and top each with a poached egg. Cut the tongue scraps into matchsticks and combine them with the gherkins, olives, carrots and celery. Pour the sauce over the eggs and sprinkle with the mixture.

6 poached eggs, trimmed
6 thick slices smoked beef tongue
2 gherkins, cut into matchsticks
4 black olives, diced
2 tablespoons finely diced cooked carrots
1 tablespoon finely diced celery
2 cups purée of tomatoes or tomato sauce

TOMATO SAUCE

Melt the tomatoes in the oil with the remaining ingredients in a small heavy pan. Half cover the pan, adjust the heat to barely simmer, and cook for 30 minutes, stirring at intervals. Correct the seasoning and blend into a smooth sauce.

9 ripe tomatoes, peeled, seeded, and chopped
6 tablespoons oil
1½ teaspoons salt
¼ teaspoon sugar
Freshly ground pepper, to taste
½ small garlic clove, crushed
3 tablespoons chopped parsley

Jellied Eggs or Eggs in Aspic

Eggs are served in aspic in many different ways. They may be prepared in one large mold or individual molds that are unmolded before they are served, or in ramekins (or individual cups) that are not unmolded. Since lining a mold with aspic is a long-drawn-out process and individual molds are more easily prepared, the following suggestions are all for hard-cooked eggs, six-minute, or poached eggs made in individual cups for unmolding or in ramekins for eating out of the ramekin.

The difference in preparation is that the egg that is going to be unmolded is dropped into a deep custard cup or similar cup so that the accompaniments may be added on top of the egg. When the egg is unmolded, it will be uppermost and look attractive. When eggs are prepared in ramekins, the accompaniments are put in first, then the egg, and then the aspic, so that, again, the egg is on top and looks attractive.

EGGS IN RAMEKINS, TYROL

Hold the poached eggs in cold water until needed. Crush the smoked trout and beat in enough of the cream to make a light mousse. Season it well, divide it over 6 ramekins, smooth it down, and chill until needed. Stir the gelatin into the wine and set it aside for 15 minutes. Heat half the consommé to boiling, take it from heat, stir in the gelatin until it is dissolved. Add the remaining consommé and cool the aspic. Arrange 1 well-drained egg on the mousse in each ramekin and pour over a tablespoon of aspic. Set the ramekins on a tray and push it into the refrigerator. As soon as the aspic has set, repeat the addition of the aspic and the chilling until the eggs are glazed and the ramekins are filled up to the edge. Chill until needed. Put a horseradish tuft on each egg and serve at once.

Amounts of aspic needed will differ with the size of the ramekins.

6 poached eggs, trimmed
2 smoked trout, skinned and boned, or
*   smoked mackerel*
½ to ⅔ cup heavy cream, as needed
Salt and white pepper to taste
1 envelope gelatin
¼ cup dry white wine
1¼ cups clear consommé
2 tablespoons freshly grated horseradish

VARIATIONS: 1. Fill ramekins with chopped cooked shrimp and diced celery bound with a little mayonnaise. Top with cold poached eggs and pour the aspic over. Garnish with a sprig of parsley.

2. Fill ramekins with diced smoked salmon and small capers. Cover with cold poached eggs and pour the aspic over. Garnish with a sprig of dill.

3. Crush canned salmon into a paste with diced pickle and a little mayonnaise. Fill the mixture into ramekins, top with cold 6-minute eggs and pour the aspic over. Garnish with slices of stuffed olives.

When 6-minute eggs or poached eggs are used, the yolk of the egg breaks and creates a sauce. When hard-cooked eggs are used under aspic, either they should cover a moister salad, or a sauce should be passed. In that case the ramekins should not be filled to the top rim.

4. Cut hard-cooked eggs in half. Place them, cut side down, on liver purée (Chicken Liver Pâté beaten until light with cream and a little sherry) and pour the aspic over. Garnish with 6 little truffle slices.

5. Grind leftover ham, stir in a little diced dill pickle and cream. Cover with half a hard-cooked egg, and pour aspic over. Garnish with 6 little truffle slices.

6. Stir smoked turkey pâté with cream and minced parsley and onion. Fill it into ramekins, cover with half a hard-cooked egg (or a poached egg), and pour aspic over. Garnish with chopped pistachio nuts.

TARRAGON EGGS

Stir the gelatin into ½ cup of the consommé and set it aside for 10 minutes. Bring 1 cup of the consommé to a boil, take it from the heat, and stir in the gelatin until it is dissolved. Add the remaining 2½ cups of consommé and set the aspic in a cool place; do not chill it. Prepare the eggs, hold them in cold water until ready to glaze. When aspic is cool and starts to thicken but not to set, dip the tarragon leaves in aspic and cross 2 on each poached egg. Pour a ¼-inch *mirror* of aspic into a flat porcelain or crystal 12-inch platter and chill it until it is set. Arrange one of the eggs in the center and place the remaining 6 around it. Brush the eggs with aspic and chill until set. Repeat until the eggs are smoothly and thickly glazed. If the aspic becomes too thick to brush, set it into a bowl of warm water and stir it until it is more liquid. When the eggs are glazed, pour the remaining aspic onto a flat plate and chill it until it is set. Then dice it finely, sprinkle it with a little tarragon vinegar, and chill it. Spoon a round of thick, cold mayonnaise into each artichoke bottom and set them in the triangles between the eggs. Cross 2 strips of pimento over each round of mayonnaise. Depending on the size of the dish, either arrange the finely diced aspic as a border or put it in the hollows between the eggs and the artichoke bottoms. Garnish with small end sprigs of cress or parsley in the 6 little hollows around the center egg. Chill until ready to serve.

2 envelopes gelatin
4 cups clarified consomme
7 cold poached eggs, trimmed
2 sprigs fresh tarragon or tarragon leaves in vinegar
1 tablespoon tarragon vinegar
1 recipe Tarragon Mayonnaise
6 artichoke bottoms
1 pimento, cut into 12 thin strips
6 little end sprigs of water cress

MOLDED EGGS IN ASPIC, MARIE

Prepare the eggs. Stir the gelatin into the sherry and set it aside for 15 minutes. Bring 1 cup of the bouillon to a boil, take it from heat and stir in the gelatin until it is dissolved. Add the remaining bouillon and cool. As soon as it is cold but not yet set, pour 1 tablespoon into each of 6 custard cups. Arrange them on a tray and set them in the refrigerator. When the aspic is set, dip a pimento round in aspic and set it against the center bottom of the cup. Chill again, pour on another spoon of aspic and add the eggs, smoothest side down. Pour aspic around the egg, but not enough to raise or move it. Repeat, adding aspic and chilling until the aspic has just covered the egg. Add a round of ham, another film of aspic, a layer of vegetable salad, and a final layer of aspic. Chill until needed. Dip the molds in warm water, invert them onto a serving platter or individual plates and garnish with water cress.

Note quantities will vary according to the size of the cups.

6 poached eggs, trimmed
1 envelope gelatin
¼ cup sherry
3 cups clear beef bouillon
6 small rounds cut from 1 pimento
6 round disks of ham
1 cup vegetable salad bound with a little Mustard Mayonnaise
6 sprigs water cress

VARIATIONS: 1. Flavor aspic with Madeira instead of sherry. Place a truffle slice in the mold, fill with 6-minute eggs, and top them with a thick layer of homemade chicken liver pâté mixed with chopped pecans.

2. Flavor aspic with tarragon, cross 2 tarragon leaves at bottom of mold, and cover with a poached egg. Fill with aspic and end with a round slice of tomato from which seeds were removed and the cavities filled with minced tongue.

A plate of ham and eggs is lovely somewhere between eleven and twelve in the morning—in the country—scrambled eggs are good after midnight, but it takes a special effort to move a cold egg into more elite circles. Most of the egg recipes are more a matter of assembling than of prolonged cooking, and the special effort is in arranging and garnishing them. It takes time to do, but it takes it at a time of the day when there is less pressure. I would rather spend forty-five minutes longer peeling tomatoes and filling eggs than to make an omelet or soufflé in my best dress and with guests waiting.

There are gala egg combinations . . . most famous of all is with caviar. While a little riced hard-cooked egg with lots of fresh caviar is not the purist's preference, a little caviar with a cold poached egg or in a stuffed egg or in an egg sauce can be heavenly. Eggs can be made worthy of the food luxuries, caviar, truffles, goose liver, lobster, or smoked salmon. And since eggs and postage stamps are almost the only things we can still buy for pennies, they counterbalance the cost of some of their accompaniments. The great chefs devoted a great deal of time to creating beautiful egg dishes for any meal and any season. Our restaurants all list eggs for breakfast, some list eggs Benedict or eggs Florentine for luncheon, and there are no eggs at all on any dinner menus. The following egg dishes can start a dinner or center a supper or luncheon. They are made for cold buffets and in hot summer they can be the main course of any refreshing, healthful meal.

COLD SCRAMBLED EGGS DUBOIS

Cold scrambled eggs are very popular in Scandinavia, where they are combined with smoked salmon, dill, cold roast beef, smoked eel, and tomatoes. Urbain-Dubois combined scrambled eggs with diced lobster, filled the mixture into lobster shells, garnished them with lobster slices, and beat the tomalley and coral of the lobsters into the mayonnaise, which was served separately. If you have empty lobster shells (Dubois used only the opened claws) and leftover lobster meat, scramble eggs, dice the meat into them and retain the best pieces for the garnish. If there is no tomalley or coral, serve with mayonnaise to which finely cut dill has been added.

COLD SCRAMBLED EGGS SULTAN

Scramble eggs beaten with 1 teaspoon heavy cream per egg and 2 teaspoons finely chopped pistachio nuts per egg. Sprinkle the top with paprika and serve cold, surrounded with tomato slices. Pass buttered pumpernickel slices.

THREE OPEN EGG SANDWICHES
For a luncheon or late Sunday breakfast

BERGEN On a slice of buttered rye bread, place a large slice of mildest smoked salmon, which can overhang the bread. On the salmon place a mound (do not spread it) of cold scrambled eggs and garnish with sprigs of dill. Accompany with a pepper mill.

COPENHAGEN On a thin slice of buttered pumpernickel bread, arrange long wedges of smoked eel. Diagonally across the sandwich arrange a strip of cold scrambled eggs and sprinkle them with finely cut chives. Garnish with very thin lemon slices.

BORNHOLM On a slice of buttered rye bread, arrange fillets of smoked herrings (Bornholmers if obtainable), center with an onion ring 3/16 of an inch thick—of suitable size—to hold 1 raw egg yolk secure on the herring. Or top with 1 cold poached and trimmed egg. The egg must be soft enough so that the yolk becomes the sauce for the smoked herring. Garnish with cut dill and a red radish.

OPEN EGG SANDWICH MARGOT

Prepare toast, beat butter with anchovy paste and spread it on the toast. Cut eggs in half lengthwise, scoop out and rice the yolks, and mix them with the tongue, olives, relish, and enough mayonnaise to bind. Refill the egg whites with the mixture and place 2 halves on each slice of toast. Garnish with parsley. Serve the remaining mayonnaise in a bowl.

6 slices crisp fried bread
7 tablespoons butter
1 teaspoon anchovy paste, or to taste
6 hard-cooked eggs, peeled
1 slice tongue, minced
3 stuffed olives, minced
1 tablespoon drained pickle relish, minced
1 recipe Herb Mayonnaise
Sprigs of parsley

RUSSIAN EGG IN TOMATOES
serve as a luncheon dish

Peel and cut eggs in half lengthwise. Rice yolks into a bowl through a coarse sieve and place whites carefully into cold water. Add mustard, lemon juice, onion, and chives to yolks and stir in mayonnaise, 1 spoon at a time, to make a smooth paste. Season to taste with salt and white pepper and pipe the paste into the drained whites. Put a little caviar onto each egg and chill them until needed. Cut tomatoes in half across and scoop out the pulp with a spoon. Do this carefully so that the tomatoes do not break. Divide the water cress and parsley over the 12 half tomatoes and set a half stuffed egg in each. Press them down sufficiently so that a rim of chopped water cress and parsley will show between the tomato and the egg. Arrange the tomatoes on a bed of lettuce leaves and serve them with a glass or china bowl of lemon mayonnaise. If tomatoes are small, the eggs can be cut across the short way to stand upright in the tomatoes.

6 hard-cooked eggs
½ teaspoon made mustard
½ teaspoon lemon juice
1 teaspoon grated onion
2 teaspoons finely minced chives (if not
*   available, substitute 1 additional*
*   teaspoon grated onion)*
2–3 tablespoons mayonnaise
Salt and white pepper
1 small jar (at least 2 ounces) good caviar
6 evenly sized medium tomatoes, peeled
1 cup finely chopped water cress
¼ cup finely chopped parsley
1 head Boston lettuce
1 recipe Lemon Mayonnaise

CURRIED EGGS BARODA
serve as a luncheon dish or as a first course at dinner

Peel and cut eggs in half lengthwise. Rice yolks into a bowl through a coarse sieve and place whites carefully into cold water. Stir mayonnaise with anchovy paste, curry powder, and salt until smooth. Add a little more of any ingredient to taste, but the anchovy flavor should predominate. Stir the mixture into the yolks and add mayonnaise, if necessary, to make a smooth paste. Pipe the paste into the drained whites and chill until needed. Stir the gelatin into ¼ cup of the consommé, heat remaining consommé to boiling, take it from the heat, and immediately stir in the softened gelatin until it is dissolved. Pour the consommé into a pie dish or shallow pan and chill it until it is firmly set, then cut it into even dice with a sharp knife. Boil the broc-

6 hard-cooked eggs
3 tablespoons mayonnaise
1 teaspoon anchovy paste
½ teaspoon curry powder
Salt to taste
1 envelope gelatin
1½ cups clear chicken consommé or 1 No. 1
*   can*
1 large bunch broccoli or 1 medium
*   cauliflower*
2 teaspoons salt
1 recipe Curry Mayonnaise

coli for exactly 15 minutes in salted water to cover and drain and chill it well. Arrange the stuffed eggs on a glass or china platter, garnish them with the diced aspic and broccoli spears, and serve curry mayonnaise separately.

If cauliflower is substituted for the broccoli, boil it until just tender, about 20 minutes for a 1½-pound head. Boil only for 10 minutes if the head is divided into flowerets.

MAIN COURSES

CHAPTER FIVE

Main Courses, Aspics, Seafood,
Meat, and Poultry

COLD FOOD has apparently nothing to do with the climate. There are few cold Mediterranean dishes, but the cookery of the Scandinavian countries leans heavily on what they call their *cold table* or smorgasbord. The cold table is part of breakfast, lunch, and dinner, and the traditional warm dishes are in the minority. As we go southward the food changes with the temperature, it becomes hotter in its preparation and its ingredients. We happily eat cold food in Norway in cold weather and hot food in Sicily in summer, but when we are home we tend toward warm food, especially when we have guests. We eat a cold luncheon when we are alone, but if guests are expected we usually go out of our way to give them something warm.

Hot foods are a habit rather than a preference; millions of Americans eat a cold lunch with hot coffee and possibly a hot soup, while millions of Europeans, with the exception of the Scandinavians, insist on a hot luncheon but do not mind a cold supper. When we eat cold food, it is more apt to be a cold fruit or shrimp cocktail at the beginning of the meal and a frozen dessert at the end of it; but when it comes to the main course, it's hot.

These habits go back to a time when hot meals indicated that cook was in the kitchen, while a cold meal, as the traditional cold Sunday-night supper, or midnight supper, meant that the cook was either having her day out or that she was asleep. Everyone looked forward to the informality of these cold meals, and it is only since there are no cooks in most homes that they have disappeared.

In order to benefit from the advantages of cold cookery, it is essential that the main course or entree should be cold. Anyone can keep a soup hot or a pie warm, but the troublesome main course and all its accompaniments are the hardest to serve hot or keep hot.

The real problem in preparing dinner is the main course, not only because it is the course with the largest number of supporting dishes, but because it is the course from which most is expected. As the name implies, the rest of dinner revolves around it, and a disappointing main course can make an unsuccessful dinner. We have come to accept cold appetizers, entrees, and desserts, but the main course at a sit-down dinner in winter or summer is supposed to be hot. Worse still, it is supposed to tower over the rest of the meal in weight and volume.

In hot cookery or cold cookery this can only be accomplished with an imposing roast, a large bird or a whole fish. The beef tenderloin, or any part of it, squabs, and small game birds do not, admittedly, rise to a peak on the platter, but they make up for it in value. The main course must have prestige. The cook-hostess has to cook it, always aware of her investment and her waiting guests, to perfection and on time.

Cold cookery can ease some of this responsibility. The main course and all its entourage—as we have stressed—can be ready the day before the guests arrive. It can look even more prestigious than its hot counterpart, and it can cost less. It must, however, be carefully selected. There are two types of cold main courses, and they should not be confused. We can serve our dinner guests a well-garnished cold roast saddle of lamb in December, from Maine to Florida to Southern California, but we cannot give a man—possibly in a dinner jacket—an Arabian chicken salad for his dinner. We can give him chicken chaud-froid in spring and fall, but main course salads are for summer and Sunday suppers.

The following recipes are for the informal meals, for hot summer, for suppers, and for luncheons. They take less cooking and preparing and they are a little less extravagant. The main course suggestions for formal meals, midwinter meals, and holidays are in Part II, Chapter 10. All of them are interchangeable, depending on the special occasion or purpose.

ASPIC

Aspic serves a triple purpose in preparing cold dishes, it adds flavor, it glazes and highlights the appearance of the dish, and it can enhance its importance.

In cold cookery we are turning many simple—and economical—dishes into main courses, and a clear aspic goes far in adding elegance. It can be used as a *glaze* over the surface, as a *mirror* on the platter on which the cold food is arranged, as a *bed* of chopped aspic, or as a *garnish* of diced aspic. It can also be used to line a mold before it is filled, or it can be poured into a shallow pan and cut into rounds or *cutouts* with which to decorate a platter.

Aspic is easy to prepare and easy to use, but it is attractive only when it is absolutely clear. If canned beef bouillon is used, always chill the can before using and lift off the few little fat globules from the top before bringing it to a boil. If beef bouillon cubes are used, strain the bouillon through a triple cheesecloth wrung out in cold water.

1. Always stir plain gelatin into a small quantity of liquid until it is no longer powdery, then set it aside for at least 10 minutes until it is puffed into a dry lump and has absorbed the liquid. Place 1 envelope plain gelatin in a ½-cup measure or into any suitable cup and stir in ¼ cup liquid. If possible do not use water; a dry white wine, sherry, and Madeira are all excellent for this purpose. If more than ¼ cup liquid is added, the gelatin will turn it into a thick mush, which is harder to empty into the boiling bouillon than the dry lump of puffed gelatin.

2. Bring the clear consommé or bouillon, or wine or clarified fish stock, which will be the base of the aspic, to a boil and take it from the heat. Immediately stir the lump of gelatin into it until it is dissolved. Do not stir in the gelatin while the liquid is still boiling over heat.

3. Depending on its purpose, the aspic can be poured into a shallow bowl to cool or onto a platter or into a mold. If it is going to be used for glazing, it should cool at room temperature, and it should be used when it is cold but not yet *set*. If it were to *set* while it is being used, place the bowl into a pan of warm water and stir until it is liquid again.

4. If you are making a quart of aspic for any purpose, it is not necessary to bring the entire quantity of bouillon to a boil. Soften the gelatin, bring 1 cup of the bouillon to a boil, take it from heat, stir in the gelatin until it is dissolved, then stir in the remaining bouillon. This saves time in cooling the aspic.

5. Use more gelatin in warm weather or when the aspic will be part of a buffet, which should look good over a longer period of time than if it is served at dinner. The recipes specify the proper amount of gelatin to use to be on the safe side, except in the hottest weather.

CRAB MEAT RING

Drop the contents of an ice tray into a 1-quart (5 cup) ring mold and set it in a cool place. Soften the gelatin in the white wine, heat the consommé to a quick boil and take it from the heat. Immediately stir in the gelatin until it is dissolved. In a bowl combine crab meat, chives or onion and the lemon mayonnaise. Add the lime and lemon juice and rind and the consommé. Chill the mixture for 10 minutes, then fold in the stiffly beaten cream. Pour ice cubes and water out of the mold but do not dry it. Pour in the mixture and place it in freezer or freezing compartment for 20 minutes, or until set. Move it to the refrigerator and chill it for at least 2 hours before serving. Fill the unmolded ring with a zucchini salad sprinkled with parsley and pass lemon mayonnaise separately.

2 envelopes gelatin
¼ cup dry white wine
½ cup clear chicken consommé
1½ cups flaked cooked crab meat or 2 8-ounce cans
3 tablespoons cut chives or 1 tablespoon minced onion
½ cup Lemon Mayonnaise
1 lime, the juice only
½ lemon, the juice and grated rind
1 cup heavy cream, whipped
1 recipe Zucchini Salad
2 tablespoons minced parsley

SALMON RING

Substitute 2 cups freshly cooked and flaked salmon for the crab meat and substitute finely snipped dill for the chives. Fill the salmon ring with a salad of cooked fresh baby green peas, bound with mayonnaise and sprinkled with chopped mint. Garnish with a ring of thin cucumber slices alternating with lemon slices.

SPRING SHRIMP

Combine shrimp with cooked and raw vegetables and bind with mayonnaise beaten with tarragon dressing. Chill and serve the shrimp mounded on a serving platter, with a circle of egg slices and a sprinkling of cut chives. Serve water cress and chive mayonnaise separately.

1½ pounds shrimp, peeled, deveined, and cooked
3 cups cooked vegetables (cauliflower, green peas, cut green beans, and diced carrots)
½ cup each diced celery and cucumber
¼ cup mayonnaise
¼ cup Tarragon Dressing
3 hard-cooked eggs, sliced
2 tablespoons finely cut chives
1 recipe Water Cress and Chive Mayonnaise

COLD SHRIMP CURRY

Arrange the rice in a wide bowl, cover it with the shrimp lightly mixed with avocado, green peppers, apples, nuts, and onions. Stir the curry powder into the soft butter until smooth, stir in the sour cream and season well. Fold in the mayonnaise and pour half the sauce over the shrimp mixture. Garnish with thin lime slices and serve very cold. Accompany the curry with a bowl of chutney and the remaining curry mayonnaise.

1½ cups rice, cooked al dente, page 145
2 pounds shrimp, peeled, deveined, and cooked
1 avocado, peeled and diced
½ green pepper, seeded and diced
2 tart apples, peeled, cored, and diced
½ cup toasted salted cashews (parched cashews in vacuum jars) chopped medium fine
¼ cup chopped spring onions or scallions
1 tablespoon curry powder, or to taste
1 tablespoon soft butter
⅔ cup sour cream
Salt and pepper to taste
1⅓ cups mayonnaise
2 limes, sliced knife-back thin
1 jar mango chutney

LOSTER VICTORIA

Combine the ingredients and marinate them in the refrigerator in the French dressing for at least 2 hours, turning them carefully a few times. Mound the mixture on a serving platter and garnish it with the halved tomatoes.

3 cups sliced and cubed cold cooked lobster meat
1 bunch asparagus spears, cut in short lengths, steamed and chilled
1 cucumber, peeled, seeded, and diced
2 peeled truffles, diced
5 large fresh mushrooms, thinly sliced
3 tablespoons minced herbs (chives, chervil, parsley, tarragon, and dill)
½ cup French Dressing

Cut tomatoes in half, scoop them out, and fill the half shells with mayonnaise sprinkled with chopped salted nuts.

GARNISH:
3 tomatoes, peeled
1 cup stiff mayonnaise
¼ cup chopped salted filberts or pecans

LOBSTER FLAMENCO

Cook the lobster lightly in the butter, add the brandy and flame. As soon as the flame dies down, stir in the cream. Add the tomato purée and the tarragon and simmer for 5 minutes. Cool the mixture, fold in the mayonnaise, the pimento strips, and the button mushrooms. Garnish the lobster with mustard stuffed eggs and serve very cold.

3 cups cold cooked lobster meat cut into large pieces
2 tablespoons butter
1 large jigger brandy, warmed
1 cup heavy cream
2 tablespoons thick tomato purée or paste
2 teaspoons chopped fresh tarragon or dried tarragon, scalded
¼ cup stiff mayonnaise
2 pimentos, cut into short strips
1 cup cooked button mushrooms, drained
1 recipe Mustard Stuffed Eggs

LOBSTER IN MUSTARD SAUCE

Split the boiled lobsters and crack the claws. Take out the green tomalley, pink coral, and white fat and retain them. Empty the bodies and remove the vein from the tail. Cool and chill the lobsters. Simmer shallots in brandy with the tarragon for a few minutes until the shallots are softened, take from heat, and stir in the mustard. As soon as the mixture is cold, fold it into the mayonnaise with the sieved tomalley, coral, and fat of the lobster. Before serving, fill the bodies with Monte Cristo salad and arrange the half lobsters on cold plates with their cracked claws. Garnish with lettuce hearts and pass the mustard sauce in a crystal or porcelain bowl.

3 2-pound lobsters, boiled
½ cup finely chopped shallots
⅓ cup brandy
2 tablespoons minced fresh tarragon or 1 tablespoon dried tarragon
2 tablespoons mild brown mustard, preferably Dijon
1 recipe homemade mayonnaise
1 recipe Monte Cristo Salad
2 heads Boston lettuce

COLD SALMON

There are four basic forms in which salmon lends itself ideally to cookery. As a whole drawn fish or a large section of it, as individual steaks, as a salmon mousse, or as a salad. The whole salmon is always gala (it can even be spectacular) for a dinner or buffet. Large pieces or individual steaks can be made very attractive and are entirely suitable as a main dinner course, while a cold salmon mousse may be served as a main luncheon or supper course or a first course at a large dinner. A salmon salad, depending on how it is garnished and presented, may be served in the same way as a mousse.

The *whole drawn salmon* means that head and tail are left intact and a fish kettle is needed to cook it. The whole drawn salmon usually has to be ordered a few days before it is needed. A large piece of *dressed salmon* means a center section, a TRONCON or a thick piece of over 1½ inches. It can also be the *darne* (center piece) or tail-piece, which has to be ordered in advance. Order approximately ½ pound of slices or steaks per person or a 6- to 8-pound salmon for 12 to 16 people. If the fish is richly garnished with shrimp, stuffed eggs, or small stuffed tomatoes, a 6- to 8-pound salmon can serve from 14 to 20. *Salmon steaks* are usually cut for individual service, and if a larger number are served, it will look better if they are of an even size. For a *salmon mousse* or *salad,* allow about ¼ to ⅓ pound of fish per person.

The salmon used for these four basic preparations has to be poached before it is cooled and chilled for final preparation. The cooking should be done on the day before it is to be served. I have often picked up a drawn salmon in the afternoon and cooked it immediately. It then cooled slowly in its own broth and was refrigerated overnight. On the following morning it was ready to be placed on its serving platter and decorated. I could put it back in the refrigerator before noon and forget about it until it was time to serve.

TO POACH A WHOLE SALMON

Wrap a 6- to 8-pound drawn salmon lightly in cheesecloth and lay it carefully into a fish kettle with the two ends of the cheesecloth folded over to act as handles when taking out the fish. Do not hang them over the side of the kettle, as they will prevent the lid from fitting securely and steam will escape. Add 3 to 4 quarts boiled and cooled Court Bouillon (given below) or enough to barely cover. Place the kettle over high heat and bring it to a boil. Reduce heat to simmer and hold the fish at simmering point until tender and done. Simmer for 6 to 10 minutes per pound, depending on size. The larger fish require more time. Bear in mind that the fish will cool in the bouillon and some cooking will continue after it is removed from the heat. A fish thermometer inserted in the thickest part would just read 140° F. Do not open the kettle to remove the fish until after it is entirely cold. Unwrap it carefully and do not be distressed if parts of the skin come away with the cheesecloth; you will undoubtedly scrape off the outside layer in any case, to reveal the salmon pink flesh, before you decorate the fish. A *darne,* or a tailpiece, is poached in the same way, allowing about 8 minutes of cooking to each pound of weight. For salmon steaks or tronçons or pieces less than 2 inches thick, allow 1 minute cooking time per ounce of weight, or 16 minutes for a 1-pound piece. A 1-inch steak will require 10 minutes in all. If a test is preferred, unwrap the fish and test, on the underside, with a fork or skewer. The fish is done if it flakes easily when tested with the fork or if the skewer comes out clean when inserted in the thickest part.

COURT BOUILLON

Simmer the bouillon for 25 minutes, strain, and cool it completely before pouring it over the fish.

3 quarts water
3 cups dry white wine
2 medium onions, sliced
2 carrots, scraped and sliced
4 sprigs parsley or dill
½ teaspoon dry or fresh thyme
1 bay leaf
6 peppercorns
1 parsley root—if you have a garden
¼ cup white vinegar

ASPIC FOR COLD SALMON

Soften 4 envelopes plain gelatin by stirring them into 1 cup light sherry. Pour the court bouillon remaining in the fish kettle into an enamel saucepan and reduce it to 4 cups by boiling rapidly. Pour it through a double layer of dense cloth, as a napkin, previously wrung out in warm water; repeat 3 times. Return the strained bouillon to the saucepan and bring it to a boil. Take it from the heat and stir in the gelatin and sherry until it is completely dissolved. Set it aside to cool but not to set. When cooled aspic starts to set and becomes too thick to flow, put the bowl into a larger bowl containing warm water. If the court bouillon is still unclear after straining, clarify it before reducing it.

TO CLARIFY COURT BOUILLON

Strain the court bouillon from the fish kettle into a clean soup kettle and cool. When it is cold lift any impurities from the surface and measure the quantity. For every 4 cups of bouillon add 1 egg white beaten slightly with 2 tablespoons of water. Add the eggshell, broken into small pieces. Place the kettle over heat and bring it slowly to the boiling point, stirring constantly. Boil for just 2 minutes, stirring. Let the bouillon stand undisturbed in a warm place or over very low heat for 20 minutes. Strain it through a triple layer of cheesecloth, wrung out in cold water and placed in a fine sieve.

Court bouillon may also be clarified with raw beef.

If time is limited, make the Aspic for Cold Salmon dishes with canned bouillon as described on page 98. The flavor of beef will not be noticeable over the sherry.

COLD SALMON RING filled with green pea salad

Stir plain gelatin into white wine or stock. In the top of a double boiler, over boiling water, melt butter, stir in flour and gradually add milk. Stir the mixture with a French wire whisk until it is thick and smooth. Take from heat and stir in the softened gelatin until it is dissolved. Let the mixture cool, stir in the salmon. Beat in the egg yolks and seasonings, onion and sugar. Fold in the cream and correct seasoning. Fill the salmon mixture into a rinsed 2-quart ring mold, cover it with foil, and chill it until set, or overnight. Before serving,

3 cups cooked salmon free of skin and bones, flaked
2 envelopes plain gelatin
¼ cup dry white wine, fish stock, or stock
3 tablespoons butter
3 tablespoons flour
1 cup milk
3 egg yolks, beaten
Salt and white pepper to taste
2 teaspoons minced onion
1 pinch sugar
1 cup heavy cream, whipped

dip the ring mold into hot water and unmold it onto a round platter. Decorate the outside of the ring with alternating lemon and tomato slices and fill the ring with Green Pea Salad with Mint. Serve with Curried Melba Toast.

SALMON STEAKS

Poach the salmon steaks in Court Bouillon or salted water for 10 minutes. Let them cool in the liquid. Take them out and chill them until needed. Stir the gelatin into ½ cup of the sherry. Heat the bouillon to boiling, take it from the heat, and stir in the gelatin until it is dissolved. Add the remaining sherry and let the aspic cool. Arrange the salmon steaks on a platter and secure the 2 ends of each to form an oval space. Fill this space with button mushrooms, heads up, and brush a coat of gelatin over the steaks. Arrange a pattern of tarragon leaves (or sliced stuffed olives) on the steaks and glaze with a second layer of aspic, always brushing the mushrooms generously. When the aspic has set and will prevent a new coat from running out of the oval space, continue to glaze the steaks and to fill the space around the mushrooms. If aspic becomes too thick, set it in a bowl of warm water. Chill the glazed steaks. Cut a lid from the tomatoes, empty them, and fill them with herbed mayonnaise. Arrange a platter or individual plates with the glazed salmon steaks, asparagus spears, and filled tomatoes. Refrigerate the platter or plates until ready to serve.

6 1-inch-thick salmon steaks of even size (do not remove skin)
2 envelopes plain gelatin
1 cup pale sherry
1 cup bouillon
1 can whole button mushrooms
Tarragon leaves
6 evenly sized tomatoes, peeled
1 recipe Herbed Mayonnaise
1 bunch cooked asparagus spears

SALMON MOUSSE PARISIENNE

Stir gelatin into the wine and set it aside. Poach the salmon, onion, and peppers in salted water to cover for 15 minutes. Take out the fish with a slotted spoon and return the skin and bones to the water the fish was boiled in. Increase heat and boil uncovered until fish stock is reduced to 1 cup. Strain and set it aside. If flaked salmon was used, substitute bouillon for fish stock. Melt the butter in the top of a double boiler over boiling water, stir in the flour until smooth, add the fish stock, and stir until it is thickened and smooth. Add the softened gelatin and continue to stir until it is dissolved. Take from heat, add the finely flaked or ground salmon, and season to taste. Cool the mixture, stir in the truffles and nuts, and fold in the whipped cream. Pour it into a 6-cup mold, rinsed in cold water, and chill for at least 2 hours. Before serving, unmold the mousse onto a large round platter and arrange 6 little wedges of overlapping shrimp around it. Intersperse the shrimp with small bunches of crisp water cress and serve with a bowl of cream or Swedish mayonnaise.

2 envelopes gelatin
½ cup dry white wine
1 pound salmon steaks or 2 cups cooked
  flaked salmon
2 onion slices
3 peppercorns
2 tablespoons butter
3 tablespoons flour
1 cup reduced stock from fish
Salt and white pepper to taste
2 peeled truffles, diced (optional)
¼ cup chopped pistachio nuts
¾ cup heavy cream, whipped

GARNISH:
1 pound cooked shrimp
½ bunch water cress, coarse stems removed
1 recipe Cream or Swedish Mayonnaise

HAM MOUSSE

Stir the gelatin into the wine and set it aside for 15 minutes. Melt the butter in the top of a double boiler over boiling water, stir in the flour until smooth, and add the bouillon. Continue stirring until the sauce is thickened and smooth. Add the gelatin and stir until it is dissolved. Take from heat, cool and add the ham, gherkins, parsley, and onion. Add salt only if the ham is very mild. Fold in the stiffly whipped cream and pour the mixture into a 6-cup mold, rinsed out in cold water. Chill it for at least 2 hours or until firmly set. Unmold the mousse onto a chilled platter and serve it with mustard mayonnaise. The mousse may also be poured into 6 individual molds. They should be unmolded to surround a Cauliflower or Asparagus Vinaigrette.

2 envelopes gelatin
½ cup dry white wine
3 tablespoons butter
3 tablespoons flour
1 cup bouillon
1 pound or 2 cups lean boiled ham, finely
  minced or ground
¼ cup minced sweet gherkins
2 tablespoons minced parsley
1 tablespoon minced onion
1 cup heavy cream, whipped
1 recipe Mustard Mayonnaise

HAM MOUSSE WITH ASPARAGUS

Stir the gelatin into ¼ cup of the stock and let it soften for 15 minutes. Bring the stock to a boil, take it from heat and stir in the gelatin until it is dissolved. Cool the mixture and stir in the ham, vinegar, mustard, relish, celery, and seasonings. Salt carefully if the ham is salty. Fold in the stiffly whipped cream and pour the mixture into a 6-cup mold, rinsed in cold water, or into 6 individual molds or custard cups. Chill the mousse for at least 2 hours. Unmold and serve it surrounded by the asparagus spears. If individual molds were used, mound the asparagus in the center of the platter and surround it with the individual mousses. Serve with Mustard or Cream Mayonnaise.

2 envelopes gelatin
1¼ cups meat stock or bouillon
2 cups ground ham, all fat removed
1 tablespoon tarragon vinegar
1 teaspoon Dijon or mild brown mustard
¼ cup well-drained sweet pickle relish
¼ cup finely chopped celery
Salt and pepper to taste
1 cup heavy cream, whipped
1 bunch asparagus, prepared and steamed,
*   page 161*

CHICKEN MOUSSE

Stir the gelatin into ¼ cup of the stock and let it soften for 15 minutes. Beat the egg yolks and remaining stock in the top of a double boiler over simmering water, until thickened. Add the gelatin and stir until it is dissolved. Take from heat and cool. Add the chicken, celery, green pepper, and parsley and season to taste. Fold in the stiffly whipped cream and pour the mixture into an 8-cup mold or ring mold, rinsed in cold water. Chill for at least 2 hours. Unmold on a lettuce-lined platter and serve with sour cream dressing or French dressing. If a ring mold was used, fill center with cold cooked green peas, lightly bound with French dressing and sprinkled with chopped mint or parsley or finely cut chives.

2 envelopes gelatin
1¼ cups chicken stock or consommé
3 egg yolks
2 cups finely chopped cooked chicken
⅓ cup chopped celery
2 tablespoons finely diced green pepper
2 tablespoons finely chopped parsley
Salt and white pepper to taste
1 cup heavy cream, whipped
1 recipe Sour Cream Dressing or French
*   Dressing*

CHICKEN CHAUD-FROID WHITE

If you usually make broth of wing tips, necks, and giblets, do not add it to the stock in this recipe as it will darken the white sauce.

Place chickens with carrots, onion, and parsley in a large kettle. Add fresh water to cover and take out the chickens. Bring the water to a rapid boil, add the chickens and salt to taste. As soon as the water returns to a boil, skim off the foam, reduce heat to a medium boil, and cook the chickens, covered, for about 20 minutes, or until tender. Pierce a drumstick with a sharp knife and if the juice that runs out is colorless, the chickens are done. Take out the pieces and cool them until they can be handled. Remove the backbones, wings, all skin that doesn't cover the breasts or second joints, and all scraps and return them to the soup kettle. Continue to simmer the stock, uncovered, until it is reduced to 6 cups. Arrange the reserved chicken pieces, meat side down, in a roasting pan, strain the reduced stock over them, cover with foil and refrigerate until needed. I usually do all this on the day before and glaze the chickens in the morning, but the whole thing can be done in 1 day. The only thing that is important is to allow enough time for the stock to become cold so that the fat can be lifted from the top.

4 fat young broilers, quartered
2 carrots, scraped and quartered
1 onion, quartered
6 sprigs parsley
Salt to taste
Butter as needed
⅔ cup flour
1 cup heavy cream
4 envelopes gelatin
¾ cup dry sherry
4 sprigs fresh or bottled (in vinegar) tarragon
4 smallest juice oranges
1 cup whole cranberry sauce
1 recipe Herbed Mayonnaise

CHAUD-FROID WHITE

Lift all fat from the stock, melt it in the top of a double boiler over boiling water, and add enough butter to make ½ cup. Stir in the flour and cook for 10 minutes longer. Gradually stir in 3 cups of the strained stock and stir until the sauce is smooth and thickened. Add the cream and cook, uncovered, stirring occasionally for 20 minutes. Stir 3 envelopes of the gelatin into ½ cup of the sherry and set it aside for 15 minutes. Stir the sauce vigorously with a French wire whisk, correct the seasoning, and stir in the gelatin until it is dissolved. Take the sauce from the heat and cool it to room temperature. In the meantime draw the skin from the chicken pieces, lift the breasts from the bones, and trim them neatly. Leave the second joints and drumsticks intact, but trim them and remove the knuckles from the end of the drumsticks. Arrange the pieces, meat side up and carefully dried, on a wire rack over a clean pan and spoon the sauce over them. The sauce will cling to the meat with the first coat. Chill chicken on the rack and repeat the spooning and chilling until the sauce is used up. Scrape the sauce that ran into the pan back into the double boiler and stir it over simmering water until it is back to flowing consistency. Coat the chicken pieces smoothly and repeat the chilling and the reheating of the sauce from the pan until the pieces are heavily covered and smooth. The 4 cups of sauce will be more than enough for the purpose. Chill the chicken until needed. Stir the remaining gelatin into the remaining sherry. Reduce the remaining stock to 1 cup, strain it through a fine sieve, and bring it back to a boil. Take from heat and stir in the gelatin until it is dissolved. Cool the aspic until it just begins to thicken. Dip tarragon leaves into the aspic and arrange 3 on each chicken breast and on the second joints. Chill again for 10 minutes and then brush aspic lightly over all the pieces. Two coats will be enough to glaze them. Return them to the refrigerator until needed.

Arrange the 8 chicken breasts on a serving tray or very large platter. Place a hollowed-out half of a small juice orange between each breast and fill it with cranberry sauce. Mound the legs in the center of the tray and garnish with parsley. Serve herbed mayonnaise in a crystal dish and serve the chaud-froid with Sunday Salad and homemade melba toast.

SUNDAY SALAD (may also be served as a main dish)

Soak the white beans overnight in 2 cups fresh water. At noon next day, add 2 cups water and 1 teaspoon salt and bring them to a boil. Boil them for 20 to 25 minutes until just tender and before the skins start to split. Drain them well and run cold water through them. There will be 2¼ to 2½ cups beans. Snap the ends off the green beans and put the beans in cold water for at least an hour. Arrange them, by the bunch, on a wooden cutting board and cut them across into ¼- to ⅓-inch lengths with a sharp knife. Boil them in salted water until they are barely tender, about 12 minutes, drain them well. There will be about 3 cups, combine them with the white beans and the cut dill and pour over enough orégano dressing to just bind. Cover and marinate in the refrigerator for at least 24 hours. Then add the minced onion, gherkins and stuffed olives and refrigerate until needed. I always prepare this salad 3 days before it is to be served. One or 2 days before serving, prepare the potatoes and zucchini. Peel and slice potatoes and boil them in salted water until *al dente*, just about 1 minute for some potatoes, so watch carefully after 1 minute and take them out while they are crisp. Drain, sprinkle with white wine, grind black pepper over them to taste, and chill. Trim and slice the zucchini and boil the slices in salted water until you can just see a small transparent circle around the seeds. Drain the zucchini at once and chill until needed.

To combine the salad, mix 2 tablespoons of the orégano dressing with 2 tablespoons of the herbed mayonnaise and pour over the potatoes. Turn them carefully and sprinkle with the cut chives. Drain the zucchini again and slice the tomatoes. Mound the beans in the center of a wide salad bowl or platter, divide the potato salad into 4 parts, and place them around the beans, alternating with the zucchini. Pour a little more orégano dressing over the zucchini and garnish with a circle of tomato slices.

Serve this salad with any of the cold meat dishes, or serve it as a main dish on Sunday night. In that case add the diced meat to the beans shortly before serving.

1 cup dried white beans
1 teaspoon salt
1 pound green snap or string beans
2 bunches dill, finely cut
1 recipe Orégano Dressing
2 tablespoons each minced onion, gherkin, and stuffed olives
1 pound new potatoes
Dry white wine
Pepper mill
1 pound zucchini
2 tablespoons Herbed Mayonnaise
Cut chives
1 pound tomatoes, sliced
1½ cups large dice of skinned bologna sausage or ham, optional

CHICKEN CHAUD-FROID BROWN

To the ingredients for the White Chaud-Froid, add 2 beef bouillon cubes, substitute truffle slices for the tarragon leaves and Madeira or port for the sherry. Follow the recipe in all other details up to chaud-froid white. At this point, brown the butter, enrich the stock, and turn it into a brown chaud-froid with different garnishes and accompaniments.

CHAUD-FROID BROWN

Brown the chicken fat and butter in the top of a double boiler. Stir in the flour over low heat and continue to stir until it is browned and absorbed. Heat 3 cups of the chicken stock and strengthen it with the 2 beef bouillon cubes. Set the top of the double boiler over boiling water in the lower section and stir the stock and cream slowly into the brown *roux* until the sauce is thickened and smooth. Correct the seasoning and, if necessary, add a dash of a gravy darkener, as Gravy Master or Kitchen Bouquet. Coat the chicken pieces with the brown chaud-froid exactly as for the white and decorate each piece with a thin truffle slice. Glaze with Madeira or port wine aspic. Serve the chicken chaud-froid brown, around Glazed Baked Apples, or around cold baked apples filled with whole cranberry or lingonberry preserve, or around Oranges Filled with Cumberland Sauce. Accompany the brown chicken chaud-froid with a Cauliflower or Asparagus Vinaigrette or a Monte Cristo Salad without lobster.

CHICKEN CHAUD-FROID WITH RICE SALAD WHITE

Prepare the chickens exactly as for Chicken Chaud-Froid, page 108. When ready to serve arrange the rice salad on a serving platter and place the chicken pieces around it. Garnish with halved tomatoes, emptied and filled with stiff mayonnaise.

3 fat young broilers, quartered
3 cups Chaud-Froid Sauce with Egg Yolk
1 recipe Herbed Rice Salad, without garnish
3 very small tomatoes, peeled
½ cup mayonnaise

CHAUD-FROID SAUCE WITH EGG YOLKS jellied white sauce

In the top of a double boiler, over boiling water, stir butter and flour into a *roux*. Stir the stock gradually into the roux and let it cook for 20 minutes. Stir the gelatin into the sherry and let it soften for 15 minutes. Take sauce from heat and stir in the gelatin until dissolved. Reduce heat so that water in lower section of double boiler is under simmering point. Return sauce and beat it over warm water until it is smooth. Beat cream with yolks, stir them into the warm sauce in a thin stream. Add salt to taste and stir until the sauce is smooth and thick. Cool the sauce until it is almost beginning to set, then use it to coat chicken breasts, whole small chickens, eggs, or any chaud-froid recipes. If the sauce sets, beat it over warm water. Never place it over boiling water.

4 tablespoons butter
5 tablespoons flour
2 cups clear chicken stock
2 to 3 envelopes gelatin (always use more gelatin in summer than in winter)
⅓ cup light sherry
1½ cups heavy cream
2 egg yolks
Salt to taste

COLD CHICKEN FRICASSEE

Put the chicken pieces into boiling salted water to cover and bring the water back to a boil. Skim off the foam, add the vegetables and herbs, and reduce heat to a slow boil. Cook covered for 20 minutes until the chicken is tender. Take it out, draw off the skin, and cut the supremes (the breast with the first wing joint) from the bones. Trim the pieces and return skin, bones, wing tips, necks, and scraps to the vegetables in the kettle. Boil uncovered until the stock is reduced to 5 cups. Strain the stock into a bowl, add the chicken pieces and refrigerate until the fat can be lifted from the surface. Put the fat into the top of a double boiler over boiling water, add enough butter to make ⅓ cup. Stir in the flour and cook for 10 minutes, stir in the strained stock and cook, stirring occasionally, for 20 minutes longer. Cook the onions in the butter in a heavy saucepan without letting the butter brown. When they are soft and transparent, add the apples and cook until they are tender but not soft. Lift the onions and apples to the sauce in the double boiler with a slotted spoon. Stir in the cream and flavor with Calvados or whiskey to taste. Season the sauce well and let it cool, add the chicken pieces and chill. Serve very cold garnished with water cress and accompany with Cauliflower or Asparagus Vinaigrette.

2 broilers, quartered
2 stalks celery
2 carrots
1 onion
1 bay leaf
2 sprigs each of thyme and parsley
Butter as needed
⅓ cup flour
⅓ cup chopped onions
3 tablespoons butter
2 apples, peeled and cut into large dice
1 cup heavy cream
Calvados or whiskey to taste
Salt and white pepper to taste
½ bunch crisp water cress

ARABIAN CHICKEN SALAD

Cut chicken meat in large pieces, combine it with the rice and shrimp in a bowl that has been rubbed with a garlic clove. Add cucumber and onion and bind the salad with a dressing of mayonnaise beaten with French dressing and strained chili sauce. Serve in a lettuce-lined bowl and circle the salad with overlapping slices of tomatoes, sprinkled with parsley.

1 frying chicken, simmered for 25 to 30 minutes and chilled
2 cups cold slightly undercooked rice
½ pound small shrimp, peeled, deveined, and cooked
½ clove garlic
1 small cucumber, peeled, seeded, and diced
½ onion, chopped
½ cup mayonnaise
¼ cup French Dressing
3 tablespoons chili sauce
Boston lettuce leaves
3 tomatoes, peeled
3 tablespoons finely chopped parsley

CHICKEN SALAD BAGRATION

Combine chicken, artichoke, celery, and macaroni with mayonnaise beaten with enough tomato purée to tint it pink. Season well and mound the salad in a shallow bowl. Cover it with the julienne of tongue, sprinkle with parsley, then with white of egg and finally with the riced yolk. Center with truffle dice and pass a separate bowl of more mayonnaise.

3 cups cubed cold cooked chicken
6 artichoke bottoms, cut into 6 wedges each
1 celery heart, scraped and diced
1 cup cooked macaroni, broken before cooking
½ cup mayonnaise
2 tablespoons tomato purée, or to taste
Salt and pepper to taste
6 slices cold smoked tongue, cut in julienne strips
3 tablespoons finely chopped parsley
2 hard-cooked eggs, yolk and white riced separately
1 large peeled truffle, diced (optional)

OPERA SALADE

Combine the meats, asparagus, and celery, bind them lightly with dressing and arrange them in a lettuce leaf-lined salad bowl. Surround the salad with overlapping slices of cucumber and the hard-cooked eggs, from which a thick lid has been cut and the yolk removed with a small coffee spoon. Use the egg yolks to make a Sauce Ravigote, and fill the sauce into the egg whites. Rice the egg white lids over the salad.

1 roasted frying chicken, skin removed, meat cut into large pieces
3 thick slices smoked tongue, trimmed and cut into dice
½ pound asparagus, steamed, tender spears cut into short lengths
1 heart of celery, scraped and diced
French Dressing to bind
1 head Boston lettuce
1 cucumber, thinly sliced
6 hard-cooked eggs, cut across the bottom to stand upright

COLD CHICKEN PIE

Put chicken pieces, including necks and giblets, into boiling water to cover. As soon as it returns to a boil, skim off the foam and add the vegetables, parsley, and salt. Boil gently for 20 minutes. Take out the pieces and draw off the skin. Trim the breasts from the bones, leaving the wings on, and return the bones, skin, and scraps to the kettle of stock. Increase heat and reduce the stock to about 3 cups. Strain the stock and slice the liver and heart. Melt the butter in the top of a double boiler over boiling water and stir in the flour. Add the strained stock and stir until the sauce is thickened and smooth. Arrange the chicken pieces in a 9×14×1¾ inch Pyrex baking dish and fill the spaces with mushrooms, onions, eggs (which should be sliced but not spread or opened). Stir the parsley and sliced liver and heart into the sauce and pour it over. Cool the ingredients and cover with the crust. Pinch it down firmly, cut vents into the top, and cut the scraps into flowers and leaves, using a fluted cookie cutter. Dip them in the beaten egg and ornament the top. Brush the top and cutouts with egg and bake the pie in a 375° F. oven until the crust is golden, about 35 to 45 minutes. Cool and serve cold with a crisp water cress salad and Cranberry Relish.

2 broilers, quartered
3 carrots, scraped and quartered
1 onion, quartered
1 celery stalk, roughly chopped
3 sprigs parsley
Salt to taste
5 tablespoons butter
5 tablespoons flour
1 6-ounce can button mushrooms
12 small white onions, trimmed and parboiled
6 hard-cooked eggs
3 tablespoons finely chopped parsley
1 recipe Golden Cheese Crust (given below)

GOLDEN CHEESE CRUST

Work butter and cheese into flour sifted with salt and paprika and work, with the lightly beaten yolk, into a smooth paste. Chill, roll out thin, and use to cover the pie. Brush with beaten egg before baking.

1½ cubes or ¾ cup butter
¾ cup sieved or grated sharp Cheddar cheese
2¼ cups flour
1 teaspoon salt
2 teaspoons paprika
1 egg yolk
1 egg beaten with 1 tablespoon cold water

GREEN CHICKEN SALAD

Cut asparagus spears into short lengths, tender part only, and combine them with the chicken, green peas, and black olives. Bind the salad lightly with mayonnaise whipped with heavy cream and serve the rest separately. Add seasonings. Arrange the salad in a bowl and garnish it with green pepper and pimento.

1 bunch asparagus spears, steamed and
   chilled
3 cups cubed cold cooked chicken
1½ cups cold cooked green peas
3 tablespoons diced black olives
⅔ cup mayonnaise
⅓ cup heavy cream
Salt and pepper to taste
⅓ green pepper, seeded and finely
   chopped
1 pimento, diced

BEEFSTEAK TARTARE

Bring the beef slices to room temperature and scrape them to obtain beef without sinews, fat, or gristle. Hold the beef down firmly on a counter or table and scrape a tablespoon or soup spoon across its surface, away from you. Hold the spoon close to the bowl and exert a light pressure in scraping it across the meat. The bowl of the spoon will fill with soft red beef, which should be placed on a plate. As enough meat accumulates, it should be covered with a small inverted bowl. Turn the slice several times until all the meat has been scraped out of it and only the edge and sinews remain. Do the same to the second slice and serve before the meat turns dark.
TO SERVE: Shape the meat into two loose nests, do not press it

2 1-inch-thick slices top round of beef
2 egg yolks
GARNISHES:
2 little mounds of finely chopped onion
2 little mounds of brown mustard
1 little mound of caraway seeds
1 little mound of paprika on a lemon slice
1 little mound of pepper
1 little mound of salt
2 little mounds of minced dill pickle
1 little mound of minced anchovies
1 little mound of minced parsley

heavily. Drop an egg yolk into each and surround the meat with little mounds of the traditional garnishes.

The more traditional or nonattainable additions are: a small jar of beluga caviar, or a splash of old sherry. The least informed add catsup, Worcestershire sauce, or oil. Serve with buttered thin slices of pumpernickel or rye bread.

COLD BOILED BEEF

Place the short ribs into a large kettle of cold water and bring them to a boil. Skim the foam from the surface and add the vegetables and seasonings. Boil for 30 minutes. Plunge the brisket into the boiling stock, and when it returns to a boil, reduce heat, skim it again, and cover the kettle, leaving a small opening. Simmer until the brisket is tender, about 2 to 2½ hours. Take out the brisket and let it cool. Strain the stock, cool it, chill it, and lift off the fat. Place the brisket in a bowl, cover it with cold stock, and refrigerate it until needed. To serve, take out the meat, trim it neatly, and slice it thinly. Use the stock for some other purpose.

1 pound short ribs of beef
2 carrots
2 onions
2 stalks celery
1 bay leaf
2 sprigs parsley
4 peppercorns
2 teaspoons salt, or to taste
3 pounds brisket of beef, tied to hold its shape

Serve the meat with:

Add onion, capers, and parsley to the dressing and serve it with the meat. Serve the remaining accompaniments on a relish dish or in several small dishes.

½ onion, chopped
2 tablespoons chopped capers
2 tablespoons minced parsley
1 recipe French Wine Dressing
2 cups Pickled Beets
2 cups Cucumber Salad
½ recipe Potato Salad
2 dill pickles, sliced
Düsseldorf mustard
Curls of freshly grated horseradish

BEEF VINAIGRETTE

Place the beef in salted furiously boiling water to cover. As soon as the water returns to a boil, skim off the scum, reduce heat to simmer, and cook the beef, covered, for 1 hour. Drain and cool. Cut the beef into 3 thick slices and lay them side by side in a casserole with a tightly fitting cover. Add 2 cups water, brought to a boil with the wine, the bouquet and bay leaf, onion, spices, and salt. Cover the casserole closely and simmer the meat for 1 hour longer. Depending on the quality of the meat, if it is tender, add the vinegar, simmer for 15 minutes longer, and cool the beef in the casserole. If the pieces are not tender, boil for approximately 30 minutes longer before adding the vinegar. When the beef is cold, place the casserole in the refrigerator until needed. Serve sliced with the boiled potatoes and the vinaigrette sauce.

Since almost everything needed for a fully rounded meal is in a *meat salad,* serve it with cheese and fruit. Either start the meal with fruit and end with cheese, or start with the salad and end with fruit and cheese.

3 pounds brisket of beef
1 cup white wine
1 bouquet of herbs (parsley, thyme, basil, rosemary, chervil)
1 bay leaf
1 onion, sliced
4 each peppercorns and cloves, roughly pounded
Salt to taste
¼ cup mild tarragon vinegar
4 to 6 cold boiled potatoes, sliced
1 recipe Vinaigrette Sauce

SALADS

CHAPTER SIX

Salad Dressings, Sauces, Relishes, and Salads

MOST combined and nonsweetened cold foods, especially when they are bound with a cold and salty sauce, are usually grouped as salads. At the same time a bowl of mixed greens is also a salad. The first group constitutes important parts of the meal or even a meal in itself, while the second group is an accompaniment, usually for the meat course, or a refresher to follow a meat course.

The word "salad" derives from *sal* (salt) and has come to mean any cold cooked or raw food combined with a piquant and salty dressing. Salad can be served as an appetizer—the hors d'oeuvre tray is a series of salads—main course, or side dish. Starting a meal with a salad is an important health and/or weight-loss measure, not just something they do in California.

The artfully arranged salads and even the molded salads are largely a thing of the past. They take too much time to create and, since we want to cook and arrange our cold dishes ahead, few of us have the refrigerator space for six or more salad plates, all arranged with rosettes of mayonnaise on picturesque compositions. Aspic is a great enhancer, whether it is a diced garnish, a *glaze*, or a *mirror*, but burying coleslaw in a mold of sweet lime jelly does not add to it.

The salad chapter is large because it combines the accompaniment salads with the separate-course salads and some of the full meal-in-one salads (others are among the entrees). All sauces, except the sweet ones, are in this chapter. There are a great many because the list of salad ingredients may be long, but it can be made endless with changes in the dressings, mayonnaises, and sauces. A lobster salad may start off with the same main ingredients, but, combined with potatoes and Mustard Mayonnaise, it is totally different from when it is served under Curry Mayonnaise with hard-cooked eggs and apples.

A Chiffonade Dressing on Belgian endive has no resemblance to endive under Roquefort Cheese Dressing and Mayonnaise, and we have only ourselves to blame when there is a certain monotony in our salads.

The directions for making French Dressings usually call for stirring or shaking to obtain the traditional thin French Dressing variations. If an emulsified dressing is preferred, any of the recipes can be made in the blender. Shake them well before using.

MAYONNAISE made in blender

Combine vinegar, egg, and seasonings in blender container. Cover and blend at top speed for 5 seconds. Uncover and add the oil in a thin stream, while the motor is running. Turn off the motor when all the oil has been added and scrape down the sides of the container with a rubber scraper. Stir the mayonnaise with the scraper to remove the oil slick from the center, cover and blend once more at top speed for 4 seconds. Pour the mayonnaise into a container, cover closely, and store in refrigerator as needed.

2 tablespoons French wine vinegar
1 egg
1 to 1½ teaspoons salt, to taste
1 teaspoon dry English mustard
¼ teaspoon white pepper
1 cup peanut oil

CURRY MAYONNAISE

Follow directions for Mayonnaise, above. Blend the curry powder with the first ingredients, then add the oil. If more curry is preferred, do not stir it into the finished mayonnaise. Take out a little mayonnaise, stir the curry into it until smooth and then blend it back into the curry mayonnaise. Serve with fish, raw or cooked cauliflower, hard-cooked eggs, or as the recipe requires.

1 tablespoon wine vinegar
1 egg
½ teaspoon salt
1 teaspoon dry mustard
¼ teaspoon pepper
½ to 1 teaspoon curry powder
1 cup peanut oil

TARRAGON MAYONNAISE

Follow directions for Mayonnaise above, blending the tarragon with the first ingredients until it is roughly chopped. Add the oil and chill before serving.

1 tablespoon tarragon vinegar
1 egg
¾ teaspoon salt
½ teaspoon dry mustard
¼ teaspoon white pepper
½ tablespoon dried tarragon, scalded, and/or
*   4 sprigs fresh tarragon, stems removed*
1 cup peanut oil

HERBED MAYONNAISE

Follow directions for Mayonnaise, blending the herbs with the first ingredients until they are roughly chopped. Add the oil and chill before serving.

1 tablespoon tarragon vinegar
1 egg
1 teaspoon salt
1 teaspoon dry English mustard
¼ teaspoon pepper
1 tablespoon finely cut chives
2 sprigs parsley, stems removed
1 sprig chervil, stem removed
1 sprig tarragon, stem removed
1 cup peanut oil

GREEN MAYONNAISE

Wilt the spinach and herbs in a little boiling water, drain them very well. Press out all liquid and mince the herbs into a rough purée in a bowl. Make the Mayonnaise as given above. When it is finished, add the green juices pressed from the purée. If preferred, part of the purée may be blended into the mayonnaise after it is completed.

1 tightly packed cup washed spinach leaves, parsley sprigs, roughly cut chives, chervil, basil, and tarragon leaves
1 tablespoon tarragon vinegar
1 egg
1 teaspoon salt
½ teaspoon dry English mustard
¼ teaspoon pepper
1 cup peanut oil

WATER CRESS AND CHIVE MAYONNAISE

Chop the cress finely and add the chives. Make the Mayonnaise as given above and fold in the chopped cress mixture after it is completed. If preferred, the cress may be added gradually to the mayonnaise in the blender with the motor running, until it is cut fine. Stir in the chives and chill before serving.

½ bunch water cress, all stems removed
3 tablespoons cut chives
1 tablespoon lemon juice
1 egg
1 teaspoon salt
½ teaspoon dry English mustard
¼ teaspoon pepper
1 cup peanut oil

ESCOFFIER MAYONNAISE I

Prepare a plain homemade Mayonnaise in the beater or the blender, page 122.

Beat the onion, mustard, and sauce into the mayonnaise and add more Escoffier sauce to taste. Chill the sauce and serve it, sprinkled with parsley, with a cold veal roast and a salad of green peas.

2 teaspoons scraped onion
2 teaspoons Dijon mustard
½ to 1 tablespoon Escoffier Sauce, to taste
1 cup Mayonnaise
1 tablespoon finely chopped parsley

ESCOFFIER MAYONNAISE II

Combine the mayonnaise with all ingredients and stir well. Chill until needed. Serve with fish, eggs, or vegetables. Also good with cold chicken.

½ recipe or 1¼ cups Mayonnaise made in the blender, page 122
5 tablespoons finely chopped unpeeled red radishes
2 teaspoons finely chopped fresh chervil
1 tablespoon finely chopped parsley
1 teaspoon finely cut chives

LEMON MAYONNAISE in the blender

Place egg, lemon juice, rind, and seasonings in blender container. Blend at high speed for 4 seconds. Remove the top, with the motor running, and add the oil in a thin stream. Turn off motor, scrape down the sides of the container, and stir the mayonnaise once with the rubber scraper. Blend for 4 seconds longer and store in refrigerator until needed.

1 egg
1 tablespoon lemon juice
Grated rind of 1 lemon
½ teaspoon salt
¼ teaspoon white pepper
¼ teaspoon dry mustard
1 cup salad oil

LEMON DILL MAYONNAISE

Cut off the soft fronds of dill and discard the coarse stems. Cut the dill finely with kitchen scissors to obtain 3 to 4 tablespoons. Stir them into the mayonnaise after the oil has been added. The blender will not cut the dill.

TARRAGON MAYONNAISE in blender

If dried tarragon is used, steep it in the vinegar for several hours before making the mayonnaise. If fresh tarragon is available, discard all stems and cut the leaves roughly with a kitchen scissors. If the tarragon from the vinegar bottle is used, it is usually very soft and can be broken into the mayonnaise before the last blending. Place egg, vinegar, and dry ingredients in the blender container, cover, and blend for 4 seconds. Uncover, with the motor running at high speed, and add the oil in a thin stream. Turn off motor and scrape down the sides of the container. Add the fresh tarragon leaves or the broken sprigs from the bottle and blend only long enough to mince them roughly. Do not blend until the tarragon is powdered. Chill until needed.

3 sprigs fresh tarragon, or 1 teaspoon dried tarragon, crushed, or the tarragon sprigs from the vinegar bottle
1 egg
1 tablespoon tarragon vinegar
1 teaspoon salt
½ teaspoon English mustard
¼ teaspoon white pepper
1 cup salad oil

CREAM MAYONNAISE in blender

Place egg, vinegar, and seasonings in blender container, cover, and blend at high speed for 3 seconds. Remove the cover with motor running and add the oil in a thin stream. Turn off the motor and scrape down the sides of the container; stir the mayonnaise once with the scraper. Cover and blend for 4 seconds longer. Chill the mayonnaise until needed, then fold in the whipped cream and serve.

1 egg
1 tablespoon wine vinegar
1 teaspoon salt
½ teaspoon English mustard
¼ teaspoon white pepper
1 cup salad oil
½ cup whipped cream

ANCHOVY MAYONNAISE

Combine all ingredients and serve over hard-cooked eggs or cold poached eggs.

1 recipe or 1 cup Mayonnaise
4 anchovy fillets, minced
1 tablespoon finely cut chives
1 tablespoon lemon juice

MUSTARD MAYONNAISE in blender

Place egg, vinegar, and seasonings in blender container and blend at high speed for 3 seconds. Open the container with the motor running and add the oils in a thin stream. Turn off the motor and scrape down the sides of the container. With the scraper, stir the mayonnaise once, add the mustard and dill, and stir once more. Cover and blend only until smooth. More mustard may be added to taste. Most blenders do not cut dill, so finely snipped dill must be added. Chill the mayonnaise until needed.

If a blender is not available, use dill-flavored vinegar in making the mayonnaise and add mustard and snipped dill as above, just before completing.

1 egg
1½ tablespoons dill vinegar
1 teaspoon salt, or to taste
¼ teaspoon freshly ground black pepper
¼ cup olive oil
¾ cup salad oil
2 tablespoons mild brown mustard, preferably Dijon or Düsseldorf
1 tablespoon finely snipped dill if available

SWEDISH MAYONNAISE

Beat or blend the mayonnaise, add the applesauce and horseradish, and beat or blend only long enough to mix well. Chill and serve with cold pork roast or with herring fillets.

1 recipe or 1 cup Mayonnaise
¼ cup thick applesauce, made of sour apples
1 tablespoon finely grated horseradish

AFRICAN MAYONNAISE

Beat or blend the mayonnaise, add the remaining ingredients, and beat or blend until smooth. Chill and serve with cold cooked asparagus or fruit salad.

1 recipe or 1 cup Mayonnaise
4 tablespoons cream cheese, riced
3 tablespoons orange juice
1 tablespoon grated orange rind
2 teaspoons port wine, or to taste

TARRAGON VINEGAR I

Place tarragon in a sterilized quart jar. Bring the remaining ingredients to a boil and pour them over the tarragon. Let steep for 2 weeks in a cool place. Pour the vinegar through a triple cheesecloth, wrung out in cold water. Boil the jar to sterilize it, fill the vinegar back into it, and return the tarragon sprigs. Cover and refrigerate or store in a cool place. Use wherever recipes call for tarragon vinegar.

6 cleaned sprigs tarragon
3 cups white wine vinegar
1 clove garlic, roughly chopped
2 shallots, minced
½ small onion, stuck with 3 cloves
4 black peppercorns, roughly crushed
1 pinch anise seeds, crushed

TARRAGON VINEGAR II

Wash and dry enough fresh tarragon to obtain 2 cups of crushed leaves. Place them in a glass jar with the cloves and peppercorns. Pour the boiling vinegar over the tarragon, seal the jar, and keep it at room temperature for 10 days, shaking well every day. Strain the vinegar into a sterilized bottle, and use it when recipes call for tarragon vinegar.

2 cups crushed tarragon leaves
2 cloves, crushed
2 peppercorns, crushed
2 cups wine vinegar, heated to boiling

FRENCH DRESSING I

Stir vinegar with salt and pepper and mustard until the salt dissolves. Stir in the oil and store in a closed jar in the refrigerator. Shake very well before using. Use this basic French dressing for marinating salads unless otherwise specified in the recipes.

⅓ cup tarragon vinegar
1¼ to 1½ teaspoons salt
¼ teaspoon freshly ground black pepper, or to taste
1 teaspoon dry or brown mustard, optional
⅓ cup olive oil
⅓ cup salad oil

FRENCH DRESSING II (made over the salad)

Over the bowl of crisp *dry* salad greens, stir the salt, pepper, and mustard with the vinegar in a large salad spoon. When the salt is dissolved and the mustard is smooth, empty the spoon over the greens. Lift the greens until all leaves have been lightly touched with the vinegar. Add the oil and continue to lift and turn the leaves lightly until the oil adheres to all of them.

¼ teaspoon salt
¼ teaspoon freshly ground black pepper
1 teaspoon Dijon mustard
1 tablespoon wine vinegar
2 tablespoons olive oil

HERB FRENCH DRESSING

Shake vinegar and seasonings until salt is dissolved. Add all other ingredients and shake well. Chill until needed and shake vigorously before using.

¼ cup tarragon vinegar
1 teaspoon salt
¼ teaspoon freshly ground white pepper
¼ cup olive oil
¼ cup salad oil
1 teaspoon minced onion
1 tablespoon minced parsley
1 teaspoon minced summer savory
1 teaspoon minced chervil or 1 teaspoon minced chives or 1 teaspoon minced basil

LEMON FRENCH DRESSING

Shake or stir the salt, pepper, and mint with the lemon juice and rind until the salt is dissolved. Add the oil and use the dressing over green salads, green pea or cauliflower salads.

1 teaspoon salt
¼ teaspoon freshly ground pepper, or to taste
2 tablespoons finely chopped fresh mint or 2 teaspoons dried mint, scalded
¼ cup lemon juice and a little of the grated rind
½ cup oil

MUSTARD FRENCH DRESSING

Stir the mustard with the dry ingredients until smooth. Beat in the parsley and lemon juice until light and foamy. Fold in the whipped cream and chill until needed. If preferred the sauce can be prepared in advance and chilled. The cold whipped cream can be added before it is served.

1 to 2 tablespoons mild mustard, preferably Dijon, to taste
1 teaspoon sugar
1 teaspoon salt
½ teaspoon paprika
Freshly ground black pepper to taste
2 tablespoons minced parsley
2 tablespoons lemon juice
½ cup heavy cream, whipped

PAPRIKA FRENCH DRESSING

Stir all dry ingredients with the vinegar until salt, mustard, and sugar are dissolved. Stir in the oil and store in a cool place. Shake before serving.

1 tablespoon sweet paprika
1½ teaspoons salt
1½ teaspoons dry mustard
½ teaspoon sugar
¼ teaspoon freshly ground black pepper
⅓ cup tarragon vinegar
⅔ cup salad oil

PROVINCIAL FRENCH DRESSING

When there are so many minced ingredients in a sauce, it is easier to cut them roughly and let the blender mince them. As the blender emulsifies the oil, it always creates a thick dressing. If a thin dressing is preferred, mince the pimento, green pepper, parsley, and onion in the blender with the vinegar, seasonings, and mustard, and stir the mixture into the oils. Pour it over the salad just before mixing and serving it.

¼ cup olive oil
¼ cup salad oil
¼ cup tarragon vinegar
¼ clove garlic, crushed
1 teaspoon salt, or to taste
¼ teaspoon freshly ground black pepper
1 teaspoon Dijon mustard
1 tablespoon minced pimento
1 tablespoon minced green pepper
1 tablespoon minced parsley
1 tablespoon minced onion

OPTIONAL ADDITIONS:
1 tablespoon minced green olives
1 tablespoon minced sweet gherkins

SOUR CREAM FRENCH DRESSING

In the top of a double boiler, away from the heat, whip the cream with the yolks and gradually add the vinegar. Combine the dry ingredients and beat them into the cream. Place *over* simmering water in the lower section of the double boiler and beat until creamy and smooth. Do not let upper section of boiler touch the simmering water. Serve cold.

1 cup sour cream
2 well-beaten egg yolks
3 tablespoons tarragon vinegar
1 tablespoon powdered sugar, or to taste
2 teaspoons salt
1 teaspoon dry mustard
½ teaspoon celery salt
½ teaspoon paprika

TARRAGON FRENCH DRESSING

Stir vinegar with salt and pepper until the salt is dissolved. Stir in the mustard until smooth and gradually add the oil and beat or stir well. Add shallots and herbs and chill until needed. Shake vigorously before using.

¼ cup tarragon vinegar
2 teaspoons salt
Freshly ground pepper to taste
1 tablespoon Dijon mustard
5 tablespoons salad oil, or half olive and half salad oil
1 tablespoon minced shallots
2 teaspoons finely cut chives
2 teaspoons finely chopped tarragon

BACON DRESSING

Cut the bacon into ⅓-inch squares with a kitchen scissors. Fry them in a small pan until they are transparent, add the butter and onion, and fry until bacon is golden. Drain the bacon and onion well and retain the fat. Add the vinegar and French dressing to the bacon and onions and stir well.

FOR CABBAGE SALAD: Finely shred 1 medium head white cabbage. Scald the shreds in boiling salted water for 3 minutes, then drain them well and pour over the bacon dressing and the bacon fat. Season with additional salt and pepper to taste and stir well with 1 teaspoon caraway seeds and 1 tablespoon minced parsley.

FOR SPINACH SALAD: Wash and dry 1 pound fresh spinach, remove the coarse stems and wilted leaves. Put the spinach in a bowl, pour over the bacon dressing and about 3 tablespoons of the bacon fat. Mix the salad gently and add a little more of the fat to taste.

FOR POTATO SALAD: Boil the sliced potatoes, as for White Wine Potato Salad. Pour over the bacon fat and the bacon dressing while they are still warm. Mix very gently and add French dressing to taste. Sprinkle the salad with finely chopped parsley and crumble 2 slices crisp bacon over the top.

12 slices bacon, chilled
1 tablespoon butter
½ medium onion, chopped
¼ cup tarragon vinegar
2 tablespoons French Dressing

FRUIT SALAD DRESSING

Fold cream into mayonnaise, combine vinegar, lemon juice, seasonings, water cress, and nuts. Just before serving, fold the mayonnaise and cream into the mixture and pour over the fruit.

½ cup heavy cream, whipped
1 cup chilled Lemon Mayonnaise
2 tablespoons tarragon vinegar
½ tablespoon lemon juice
Salt and freshly ground black pepper to taste
½ cup finely chopped water cress leaves
¼ cup finely chopped pistachio nuts

ITALIAN DRESSING

Shake and stir the vinegar and salt until the salt is dissolved. Add the oils and mix well. Add all other ingredients and shake for 3 minutes. Chill and serve over tuna fish, tomato, or mushroom salad, or as the recipes require.

¼ cup wine vinegar
1 teaspoon salt
¼ cup olive oil
½ cup salad oil
½ teaspoon paprika
¼ teaspoon pepper
1 tablespoon minced parsley
1 tablespoon minced onion
1 tablespoon minced stuffed olives
½ tablespoon minced green pepper

LEMON CREAM DRESSING

Beat the eggs until thick and creamy in the top of a double boiler away from heat. Add the lemon juice and rind and beat very well. Beat in the salt, paprika, and mustard and place *over* simmering water in the lower section of the double boiler. Immediately beat in the butter in 2 pieces. Beat only until the sauce is smooth. It will curdle if it is overbeaten and if the upper section of the boiler touches the simmering water. Add the chives and serve cold.

3 eggs
1 lemon, juice and grated rind
1 teaspoon salt
½ teaspoon paprika
½ teaspoon brown mustard
2 tablespoons cold butter
2 tablespoons finely cut chives

ORÉGANO DRESSING

Beat vinegar with salt until salt is dissolved. Stir pepper, mustard, and Maggi seasoning with the garlic until the mustard is smooth, then beat in the vinegar and add the oil gradually. Add the orégano and chill the dressing until needed. Shake well before using.

2 tablespoons vinegar
½ tablespoon salt
½ teaspoon roughly ground pepper
½ teaspoon dry mustard
½ teaspoon Maggi seasoning
½ clove garlic, crushed
1 cup salad oil
*2 tablespoons dried orégano, scalded and
    drained*

RED WINE VINEGAR DRESSING

Make this dressing a little tarter than usual.

Stir vinegar with the dry ingredients until the mustard is smooth. Beat in the oils and chill until needed.

⅓ cup red wine vinegar
1 teaspoon salt
¼ teaspoon pepper
1 pinch sugar
½ teaspoon dry mustard
⅓ cup salad oil
2 tablespoons olive oil

ROQUEFORT DRESSING

Rice the cheese into a bowl through a coarse sieve. Stir in the oil slowly until smooth and light. Stir the vinegar with the mustard, paprika, salt, and sugar until the salt and sugar are dissolved. Stir the vinegar mixture into the cheese and serve on lettuce or mixed green salads. To thin the dressing, stir in mayonnaise to taste.

½ cup crumbled Roquefort, tightly packed
½ cup salad oil
2 tablespoons vinegar
1 teaspoon brown mustard
½ teaspoon paprika
¼ teaspoon salt, or to taste
1 pinch sugar, optional
Mayonnaise

ROQUEFORT PIMENTO DRESSING

Rice the cheese over a bowl of crisp lettuce or over a bowl of sliced tomatoes. Sprinkle over the pimento. Shake the remaining ingredients except parsley well, pour them over the salad, and sprinkle with parsley.

¼ cup crumbled Roquefort cheese
3 tablespoons diced pimento
¼ cup vinegar
6 tablespoons salad oil
1 teaspoon salt
2 grindings of pepper
½ teaspoon paprika
2 tablespoons chopped parsley

ST. REGIS DRESSING

Combine all ingredients except the beets and shake the dressing well. Add the beets, chill until needed, and shake well before serving over romaine, endive, or egg salad.

1 recipe Lemon French Dressing
1 tablespoon minced onion
1 tablespoon minced chervil or parsley
1 teaspoon minced capers
1 tablespoon finely chopped stuffed olives
2 tablespoons finely chopped pickled red
    beets

SALAD DRESSING FOR ZUCCHINI

Place all ingredients except the grated lemon rind in blender, cover, and blend until parsley and mint are finely chopped and oil is emulsified. This yields about 1¼ cups or enough for 2 zucchini salads made with 1 pound zucchini each. Sprinkle lemon rind over dressed salad.

2 lemons, juice and grated rind
¾ cup salad oil
½ teaspoon salt
4 to 5 parsley sprigs, stems removed
4 to 5 mint sprigs, stems removed, or ½
*   teaspoon dried mint*
5 peppercorns
½ teaspoon sweet paprika
Less than a pinch of powdered sugar
1 clove garlic, sliced
2 tablespoons roughly chopped sweet onion

AVOCADO SALAD

The same dressing is suitable for avocado salad. Peel ripe avocados, allowing ½ for each person. Cut them in half lengthwise and remove the stone. Lay the half avocados, cut side down, on crisp Boston lettuce leaves on 6 salad plates and cut them across into ½-inch slices, leaving them intact. Pour over the dressing and serve.

DRESSING FOR VEGETABLE SALADS

Put peppercorns, onion, dill seed, and salt in blender. Cover and blend until pepper is roughly broken. Add the dressing and blend for 4 seconds longer. Pour the dressing into a bowl, stir in the mayonnaise, sour cream, and finely cut dill. Use to bind vegetable salads or a Russian Salad of mixed vegetables.

3 peppercorns
½ slice onion
⅛ teaspoon dill seed
1 pinch salt
¼ cup French Wine Dressing
½ cup mayonnaise
3 tablespoons sour cream
1 teaspoon finely cut fresh dill

MINTED APPLE JELLY

Melt the jelly in the top of a double boiler over boiling water. Stir in the mint, cover, and cook for 12 minutes. Stir in crème de menthe to taste and chill the sauce before serving.

1 10-ounce jar apple jelly
4 tablespoons finely chopped fresh mint
*   leaves*
1 teaspoon white crème de menthe, or to
*   taste*

LIME AND APPLE RELISH

Scrub limes and soak them in cold water for 24 hours. Drain and cover them again with fresh water in the upper section of a double boiler. Set them over direct heat and boil for 20 minutes. As soon as they are cool enough to handle, drain them and cut them into quarters and cut the quarters into 3 pieces over the double boiler in order to catch all the juice. Remove seeds and drop the lime pieces into the juice. Set the top over the double boiler over boiling water and add the apple jelly. Stir slowly until it is dissolved. In a heavy pan, boil sugar and water until the sugar is dissolved. Add the vinegar and boil for 15 minutes longer or until the mixture is thickened. Add it to the jelly and limes and cook uncovered over boiling water until the liquid is syrupy and the limes are very soft. Pour into hot sterilized jars, seal, and cool. Makes between 5 and 6 cups depending on the size of the limes.

16 limes
1 10-ounce jar apple jelly
1 cup sugar
⅓ cup water
¾ cup tarragon vinegar

CRANBERRY RELISH

Pick over cranberries and rinse them. Melt the sugar with the vinegar in a small heavy kettle over low heat. Chop the orange finely, skin and all, and add it with its juice to the sugar. Bring it to a boil, add the cranberries and spices, and stir with a wooden spoon until all of the cranberries have burst. Chill the relish and serve. Leftover relish may be stored in a covered jar in the refrigerator.

1 pound box cranberries, 4 cups
1⅔ cups sugar
½ cup cider vinegar
1 small eating orange, pitted
1 cinnamon stick about 2 inches long
12 whole cloves
¼ teaspoon ground ginger

SAUCE ALEXANDRA

Rice the yolks into a bowl and prepare the sauce exactly like Sauce Gribiche. At the end fold in the egg whites cut to short matchsticks and the truffles. Serve with cold meat, poultry, or fish.

3 hard-cooked large eggs, separated
2 teaspoons dry English mustard
2 teaspoons tarragon vinegar
Salt and pepper to taste
1 cup salad oil
1 tablespoon minced chervil
½ tablespoon minced tarragon
1 tablespoon finely chopped pickle
1 tablespoon finely diced truffle

APPLE CHUTNEY

Spread tomatoes in a wide enamel or porcelain dish and sprinkle with 1 tablespoon of the salt. Let stand for 12 hours or overnight, drain well. Dissolve the remaining salt and sugar in the vinegar over low heat in a large kettle. Add the tomatoes and remaining ingredients and boil slowly, stirring occasionally for about 35 minutes, or until the apples and onion are soft and the volume is reduced to about 8 cups. Pour into hot sterilized jars and seal.

3 cups peeled, chopped green or ripe
 tomatoes
3½ tablespoons salt
1¼ cups dark brown sugar, tightly packed
4½ cups cider vinegar
18 sour green cooking apples, peeled and
 thinly sliced
2 Spanish onions, thinly sliced
2 tablespoons ground ginger, or to taste
5 shallots, minced
1 3-ounce hot chili pepper, seeded and
 minced
3 tablespoons mustard seed
2½ cups raisins
1 cup chopped fresh mint leaves

COLD BÉARNAISE SAUCE

Cook the wine, vinegar, shallots, herbs, and pepper in a heavy saucepan over low heat. Watch carefully and shake at intervals until the mixture is reduced to a jellylike paste. Take from heat and beat the paste with 1 tablespoon tepid water and the egg yolks in the top of a double boiler until smooth. Set the top over the lower section of the double boiler *over*, not touching, barely simmering water; the sauce should cook in the steam. Beat the sauce slowly with a French wire whisk, adding the cold butter, little by little, until the sauce is thick and smooth. Take from heat and add salt to taste. Let the sauce cool slowly, whisking it at intervals. Serve cold but not chilled. *If* the sauce were to show signs of separating, whisk in a little cold water, energetically, until the sauce is smooth.

6 tablespoons dry white wine
6 tablespoons tarragon vinegar
3 shallots, minced
3 sprigs tarragon minced, or ½ teaspoon
 dried
3 sprigs chervil minced, or 1 teaspoon dried
Freshly ground black pepper to taste
3 large egg yolks
1 cup butter
Salt to taste

CUMBERLAND SAUCE

Melt the jelly in the top of a double boiler over boiling water. Stir in the raspberry jam and let them cook uncovered to reduce them slightly. Cut the entire outside rind from a large eating orange with a potato peeler. Scald it in the port wine for 3 minutes. Take out the rind, add the port wine and the orange juice to the jelly in the double boiler. Sliver the orange rind as thinly as possible with kitchen scissors. Stir the sauce and put a tablespoonful into a cup. Stir in the mustards until smooth and stir them back into the sauce. Repeat the addition of mustard to taste. Take sauce from heat and stir in the slivered orange rind. Add a little more port wine to taste. Chill the sauce in the refrigerator and serve with ham, any cold meats or game.

1 jar red currant jelly
½ cup strained or seedless thick raspberry jam
1 orange, thinly peeled rind and juice
¼ cup port wine
1 to 2 tablespoons Dijon or Düsseldorf mustard to taste
½ teaspoon dry yellow mustard

CUMBERLAND FRUIT

Wash, dry, and hull the strawberries and chill them until needed. Place them in a bowl and pour over the sauce. Serve them with ham or game. The fruit serves as a combination sauce and refreshing accompaniment to the meat. Ripe peaches may be substituted for the strawberries. Scald them in boiling water, draw off their skins, and halve them or slice them into the Cumberland sauce while it is still cooking over boiling water. Allow the peaches to poach in the sauce for 5 minutes before taking it from the heat.

1 quart large ripe strawberries or 4 large ripe peaches
1 recipe Cumberland Sauce

FILBERT ORANGE BUTTER

Cream the butter, add the nuts and the orange juice and rind, and whip until well combined. Salt to taste and put the mixture into a butter dish and chill. Either serve with marmalade and toast for tea, or spread on dark bread as a base for open cheese sandwiches, or spread on toasted cheese bread.

½ cup or 1 cube butter
¼ cup filberts, finely chopped
½ orange, juice and grated rind
Salt to taste

SAUCE GRIBICHE

Rice the egg yolks into a bowl and stir them to a dry paste with the mustard and vinegar. Season and stir in the oil, drop by drop, as for mayonnaise. When the sauce is thick and creamy, the oil should be added in a very thin stream. Stir in the herbs, gherkins, and capers. Finish by folding in the hard-cooked egg whites, cut into short matchsticks. Serve with cold meat or fish as the recipes and menus specify.

3 hard-cooked large eggs, separated
2 teaspoons mild brown or Dijon mustard
2 teaspoons tarragon vinegar
Salt and pepper to taste
1 cup salad oil
½ tablespoon each minced parsley, chervil, and tarragon
½ tablespoon minced gherkins
1 teaspoon minced capers

HERB SAUCE

Combine all ingredients and let the sauce *draw* for at least 1 hour. Stir it well before serving it with cold meats or with fish or eggs in aspic.

1 cup salad oil
½ cup tarragon vinegar
¼ cup soda water
2 tablespoons white wine
1 pinch powdered sugar
1 teaspoon salt, or to taste
½ teaspoon dry mustard
¼ teaspoon black pepper
3 hard-cooked eggs, chopped
1 tablespoon small capers
4 shallots, finely chopped
½ clove garlic, crushed
⅓ cup minced parsley
¼ cup finely cut chives
2 tablespoons finely snipped dill

HORSERADISH SAUCE

Stir cream and melted jelly until smooth. Place 2 teaspoons of the mixture into a cup with the mustard and stir it against the side of the cup with the back of a spoon until the mustard is smooth. Add it to the cream with the grated horseradish. Season the sauce to taste and serve it very cold with smoked salmon, trout, mackerel, or any smoked fish.

⅓ cup thick, 2-day-old cream
2 tablespoons melted red currant jelly
1 teaspoon dry English mustard
¼ cup freshly grated horseradish
Salt and freshly ground black pepper to taste

HORSERADISH SAUCE FOR APPRECIATORS

With 1 tablespoon of the cream, stir the mustard until smooth. Whip the cream until stiff, adding mustard and sugar just before it is entirely stiff. Fold in the grated horseradish, fill the sauce into a small sauceboat or bowl, and spoon the jam into the center of it. Serve at once and turn the jam into the horseradish cream at the moment of serving it at the table.

⅔ cup heavy cream, chilled
½ to 1 teaspoon English mustard
1 pinch sugar or to taste
⅓ cup freshly grated horseradish
2 tablespoons lingonberry, Preiselbeeren, or
    black currant jam

HOT CATSUP, MUSTARD, AND HORSERADISH SAUCE

Stir the catsup into the dry mustard until smooth, stir in the brown mustard and the horseradish. Store the sauce in a covered jar in the refrigerator and do not eat too much at once. Serve with cold meats or boiled meats. Add catsup if it is too hot.

⅓ cup catsup
3 tablespoons dry yellow mustard
2 tablespoons mild brown mustard
⅓ cup freshly grated horseradish

SAUCE RAVIGOTE I

Crush yolks, salt, pepper, mustard, and vinegar together with the back of a spoon. Put them in an electric beater and beat in the oil, a drop at a time, as for mayonnaise. When about ⅓ cup of the oil has been used, add the rest in a thin stream until the sauce has reached the desired consistency. Add herbs and gherkins and fill the sauce into the egg whites. Pass the rest separately.

6 hard-cooked egg yolks, riced through a
    sieve or blended
Salt and pepper to taste
½ tablespoon mild brown mustard
3 tablespoons wine vinegar
1½ cups salad oil
2 tablespoons minced herbs (tarragon,
    chervil, and parsley)
1 tablespoon minced gherkins
1 tablespoon minced capers
1 tablespoon minced shallots

SAUCE RAVIGOTE II

Into the mayonnaise fold all the finely chopped ingredients and chill until needed. Serve with meat, eggs, fish, and some vegetables, as cold cauliflower.

1 recipe homemade Mayonnaise
1 teaspoon minced tarragon
2 teaspoons minced chervil
1 tablespoon minced parsley
1 tablespoon finely chopped capers
1 anchovy fillet, minced
1 tablespoon finely chopped shallots
2 tablespoons finely chopped and drained pickle

SAUCE RÉMOULADE (cooked)

Whip yolks, vinegar, mustard, oil, and wine in the top of a double boiler over, not touching, boiling water until thickened. Take from heat and stir every 5 minutes until the sauce is cold. Beat in the capers, gherkins, parsley, pickle, and seasonings and chill the sauce until needed. If a thinner sauce is preferred, add a little water to the yolk mixture while whipping it.

5 egg yolks
¼ cup wine vinegar
2 teaspoons brown mustard, preferably Dijon
½ cup salad oil
½ cup dry white wine
1 tablespoon minced capers
1 tablespoon minced gherkins
2 tablespoons minced parsley
1 tablespoon seeded and finely chopped dill pickle
1 pinch each cayenne pepper, sugar, and salt to taste

SAUCE RÉMOULADE (uncooked)

Stir the riced yolks with the raw yolk into a smooth paste, add mustard and stir in the oil, drop by drop. Add anchovy, capers, and parsley and chill the sauce for several hours before using. For a thinner sauce, add oil to taste.

3 hard-cooked egg yolks, riced
1 raw egg yolk
1 tablespoon brown mustard, preferably Dijon
3 tablespoons salad oil, or to taste
3 anchovy fillets, minced
1 tablespoon minced capers
2 tablespoons minced parsley

TRIANON SAUCE

Stir the mayonnaise and the tomato purée and fold in the remaining ingredients. Serve with fish, vegetables, or eggs.

1 recipe Tarragon Mayonnaise
2 tablespoons thick tomato purée
1 tablespoon minced onion
1 tablespoon finely diced dill pickle
1 tablespoon finely diced pimento

GLOUCESTER SAUCE

Make the mayonnaise in the blender as directed on page 122. When it is completed, fold in the fennel and lastly add the sour cream which should be stirred until light before it is added. Serve with cold roast beef, lamb or veal.

1 tablespoon wine vinegar
½ teaspoon Worcestershire sauce
1 egg
1 teaspoon salt
1 teaspoon dry English mustard
¼ teaspoon pepper
1 pinch cayenne pepper
1 cup peanut oil
2 tablespoons finely chopped fennel, or to taste
3 tablespoons sour cream, stirred

LEMON MAYONNAISE COLLÉE Aspic Mayonnaise

A mayonnaise collée is supported with gelatin and is suitable for masking some cold dishes, namely hard-cooked eggs, fish, meat, and chickens. When a heavier coating is required, use Chaud-Froid Sauce, either white or brown or tinted with tomato juice.

Prepare the lemon mayonnaise and leave it at room temperature until needed. If the room is cold, set it near warmth. Stir the gelatin into the wine or stock and set it aside for 15 minutes. Stir it over hot water until it is completely dissolved, then beat it slowly into the mayonnaise. Let it cool, and when it is cold but not yet set, pour it over the cold eggs, fish, or meat for which it is intended. Pour it from a wide spoon or bowl, since it cannot be patched and the surface is smooth only if it is not spread or repaired in any way.

1 recipe Lemon Mayonnaise, about 1⅓ cups
1 envelope gelatin
6 tablespoons white wine or white stock

MUSTARD CREAM SAUCE

Stir mustard with lemon juice and seasonings until smooth. Half whip the cream until it is slightly increased in volume and very smooth. Stir it into the mustard sauce and serve with ham, tongue, fish, or shellfish. If preferred the cream may be beaten slowly into the mustard without being whipped.

¼ to ⅓ cup brown mustard, preferably Dijon
1 tablespoon lemon juice
1 pinch each of salt and pepper
1 cup heavy cream

VINAIGRETTE SAUCE

Stir vinegar, salt, and pepper until salt is dissolved. Stir in mustard and add the oils gradually. Add the remaining ingredients and store in refrigerator for 30 minutes. Shake or beat well and serve.

3 tablespoons wine vinegar
1 teaspoon salt or to taste
Freshly ground pepper to taste
1 tablespoon mild brown mustard, preferably Dijon
2 tablespoons olive oil
¼ cup salad oil
1 tablespoon finely chopped onions
2 teaspoons finely chopped capers
½ tablespoon each minced parsley and chervil
½ tablespoon finely cut chives

THE VINAIGRETTE SALADS

Vinaigrette is French dressing, but we think of it as being a specific dressing usually served over cold cooked asparagus, artichokes, cauliflower, leeks, long green snap beans, meat in aspic, or eggs.

Steam, drain, and cool the vegetable, which should be slightly undercooked. When it is cold, pour over Vinaigrette Sauce, and just before serving drain again, add more vinaigrette, and sprinkle with various additions.

ASPARAGUS VINAIGRETTE

Arrange the cooled and very well-drained asparagus, with all spears running in the same direction, in a small pan and pour over a little of the vinaigrette sauce. Chill until shortly before it will be served, then drain and mound the asparagus on an oblong platter. Either pour over the remaining vinaigrette sauce or serve it in a glass or porcelain bowl. Arrange strips of hard-cooked riced egg white across the asparagus about 1 inch from the tips. Follow with strips of egg yolk,

2 bunches asparagus, trimmed, steamed, and chilled, page 161
2 recipes Vinaigrette Sauce
2 hard-cooked eggs, yolks and whites riced separately
1 small onion, finely chopped
¼ cup finely chopped parsley
2 tablespoons capers, finely chopped

onion, parsley, capers, and another row of egg white. If preferred a miniature version of the above can be arranged on 6 individual plates.

CAULIFLOWER VINAIGRETTE: Arrange the whole cauliflower in a lettuce-lined salad bowl. Pour over a little of the dressing, sprinkle with onions, egg white, capers, egg yolk, and parsley in that rotation. Serve the remaining dressing separately.

ARTICHOKE VINAIGRETTE: Cut cooked and cooled artichokes in half, pull out the center leaves, and take out the *choke* with a small spoon, according to directions on page 53. Drain them well, cut side down, then turn them over and fill a little of the vinaigrette sauce into the cavities. Chill them until shortly before serving, then drain them again, arrange them, cut side up, on 6 salad plates, and fill the cavities with the vinaigrette sauce. Reduce the capers and onion to 1 teaspoon for each artichoke and add them to the sauce. Rice only 1 hard-cooked egg over the cavities and sprinkle with 1 teaspoon parsley for each artichoke.

LEEK VINAIGRETTE: Cooked and chilled leeks are served in the sauce with a sprinkling of onion, capers, and parsley over the top. The egg is omitted.

MEAT IN ASPIC VINAIGRETTE: Add 1 hard-cooked egg, riced, 2 tablespoons finely chopped onion or shallot, 2 tablespoons each finely chopped gherkins and capers, and 1 tablespoon minced parsley to 1¼ cups French Dressing and serve it with any meat in aspic.

EGGS VINAIGRETTE: Serve the same vinaigrette sauce as above, omitting the hard-cooked egg and substituting 3 stuffed olives, finely chopped, with cold poached eggs or cold 6-minute eggs.

GREEN BEANS VINAIGRETTE

Make this salad when there are long, straight, tender green snap beans on the market, and then treat them as well as you would treat asparagus.

Wash and chill the beans, snap off the ends, and arrange the beans all in a row. Trim the ends off any exceptionally long ones and tie

2½ pounds string or snap beans
2 sprigs summer savory or 1 teaspoon dried
1 cup Red Wine Vinegar Dressing
½ teaspoon dried summer savory
¼ teaspoon dried dill weed
2 hard-cooked eggs, yolks and whites riced
    separately
1 medium onion, finely chopped
¼ cup finely chopped parsley
3 tablespoons finely chopped capers

them loosely into 6 even bunches with kitchen string. Boil them rapidly until they are bright green and barely tender in salted water with the summer savory. Drain them well on a folded napkin and let them cool. When they are cold, arrange them in a long mound down the length of a narrow dish and pour over the dressing, blended with the dried herbs. Shortly before serving, garnish the beans with 2 narrow lines of riced hard-cooked egg whites running down the length of the mound of beans at its outside edges. Run a line of riced egg yolk, a line of chopped onion, a narrow line of capers, and a line of chopped parsley down between the 2 lines of egg white. Chill the salad until needed.

CAULIFLOWER VINAIGRETTE

Place trimmed cauliflower, stem down, in a deep kettle. Add enough water to half cover it and take out the cauliflower. Bring the water to a rapid boil, add the salt, and return the cauliflower, stem down, to the water. Cover and, when it comes back to a rapid boil, reduce heat to simmer and steam the cauliflower until just tender. Depending on its age, it can take from 12 to 16 minutes. Pour off the water and pour a little of the French dressing over the cauliflower while it is warm. Cool and chill it until the garnishes are prepared. Arrange the well-drained cauliflower on a salad platter, surrounded by Boston lettuce leaves. Push the lettuce leaves under the cauliflower and let them come up around it. Pour ½ cup of the remaining French dressing over the cauliflower and sprinkle it heavily with onion, egg white, capers, and egg yolk, in that rotation. It should be quite overloaded. Grind the parsley over the whole through a parsley grinder. If none is available, sprinkle chopped parsley over the egg yolk. Pass the remaining French dressing in a bowl.

1 large white cauliflower, about 1½ pounds
2 teaspoons salt
1 recipe French Dressing I
1 small onion, finely chopped
2 hard-cooked eggs, whites and yolks riced
*   separately*
3 tablespoons smallest capers, or chopped
*   large capers*
Boston lettuce leaves for garnish
4 sprigs parsley, stems removed

DILLED NEW POTATO SALAD

Peel potatoes, hold them in cold water until all are done. Slice them sideways on a cucumber slicer to obtain long oval slices about 3/16 inch thick. Put them, all at once, into boiling salted water and boil them until they are *al dente*. In other words cook the potato slices until they still have a resistance but no longer taste or look raw. New potatoes differ; it will take between 7 and 10 minutes, watch them carefully and try a slice every minute until the proper instant. Drain them at once and leave them in the strainer to drain further until they are just warm. Put them in a bowl and pour over the dressing and add the dill. If they were boiled to the right point, the slices will not break. The salad can be covered and stored in the refrigerator until the next day.

1½ pounds small new potatoes
½ cup French Dressing
1 bunch fresh dill, or ¼ cup loosely filled with snipped dill

POTATO SALAD with FRENCH DRESSING

Peel potatoes and cut them into even slices on a vegetable slicer. The slices should not be more than ⅛ inch thick. Drop the freshly sliced potatoes into boiling salted water and cover until water returns to a boil. Uncover and stand by with a slotted spoon. The length of time the sliced potatoes boil depends on their thickness and on the quality of the potato. Take out a slice after 5 minutes and test it. Continue to test until the slices are barely tender; the salad should have an *al dente* consistency. Take out the potato slices with a slotted spoon and transfer them to a bowl. While they are hot, add salt if needed, grind pepper over them to taste, and pour over the wine. When the potatoes are cold, mix oil, vinegar, shallots, and onion and pour the mixture over the potatoes. Marinate the salad at room temperature for 3 hours, turning it carefully with 2 wooden spoons each hour. Turn the salad into a bowl, sprinkle it with parsley or chives, and chill.

8 medium potatoes, peeled
2 teaspoons salt
Freshly ground pepper
6 tablespoons dry white wine
10 tablespoons salad oil
3 tablespoons tarragon vinegar
2 shallots, finely chopped
2 tablespoons finely chopped onion, or to taste
2 tablespoons finely chopped parsley or finely cut chives

POTATO SALAD STEPHAN—WHITE WINE POTATO SALAD

Boil potatoes in salted water until they are just tender but not soft, about 15 minutes. Draw off their skins as soon as they are cool enough to handle, and slice them into a wooden bowl rubbed with garlic. Sprinkle them with salt and pepper and pour over the wine while they are still warm. Add oil and vinegar and shallots, beaten together, and let them marinate for 1 hour. If the potatoes are very mealy, they may absorb all the marinade and be too dry. In that case add a mixture of 3 tablespoons wine, 2 tablespoons oil, 1 tablespoon vinegar, and salt and pepper to taste. Clean edges of bowl, garnish with a border of lettuce leaves, and sprinkle the potatoes with parsley.

8 medium potatoes, scrubbed
½ garlic clove
1 teaspoon salt
½ teaspoon white pepper
⅔ cup dry white wine
6 tablespoons salad oil
3 tablespoons tarragon vinegar
⅓ cup chopped shallots
Boston lettuce leaves for bowl
¼ cup finely cut parsley

COOKING DIRECTIONS FOR RICE FOR SALADS

Put water, salt, and lemon juice in an enameled kettle and bring it to a fast boil. "Rain" the rice slowly into the boiling water so that it will not stop boiling. Stir across the bottom of the kettle with a fork, reduce heat to simmer, and cover the kettle tightly. Cook for 16 to 18 minutes. Take off lid, test a kernel of rice; it should be barely tender, *not soft*. Continue to cook uncovered, until just *al dente*, about 5 more minutes. All the water should be absorbed, add a very little hot water. When rice is *right*, turn off the heat and stir it before taking it off to cool.

2¼ cups cold water
1 teaspoon salt
1 squeeze lemon juice
1 cup long grain rice

RICE AND CHICKEN SALAD

Cook the rice in salted water, according to directions above, reduce cooking time slightly so that the rice is *al dente* and not soft. Drain it well and let it cool. When rice is cold, combine it with the chicken and cucumbers. Line a salad bowl with crisp lettuce leaves. Mound the rice in the center of the bowl. Slice the tomatoes and cut each slice in half. Arrange an overlapping arch of tomatoes around the rice and sprinkle them with the onion and parsley. Just before serving pour as much dressing (given below) as wanted over the salad and mix it gently at the table.

2 cups rice
*1½ cups cold cooked chicken pieces cut as
    for chicken salad*
*2 cucumbers, peeled, seeded, and cut into
    large dice or lozenges*
1 small head Boston lettuce
3 tomatoes, peeled
⅓ cup finely chopped onion
¼ cup finely chopped parsley

DRESSING

Note that dressing is sharp to offset blandness of rice. If preferred add ¼ cup oil and 1 pinch sugar.

Combine in blender container and blend until smooth.

¼ cup tarragon vinegar
¾ cup salad oil, preferably peanut oil
2 teaspoons salt, or to taste
1 teaspoon dry mustard
1 teaspoon dried orégano
½ teaspoon Maggi seasoning
½ teaspoon roughly ground black pepper
1 garlic clove, crushed

CHIFFONADE SALADS

In France a *chiffonade* is a leaf vegetable cut in julienne strips and sautéed in butter. For us a chiffonade salad is a combination of finely cut lettuce and celery with tomatoes and cress. I usually add finely cut beets at the last moment so that they will not bleed into the salad and turn it pink.

Arrange the best Boston lettuce leaves around the edge of a salad bowl. Break the remaining leaves and the romaine into small pieces; separate the endive slices and place them in the bowl. On them arrange celery, eggs, tomatoes, and water cress. Just before serving top with the beets and parsley. Mix with the French dressing at the table.

Another way of preparing chiffonade salad is to prepare the salad greens in a salad bowl and serve Chiffonade Dressing (given below) separately. Pour the dressing over the salad at the table and mix it before the guests.

1 small head Boston lettuce
1 heart romaine
3 stalks endive, trimmed, cut across in 1-inch slices
1 celery heart, scraped and cut into julienne strips
1 to 2 hard-cooked eggs, sliced
2 large tomatoes, peeled and cut into wedges
½ bunch water cress, all coarse stems removed
2 cold boiled medium beets, or ½ cup well-drained pickled beets cut into julienne strips
2 tablespoons chopped parsley
1 recipe French Dressing

CHIFFONADE DRESSING

Stir salt and pepper with vinegar until salt is dissolved. Beat in the oils. Shortly before serving, shake the dressing vigorously, add the remaining ingredients, and pour it over a mixed green salad or over an endive salad.

1 teaspoon salt
⅓ teaspoon freshly ground pepper
¼ cup vinegar
¼ cup olive oil
⅓ cup salad oil
1 teaspoon finely cut chives or minced parsley
2 tablespoons finely diced cooked beets
1 hard-cooked egg, riced
½ tablespoon each finely diced green pepper, pimento, and onion

The Mixed and Combined Salads

There is a group of salads and cold dishes that have a wonderful combination of flavors but do not look very attractive after they are mixed. There are only two ways of overcoming this handicap: either bring them to the table when the ingredients are at their best and mix them at the table or mix them before they are served and mask them under a sauce or under riced eggs and other garnishings. In some cases, as in Caesar Salad, the ingredients are brought to the table separately and are combined only when the host prepares the salad. In other cases, as in the Bird's Nest, the ingredients are painstakingly arranged like a still-life and then stirred into a pink concoction before the eyes of the guests. It is then spread on buttered black bread. Garnished Beefsteak Tartare, Garnished Liptauer Cheese, and Garnished Cold Boiled Beef Salad are all presented in this way.

The visual impression is made first, and when the dish no longer looks good, it tastes good. The host- or hostess-mixed salads and cold dishes have the advantage that the guests can participate; they can even express their preferences. I always serve the guest who does not eat onions—or anchovies—with his portion of the beefsteak tartare before I add them to the remaining beef for the other guests. With the Liptauer cheese there is always someone who does not want the caraway seeds.

Bird's Nests, Chiffonade Salad, Lorette, Caesar, and Boiled Beef Salads, Tartare and Cold Curry Salad are all in the SHOW FIRST-MIX LATER group. Russian Salad, Italian, Lentil, and most of the combined salads should be mixed in advance so that their flavors can blend and enhance each other. Their presentation and garnishing go far to hide their MIXED LOOK. Among the combination salads are some that look good, as Risi Pisi or Merry Widow Salad, and they should be served just as they are.

The following mixed salads should be combined and chilled. Each short recipe explains how they should be *dressed* and *garnished,* but the amount of dressing is left to taste:

ALLEMANDE OR GERMAN SALAD

Slice 4 medium boiled and peeled potatoes. Add 2 peeled and cored sliced apples, 2 herring fillets cut in short strips, 1 diced dill pickle, ¼ cup finely chopped onion, and 2 tablespoons finely chopped parsley. Bind the ingredients lightly with 3 tablespoons mustard mayonnaise beaten with 2 tablespoons heavy cream. Arrange the salad in a lettuce-leaf-lined salad bowl and rice the white and then the yolk of 1 hard-cooked egg over it. Just before serving, sprinkle top with 1 small cooked beet finely diced, and serve with a bowl of mustard mayonnaise. For a meal-in-itself salad, increase quantities proportionately and increase the amount of herring fillets to ½ fillet per person. Serve with thin buttered black bread.

4 potatoes, medium-sized, boiled and peeled
2 apples, peeled, cored, and sliced
2 herring fillets, cut in short strips
1 dill pickle, diced
¼ cup finely chopped onion
2 tablespoons finely chopped parsley
3 tablespoons Mustard Mayonnaise
2 tablespoons heavy cream
Lettuce
1 egg, hard-cooked
1 small beet, finely diced

ANDALUSIAN SALAD I

Combine 4 cups cold cooked dry rice with ¼ cup each diced green pepper and diced pimento. Add 2 tablespoons each finely chopped onion and parsley. Invert the salad into a Boston-lettuce-leaf-lined salad bowl and surround it with a circle of 1 pound—or 5 small—tomatoes, peeled and thinly sliced. Sprinkle 6 large stuffed olives, chopped, over the rice. Serve with a bowl of orégano dressing.

4 cups rice
¼ cup green pepper
¼ cup pimento, diced
2 tablespoons finely chopped onion
2 tablespoons finely chopped parsley
1 head Boston lettuce
5 small tomatoes, peeled and thinly sliced
6 large stuffed olives, chopped
Orégano Dressing

ANDALUSIAN SALAD II

Prepare 1 small head of Boston and 1 small head of romaine lettuce. Spread them in a shallow salad bowl and bring them up around the edge to decorate the bowl. In the center arrange 1 thinly sliced onion, separated into rings, over that spread half a cucumber, peeled and very thinly sliced. Cover the cucumber with 3 tomatoes, peeled and sliced, and cover the tomatoes with 1 cup toasted bread crumbs. Serve with French Dressing and mix the salad at the table.

APPLE SALAD—MERRY WIDOW I

Peel and core 3 red eating apples and cut them in thin wedges. Immediately sprinkle them with lemon juice and combine them with the sections of 2 oranges, free of all white membrane, 1 scraped and sliced celery heart, and 3 endive stalks cut across into 1-inch slices and separated. Add 2 tablespoons each diced green pepper and pimento and ½ cup toasted walnuts. Transfer the salad to a salad bowl and pour over herb French dressing. Mix the salad at the table.

3 red eating apples, cut in thin wedges
Lemon juice
2 oranges, free of all white membrane
1 celery heart, scraped and sliced
3 endive stalks, cut across into 1-inch slices and separated
2 tablespoons green pepper, diced
2 tablespoons pimento, diced
½ cups walnuts, toasted
Herb French Dressing

DANISH COLESLAW

Shred 1 small white cabbage and combine the shreds with ¼ pound firm white mushrooms, sliced paper thin. Add 2 teaspoons each finely cut dill and caraway seeds and stir the cabbage shreds with just enough lemon French dressing to bind. Chill it until ready to serve. Stir the salad with additional dressing and transfer it to a bowl. Grind black pepper over the top and serve. Stir once at the table.

1 small white cabbage
¼ pound mushrooms, sliced paper thin
2 teaspoons dill, finely cut
2 teaspoons caraway seeds
Lemon French Dressing
Black pepper

CAESAR SALAD

Prepare the ingredients around a large salad bowl previously rubbed with a split clove of garlic and filled with the broken leaves of 2 large or 3 small heads of romaine lettuce. Grind pepper over the leaves to taste and rub a pinch of dry mustard through the fingers over the bowl with ½ teaspoon salt. Add ½ cup grated Parmesan cheese, ¼ cup salad oil, 2 tablespoons olive oil, and ream 2 lemons, cut in half, over the bowl. Break 2 eggs over the bowl—some chefs boil the eggs

Garlic, split clove
2 large heads romaine lettuce
Pepper
Dry mustard, a pinch
½ teaspoon salt
½ cup Parmesan cheese, grated
¼ cup salad oil
2 tablespoons olive oil

for 1 to 2 minutes—and add a dash of Worcestershire sauce. Mix the salad gently until the eggs are absorbed. Just before serving the salad, add 2 cups garlic salad croutons (given below), stir once more, and serve. Host and hostess need an audience when they make this salad; guests are supposed to watch.

2 lemons
2 eggs
Worcestershire sauce, a dash
2 cups Garlic Salad Croutons

GARLIC SALAD CROUTONS

Cut enough slightly stale white bread into ½-inch croutons to fill 2 cups. Fry them in a heavy pan with ¼ cup oil to which 1 crushed clove garlic has been added. Turn the croutons to brown all sides, drain them on paper towels, and—if you like—parch them slightly in a very low oven.

White bread, slightly stale, cut into ½-inch
   croutons
¼ cup oil
1 clove garlic, crushed

CASANOVA SALAD

Fill a salad bowl with crisp romaine lettuce broken into pieces. Sprinkle over ½ cup each scraped and diced celery, peeled and diced tart apple, and sprinkle at once with a little lemon juice. Add 2 chopped hard-cooked eggs and 2 tablespoons each of finely chopped shallots and pimento. Serve the salad, pour over herb French dressing, and mix it at the table. If the salad has to be prepared long in advance, add the apple shortly before serving. If fresh chervil is available, sprinkle the salad with chopped chervil and use plain French dressing.

Romaine lettuce
½ cup celery, scraped and diced
½ cup tart apple, peeled and diced
Lemon juice
2 eggs, hard-cooked and chopped
2 tablespoons finely chopped shallots
2 tablespoons finely chopped pimento
Herb French Dressing
Fresh chervil, chopped

CUMBERLAND SALAD

Break crisp Boston lettuce leaves in a salad bowl, slice 2 ripe, peeled pears over the salad, and serve with a French dressing to which 1 teaspoon grated lemon rind and 1 small jar red Bar-le-Duc conserve have been added (if not available, use 3 tablespoons melted red currant jelly). Shake the dressing well and mix the salad at the table.

Boston lettuce
2 ripe pears, peeled
French Dressing
1 teaspoon lemon rind, grated
1 small jar red Bar-le-Duc conserve or 3
   tablespoons melted red currant jelly

GERMAN CAULIFLOWER SALAD

Fry 6 slices bacon until crisp. Drain them well on paper towels and set the bacon fat aside. Mix a French dressing and substitute the bacon fat for some of the oil—measure for measure. Arrange a cold cooked cauliflower in a salad bowl, and surround it with lettuce leaves. Add ¼ teaspoon crushed caraway seeds to the dressing and pour it over the cauliflower. Crumble the bacon over the top.

6 bacon slices
French Dressing
1 cauliflower, cold cooked
¼ teaspoon caraway seeds, crushed

ITALIAN SALAD

Combine 4 cups cold cooked vegetables, small lima beans, green peas, a few diced carrots, and tender green snap beans, cut into ¼-inch lengths before cooking, with 1 cup each cooked dry white beans and cooked lentils. Add ½ cup each diced celery and cucumbers and bind the salad with mayonnaise. Mound it in the center of a large lettuce-leaf-lined salad bowl and garnish it with thin slices of salami, alternating with 3 hard-cooked eggs, sliced, and 3 tomatoes, peeled and sliced. Sprinkle 6 large stuffed olives, chopped, over the top and serve more mayonnaise and Italian dressing separately.

4 cups cold cooked vegetables, small lima beans, green peas, diced carrots, tender green snap beans, cut into ¼-inch lengths
1 cup dry white beans, cooked
1 cup lentils, cooked
½ cup celery, diced
½ cup cucumbers, diced
Mayonnaise
Lettuce
Salami, thin slices
3 eggs, hard-cooked, sliced
3 tomatoes, peeled and sliced
6 large stuffed olives, chopped
Italian Dressing

LORETTE SALAD

There are many versions of this salad, which can be adjusted to its purpose. The basic ingredients are always the same: small cooked beets, sliced; hearts of celery, sliced or cut in julienne strips; and cold cooked lobster. It is garnished with hard-cooked eggs, sliced, and anchovies. The greens are field lettuce, cos lettuce, and/or bibb lettuce. When it is served as a main course, the lobster should predominate. As a regular salad, the greens, beets, and celery predominate and the lobster is only a garnish. I arrange all the ingredients on the greens, pour French dressing over it, and mix the salad at the table.

Beets, small, cooked, sliced
Hearts of celery, sliced or cut in julienne strips
Lobster, cold cooked
Eggs, hard-cooked, sliced
Anchovies
Field lettuce
Cos lettuce
Bibb lettuce
French Dressing

MERRY WIDOW SALAD

In a border of romaine lettuce leaves, in a narrow deep salad bowl, layer slices of 3 peeled and cored ripe pears and 2 large or 3 small avocados. Sprinkle the top with 2 tablespoons each minced green pepper, diced pimento, and finely chopped parsley. Pour over lemon cream dressing and mix the salad at the table.

Romaine lettuce
3 ripe pears, peeled and cored
2 large avocados
2 tablespoons green pepper, minced
2 tablespoons pimento, diced
2 tablespoons finely chopped parsley
Lemon Cream Dressing

POTATO SALAD

Slice 6 cold boiled large potatoes thinly and combine them with ¼ cup finely chopped onions and 2 tablespoons of small capers. Bind the mixture carefully with mayonnaise thinned with a little heavy cream. Turn the potatoes with wooden spoons and try not to break them. Chill the salad until needed. Transfer it to a salad bowl, arrange crisp sprigs of water cress around it. Sprinkle generously with finely cut chives and crumble 6 slices crisp bacon over the top.

6 large potatoes, boiled, thinly sliced
¼ cup finely chopped onions
2 tablespoons small capers
Mayonnaise
Heavy cream
Water cress
Chives, finely cut
6 bacon slices, crumbled

WATER CRESS SALAD

Prepare 1 bunch crisp water cress and remove all coarse stems. Arrange it around the edge of a wide, shallow salad bowl and cover the bottom with 1 large sweet apple, peeled and cored and sliced knife-back thin. Over the apple spread 3 or 4 large white mushrooms, sliced just as thin, and over the mushrooms sprinkle ⅔ cup dry bread crumbs fried in 2 tablespoons butter. Over the crumbs, rice the white of 1 hard-cooked egg and serve. Pour over tarragon dressing and mix at the table.

1 bunch crisp water cress, coarse stems removed
1 large sweet apple, peeled, cored and sliced knife-back thin
4 large white mushrooms, sliced knife-back thin
⅔ cup dry bread crumbs
2 tablespoons butter
1 egg, hard-cooked
Tarragon Dressing

GERMAN COLESLAW

Trim and cut out stem of cabbage and shred; yield will be about 10 cups. Pack the shreds down in a large kettle, sprinkle over the salt, and add just enough water to cover. Cover the kettle, place it over high heat, and bring to a boil. Take from heat the moment it boils and drain it well in a colander. Cut red grapes across lengthwise and remove seeds with a pointed knife. Stir slaw, red grapes, onion, and lemon dressing in a large salad bowl and chill. Before serving beat mayonnaise, yolk, lemon juice, sugar, and salt together. Drain any superfluous lemon dressing from the salad bowl and stir the mayonnaise into the slaw. Wipe sides of bowl and garnish with a ring of green grapes. If the grapes are not seedless, cut them in half and remove pips as with the red grapes.

1 medium-large head white cabbage, about 2½ pounds
2 teaspoons salt
½ pound thin-skinned red grapes
¼ cup minced onion
½ cup Lemon Dressing or as much as the slaw will absorb
¼ cup mayonnaise
1 egg yolk
1 tablespoon lemon juice
¼ teaspoon sugar
¼ teaspoon salt, or to taste
½ pound seedless grapes

ASPARAGUS AND HAM SALAD

Cut the asparagus across into ¾-inch lengths, use only the tenderest part. Combine it with the next 5 ingredients in a lettuce-leaf-lined salad bowl. Pour over the dressing and let the salad marinate for about 1 hour, sprinkle with onion and parsley. If prepared earlier, the salad can marinate overnight, but the lettuce and onion and parsley should be added shortly before serving.

1 bunch steamed asparagus spears, tender green part only
1½ cups diced cooked ham
1 cup diced celery heart
2 hard-cooked eggs, chopped
2 sweet gherkins, chopped, or 2 tablespoons drained sweet relish
2 tablespoons diced pimento
1 small head Boston lettuce
⅔ cup Paprika French Dressing
3 tablespoons each chopped onion and parsley, mixed

SALADE BEAUCAIRE

On all salads that contain beets, the red color bleeds through the salad as soon as it is mixed. It is best to arrange the salad in advance and then mix it at the table just before serving.

Arrange the first 5 ingredients attractively in a salad bowl. Put the mayonnaise into a crystal or procelain bowl and sprinkle it with the chervil. Arrange the beets in a circle around the other ingredients. At the table, add mayonnaise to taste and mix the salad just before serving.

⅔ cup diced celery
2 sour apples, peeled, cored, and diced
3 stalks endive, cut across into ¼-inch-thick
*   slices*
4 medium mushrooms, thinly sliced
3 small cooked potatoes, thinly sliced
1 recipe Tarragon Mayonnaise
2 tablespoons minced chervil or, if not
*   available, parsley*
6 small cooked beets, thinly sliced or cut into
*   shoestrings*

CUCUMBER SALAD Norwegian

Peel the cucumbers and slice them very thinly on a pickle slicer. Place the slices in a bowl and sprinkle them with the salt. Cover the cucumbers with a plate and put a heavy jar or weight on the plate. Set the bowl aside for 4 to 5 hours, pouring off the water that is extracted from the cucumbers at intervals. When they are wilted, stir the vinegar with the pepper and sugar until the sugar is dissolved. Pour the mixture over the well-drained cucumbers and sprinkle the salad with the dill.

3 cucumbers
2 tablespoons salt
⅓ cup vinegar
Freshly ground pepper
1 tablespoon sugar
1 tablespoon finely cut dill

DUTCH APPLE SALAD

Cut apples into very thin slices, combine them with the onion slices in a salad bowl. Sprinkle at once with lemon juice and the grated rind. Beat the remaining ingredients into a dressing and pour it over the apples and onions. Chill the salad for at least 1 hour before serving.

2 pounds sour apples, peeled and cored
2 onions, sliced paper thin
1 lemon, juice and grated rind
4 tablespoons vinegar
6 tablespoons oil
1 teaspoon salt
Freshly ground black pepper to taste
1 teaspoon sugar

GRAPEFRUIT AND ENDIVE SALAD

Cut skin from grapefruit with a very sharp knife, going down to the meat. Separate the sections carefully, over a bowl, discard the membrane, and retain the juice. Trim and separate the endive stalks into leaves. When the leaves become too close to separate, cut the hearts into quarters, lengthwise, and add them to the leaves. Cut cheese into long strips and mix them with the endive. Arrange them—all running in the same direction—on 6 salad plates. Place overlapping grapefruit sections on the endive. Pour over the dressing, sprinkle with paprika, and serve.

2 large grapefruit, separated into sections, and the retained juice
6 thick stalks Belgian endive
1 unsliced piece Swiss cheese, at least 4 inches long
1 recipe Grapefruit Dressing (given below)
Paprika to taste

GRAPEFRUIT DRESSING

Mix grapefruit and lemon juice with mustard and stir in the salt and pepper until the salt is dissolved. Stir in the oils gradually, add the remaining ingredients, and beat or shake until smooth.

3 tablespoons grapefruit juice
1 tablespoon lemon juice
1 tablespoon Dijon mustard
2 to 3 teaspoons salt to taste
Freshly ground white pepper to taste
2 tablespoons olive oil
6 tablespoons salad oil
1 tablespoon finely chopped chervil
1 tablespoon finely chopped onion
1 tablespoon finely chopped parsley

HOLLANDAISE SALAD

Combine the cold potato slices with the smoked salmon and onion. Sprinkle with lemon juice and rind and mound the salad in a salad bowl. Sprinkle the cut chives over the salad and make a small hollow at the top to hold the caviar. Serve the salad with the lemon mayonnaise. Add mayonnaise and mix the salad at the table in such a way that caviar and chives are well distributed through the salad. Try not to break the potato slices too badly.

8 peeled large potatoes, sliced and cooked as for White Wine Potato Salad
3 slices smoked salmon, mild, cut into short strips with kitchen scissors
¼ cup finely chopped onion, or more to taste
1 lemon, juice and grated rind
3 tablespoons finely cut chives
1 smallest jar good black caviar
1 recipe Lemon Mayonnaise

MONTE CRISTO SALAD

Make this salad to fill into lobster shells for Lobster with Mustard Sauce, or turn it into a Lobster Salad Monte Cristo by adding cold cooked lobster to the salad and mixing it with Mustard Mayonnaise.

Combine all ingredients and fill them into the lobster shells.

3 hard-cooked eggs, chopped
6 new boiled potatoes, skins drawn off while
 still hot
2 truffles, peeled, diced
6 medium mushrooms, thinly sliced
½ cup chopped heart of celery
½ cup chopped tart apple

LOBSTER SALAD MONTE CRISTO

To the above ingredients add 2 cups cooked lobster meat and, if necessary, add 2 potatoes, ¼ cup celery, and ¼ cup apple to increase into a main course salad. Bind with Mustard Mayonnaise and serve from a lettuce-leaf-lined salad bowl.

SALADE NIÇOISE I

Boil the eggs and let them cool. Bring salted water to a boil in 2 saucepans. Add the potatoes and beans and cook them separately until just tender but not soft. Slice the potatoes and set them aside. Cut tomatoes across, press out all the seeds, and cut them into large pieces. Prepare the ingredients and chill them until time to prepare the salad. Do not let a mixed salade niçoise stand longer than necessary. The flavors are best when it is freshly mixed. Combine the anchovies and olives with the above ingredients, pour over the dressing, mix lightly, and sprinkle with the herbs and capers. Serve with buttered dark bread.

4 hard-cooked eggs
4 firm potatoes, peeled
½ pound green snap beans, cut across into
 ¼-inch lengths
4 ripe tomatoes, peeled
1 2-ounce can anchovy fillets, chopped
1 7-ounce can tuna fish, drained and flaked
8 large or 16 small stuffed olives, diced
½ cup Orégano French Dressing
¼ cup each finely chopped parsley and
 finely cut chives
2 tablespoons smallest capers or chopped
 capers

SALADE NIÇOISE II

Boil the beans in salted water until just tender. Drain them well. Boil the sliced potatoes in salted water, watching them carefully after the first 3 minutes. The advantage of boiling them in this way is that they can be taken out with a slotted spoon when they are tender but still crisp. Combine beans, potatoes, tomatoes, olives, and capers and add just enough dressing to bind. Garnish top with anchovies and sprinkle with herbs and radishes.

1 pound green snap beans cut into ¼-inch lengths
4 potatoes, peeled and evenly sliced (use a slicer if possible, set at ³⁄₁₆ of an inch)
4 tomatoes, peeled, seeded, and sliced
8 pitted ripe olives, sliced
1 tablespoon smallest capers
¾ cup French Dressing
1 2½-ounce jar rolled anchovies
2 tablespoons each chopped chervil and parsley
3 red radishes, chopped

SALADE NIÇOISE III

Prepare and combine all the ingredients shortly before serving. Bind the salad with as much of the French dressing as necessary. Arrange it in a salad bowl and sprinkle with the parsley. Surround the salad with overlapping slices of tomatoes and serve.

2 cups cold cooked rice, must be dry and cooked "al dente"
1 pimento, diced
1 green pepper, seeded and diced
3 hard-cooked eggs, cut into sixths
1 7-ounce can tuna fish, drained and flaked
12 anchovy fillets, drained and chopped
½ cup pitted ripe olives, sliced
4 green olives, pitted and chopped
1 cup French Dressing
½ cup finely chopped parsley
4 tomatoes, peeled and sliced

PROVINCIAL SALAD

Prepare the tomatoes, artichokes, mushrooms, and olives and arrange them in a wide salad bowl. Chill until needed. Before serving, surround the salad with the crisp water cress and pour over the dressing.

3 tomatoes, peeled and sliced
6 artichoke bottoms, cut in half and sliced
8 medium mushrooms, very thinly sliced
8 large black olives, pitted and chopped
½ bunch water cress, coarse stems removed
½ recipe Provincial French Dressing

RUSSIAN SALAD

For an informal Sunday lunch or a late supper, prepare an enormous Russian salad on the day before the party and serve it with various kinds of breads.

Drain and chill all the vegetables and combine them with radishes, pickle, meats, and lobster. Wash and dry the raw mushrooms, break out the stems, and fill the caps high with a mixture of caviar, 2 of the riced eggs, half the parsley, and the chopped mushroom stems. Bind the salad ingredients with mayonnaise. Mound them in a large bowl or on a platter and sprinkle the salad with remaining riced egg white, egg yolk, and parsley. Arrange the filled mushrooms around the salad, alternating with anchovies.

4 medium potatoes, cooked and diced
2 cups carrots, diced, cooked, and chilled
2 cups snap beans, cut into ½-inch lengths, cooked and chilled
1 package frozen baby lima beans, prepared according to package directions
4 radishes, sliced
2 dill pickles, chopped and drained
6 thick slices tongue, trimmed and diced
3 thick slices ham, fat removed and diced
3 frankfurter sausages, skinned and sliced
1 pound lobster meat, cut into pieces
12 medium mushrooms
1 small jar red caviar
4 hard-cooked eggs, yolks and whites riced separately
½ cup minced parsley
Mayonnaise
1 can rolled anchovies, drained

SPANISH SALAD

Prepare the tomatoes, onion, and cucumber and marinate them lightly in dressing in 3 small bowls. Transfer the tomatoes to the center of a wide salad bowl and arrange the onion rings and cucumbers around them. Sprinkle the border with the combined pimento and parsley. Toast the bread crumbs with the butter in a 250° F. oven, stirring them several times, until they are golden, about 20 minutes. Sprinkle them over the tomatoes just before serving. Mix the salad at the table and pass a little more French dressing in a sauce bowl.

5 large ripe tomatoes, peeled and sliced
1 onion, very thinly sliced and divided into rings
1 cucumber, seeded or scored and thinly sliced
½ recipe French Dressing
1 pimento, diced
¼ cup chopped parsley
1 cup bread crumbs
2 tablespoons butter

STROGANOFF SALAD

Combine the carrots, peas, mushrooms, and truffles. Arrange the salad in a lettuce-lined bowl and surround it with egg slices or quail eggs. Pour over the dressing and sprinkle the salad with diced aspic. Mix it at the table just before serving.

1 cup diced, undercooked carrots
2 cups cooked green peas
10 medium mushrooms, trimmed and thinly sliced
2 truffles, peeled, diced, optional
1 head crisp Boston lettuce
3 hard-cooked eggs sliced, or 1 jar quail's eggs, halved
½ cup Vinaigrette Sauce
½ cup diced aspic, page 98

TONGUE SALAD I

Break the crisp Boston lettuce leaves into a large salad bowl and cover them completely with the tongue, cucumber, cheese, pimento, and capers, in that order. Just before serving at the table, pour over the dressing, mix the salad lightly, and serve as you would a chef's salad. The tongue and other ingredients can also be bound with the dressing and arranged in a lettuce-leaf-lined salad bowl.

1 head Boston lettuce
1½ cups julienne (thin strips) cold boiled tongue
1 cup peeled and seeded cucumber cut into strips
½ cup Swiss cheese, cut into strips
2 tablespoons diced pimento
1 tablespoon smallest capers, or chopped capers
1 cup French Dressing

TONGUE SALAD II
(Ham may be substituted for the tongue)

Combine the first 8 ingredients and bind with the dressing. Arrange the salad in a shallow dish and garnish with water cress.

2 cups diced boiled tongue or ham
1 cup diced celery
1 cup peeled, cored, and diced apple
2 hard-cooked eggs, chopped
3 tablespoons chopped gherkins
3 tablespoons chopped stuffed olives
Salt and paprika to taste
2 tablespoons finely chopped parsley
1 cup Mustard French Dressing
½ bunch crisp water cress

SALADE TOURANGELLE

Cut the beans into ⅓-inch lengths and cook them separately in salted water until just tender. Drain and cool them. Cook the potato dice in salted water until barely tender; watch them carefully, they will only take a few minutes. Drain the potatoes and sprinkle them immediately with a little of the French dressing. When they are cold, combine them with the savory and beans and add just enough dressing to bind and marinate. When ready to serve, stir gently with mayonnaise, transfer to a lettuce-lined bowl, and serve.

½ pound tender green snap beans
½ pound wax beans, strings removed
4 medium potatoes, peeled and cut into ½-inch dice
⅓ cup French Lemon Dressing
1 tablespoon finely chopped summer savory or dried summer savory scalded
4 to 5 tablespoons mayonnaise to bind
Boston lettuce leaves for the salad bowl

COLD STEAMED ASPARAGUS

Wash asparagus in cold water and trim the tough ends off the stalks evenly. Scrape off any scales or woody parts from the sides of the stalks with a potato peeler. Tie the stalks into loose bunches with kitchen string and stand them upright in 1 to 1½ inches of boiling salted water in the lower section of a double boiler. Invert the upper section of the double boiler over the asparagus and steam them for about 15 minutes, depending on the size and age of the asparagus. The stalks should be *just* tender and *very green*. Take them out with kitchen tongs, drain them well on a napkin, and chill them after they are cool. Do not overchill or they will look shriveled. Serve with sauces and garnishes, as the recipes require.

1 to 2 large bunches fresh asparagus

ASPARAGUS WITH HAM SAUCE

Arrange the chilled asparagus stalks on 6 salad plates. Combine the ham, celery, egg whites, gherkins, and pimento and spoon the mixture in a thick strip over the center of the asparagus stalks. Pour over the dressing and rice the egg yolks over the top.

1 3-pound bunch asparagus, prepared and steamed (given above)
1 cup chopped boiled ham, free of fat
1 cup diced celery
2 hard-cooked eggs, chopped whites and riced yolks
3 tablespoons chopped sweet gherkins
3 tablespoons pimento
⅔ cup Paprika French Dressing

SHRIMP IN DILL MAYONNAISE

Bring celery, bay leaf, pepper, salt, and dill to a boil in a deep sauce-pan half full of water. Boil for 10 minutes. Add the peeled shrimp all at once and bring back to a boil. Boil for exactly 3 minutes after the water returns to a boil, and take from heat. If shrimp are very large, allow 4 minutes, but no more. Drain the shrimp and sprinkle with vinegar. Chill the shrimp until ready to serve. Cut the tomatoes into thin slices and drain them well. Overlap the tomato slices around the edge of a glass dish or hors d'oeuvre dish. Mix the shrimp with dill mayonnaise to bind, put them into the tomato ring, and sprinkle heavily with finely cut dill.

4 celery stalks with leaves, cut into short lengths
1 bay leaf
4 peppercorns
½ tablespoon salt
4 sprigs fresh dill
1½ pounds large shrimp, peeled and deveined
1 tablespoon tarragon vinegar
4 medium or 1 pound tomatoes, peeled
Dill Mayonnaise (given below)

DILL MAYONNAISE

Crush dill seeds and stir them into sour cream. Combine with the mayonnaise and season to taste. Peel and seed a cucumber and cut the solid flesh into small dice. Add them to the mayonnaise. Pour over shrimp and sprinkle with the fresh dill.

½ teaspoon dill seed
½ cup sour cream
1 cup mayonnaise
Salt and a pinch of sugar to taste
½ cup well-drained cucumber dice
3 tablespoons finely cut fresh dill

DESSERTS

CHAPTER SEVEN

Desserts, Fruits, and Dessert Sauces

AMERICANS have seemingly always felt a preference for cold desserts. We have a history of chilled creams, custards, sillabubs, and trifles that goes back to colonial days. In recent years we have leaned more and more toward hot meals with cold endings. In the past these endings had to be cooked or baked before they were chilled. Now they have been arranged so conveniently that most of them require nothing more serious than mixing or whipping before they are chilled and served.

Our kitchen appliances enable us to prepare and store cold desserts for long periods. Our communications are such that we can eat fresh fruit within a short time after it has ripened thousands of miles away. The possibilities are enormous, but the results are often monotonous. We serve the same desserts over and over again.

While we do not have to urge the idea of serving cold desserts, we do have to find new ones, or old ones with new faces. The day is past when frozen desserts disappeared from restaurant and home menus as soon as the weather turned cold. Ice-cream parlors and stands no longer close in autumn and reopen in spring; cold desserts have nothing to do with seasons. We do not even go on ice-cream and fresh fruit binges in June. We can say of ourselves that neither cold, nor snow, nor sleet, can deter us from our daily consumption of ice cream (but it need not always be vanilla, chocolate, and strawberry).

The popularity of cold desserts is, of course, due to their lovely taste. But no food that was hard to prepare has ever become truly popular. Of the cold desserts suggested in this chapter, some of the peaches have to be poached, and the *sabayon* is beaten over simmering water, but no cooking of any kind is needed for the rest. Preparing them is child's play, and, since everyone loves them, even in zero weather, they are a pleasant change from the usual pies, layer cakes, and plain ice creams.

Every hostess who is going to serve cold desserts, all year round, should have stemmed dessert glasses or crystal dishes. They will sparkle and enhance the cold endings.

STRAWBERRY MÉLANGE I

Most dessert mélanges, like some of the salads, look better before they are mixed than after, which does not detract from the lovely combination of flavors and textures.

Arrange the strawberries on the ice cream, cover with the other ingredients, and mix at the table just before serving. The ice cream must be at room temperature before mixing.

1 quart ripe strawberries, hulled
1 quart vanilla ice cream
2 tablespoons freshly grated orange rind
½ cup port wine
¼ cup kirsch
1 cup crushed macaroon or cookie crumbs
¼ cup broken marrons glacés

STRAWBERRY MÉLANGE II

Arrange the strawberries on a 1-inch-thick layer of vanilla ice cream in a serving bowl. Add Grand Marnier to apple jelly and pour over the strawberries. Top them with a bonnet of whipped cream and serve. Mix the ingredients lightly at the table and serve. If there is no time to arrange, place ice cream in the dish in the freezing compartment, cover strawberries with the Grand Marnier-apple jelly mixture, and refrigerate. Chill the whipped cream separately and combine about 20 minutes before serving. Store in refrigerator after the dish is combined.

1 quart strawberries, hulled
1 quart vanilla ice cream
2 jiggers Grand Marnier
⅔ jar apple jelly, melted over hot water
1 cup heavy cream, whipped

RUM MOUSSE with STRAWBERRIES OR RASPBERRIES

Chill all ingredients and utensils. Beat the sugar with the egg yolks until pale yellow and very thick. Stir in the fruit and nuts and chill the mixture for 30 minutes. Fold in the cold whipped cream and flavor with the rum. Pour the mousse into a chilled 1½-quart soufflé dish and freeze it in the freezing compartment of the refrigerator for about 40 minutes. Whip the mousse once more with a French wire whisk and freeze it for at least 6 hours longer. About 30 minutes before serving, move it into the refrigerator and cover it with the berries. Sugar them very lightly and serve.

⅓ cup sugar
4 large or 5 small egg yolks
4 tablespoons finely diced candied peel
4 tablespoons finely chopped toasted filberts
1½ cups heavy cream, whipped
1 tablespoon dark rum
1 quart strawberries or raspberries, hulled

RIPE RASPBERRIES

Ripe raspberries are lovely with Thick Cream, or with softened and beaten vanilla ice cream. They lose their velvety look when they are served *under* any sauces, so serve sauces separately or serve the raspberries *on top* of any accompaniments.

Place softened ice cream in a dessert bowl. Whip the cream, perfume it with liqueur, and sweeten it to taste. Put cream over ice cream, macaroons over the cream, and the raspberries on top. Mix at the table and serve in dessert bowls.

1½ pints vanilla ice cream
1 cup heavy cream, whipped
Kirsch or framboise to taste
Powdered sugar to taste
1 cup crushed macaroons
2 baskets ripe raspberries

RASPBERRIES UNDER SABAYON SAUCE

Pick over raspberries. Let ice cream soften slightly in refrigerator, then whip it into a soft mound. Place it in the center of a chilled dessert bowl. Arrange berries against the ice cream and sprinkle them with crushed amaretti. Place bowl in freezer. Beat yolks and sugar until light and creamy in the top of a double boiler. Add the wine and orange rind and set the boiler over 1 inch of simmering water in the lower section of the double boiler. Beat until the sabayon is light and creamy, take it from heat and beat until it is cold. Pour the sauce over the berries and serve. To speed the chilling, the lower section of the double boiler can be cooled under cold water and half filled with ice cubes. Set the upper section over it and beat until cold.

1 quart raspberries
1 quart vanilla ice cream
16 to 20 Italian amaretti (macaroons),
*   crushed*
4 egg yolks
2 to 4 tablespoons sugar, to taste
½ cup dry white wine
½ tablespoon grated orange rind

SABAYON SAUCE

Beat egg yolks and sugar until they are an almost white, solid cream. Put them into the top of a double boiler over (not touching) barely simmering water with half the Marsala. Beat with an electric beater until the sauce thickens. Add the remaining wine gradually. Take from heat when the sauce is thick and creamy. Beat in the vanilla and continue to beat the sauce over a bowl of ice until it is cold. For a thinner sauce, use 1 cup Marsala.

4 egg yolks
½ cup granulated sugar
⅔ cup Marsala
1 teaspoon vanilla extract

SABAYON À LA CRÉOLE

Whip the yolks, sugar, and curaçao in the top of a large double boiler *over* (not touching) 1 inch of boiling water, as for Sabayon Sauce (given above). When the mixture is thick, pale, and smooth, and when it has stopped increasing in volume, take it from the heat and continue beating until it is cold. If possible, beat the sabayon over a bowl of ice or ice water to chill it more rapidly. When it is cold, beat in the orange rind and fold in the stiffly whipped cream. Pour the mixture into sturdy stemmed glasses and refrigerate. Decorate with strawberries and serve.

4 egg yolks
3 tablespoons sugar
3 tablespoons curaçao or Triple Sec
2 teaspoons grated orange rind
1 cup heavy cream, whipped
1 cup strawberries, hulled

COLD ORANGE SABAYON

Beat all ingredients in the top of a large double boiler, *over* (not touching) simmering water, with an electric hand beater or rotary beater until mixture becomes frothy and increases in volume. When it stops rising, pour it into 6 stemmed glasses and chill until needed. Garnish with ripe strawberries.

3 large egg yolks
2½ tablespoons sugar
⅓ cup orange juice
¼ cup orange liqueur (curaçao or Cointreau)
2 teaspoons grated orange rind
Ripe strawberries

RUM ORANGE PARFAIT

Set a mixing bowl into a pan of ice and whip the cream with an electric hand beater until it is half stiff. Gradually add half the sugar and beat until cream is very stiff. In a second bowl, beat yolks with the remaining sugar until pale and thick. Add the rum and candied peel and fold the whipped cream into the mixture. Pour the cream into a shallow pan or into ice trays and put them into the deep freezer or the freezing compartment of the refrigerator. When the cream is beginning to freeze and is getting firm around the edges, beat it again with a French wire whisk, then pour it into the chilled dish or dishes from which it will be served. Cover the top deeply with a mixture of crushed spritz tongues and praline powder. Freeze for at least 2 hours.

3 cups heavy cream
¾ cup superfine sugar
3 large egg yolks
1 to 2 tablespoons heavy rum, to taste
3 tablespoons finely diced candied orange peel
¾ cup cookie crumbs
Spritz Tongues
¼ cup Praline Powder

RUM CREAM

A 5-minute dessert that must be served soon after it is made.

Beat the yolks and sugar until they are as light and thick as they can be. Beat in the rum and fold in the stiffly whipped cream. Divide the cream over 6 chilled stemmed glasses. To grate the chocolate, chill a dark chocolate bar, preferably orange flavored, and grate it while it is very cold. Sprinkle over the glasses and serve.

3 egg yolks
½ cup sugar
1 tablespoon rum, or to taste
1½ cups heavy cream, whipped
3 tablespoons grated dark chocolate

FILLED PEACHES WITH CHESTNUT PURÉE AND RASPBERRY SAUCE

Scald peaches in boiling water, draw off the skins, cut them in half, and discard the stones. Arrange the halves closely together in a shallow baking dish from which they can be served. Sprinkle them with lemon juice and fill the centers with the chestnut purée. Pour half the sherry and rum over the peach halves and bake them in a 375° F. oven for 20 minutes, basting them with the remaining sherry and rum every 5 minutes. Depending on the ripeness of the peaches, baking time may take less or more than 20 minutes. Test them with a fork and bake until they are tender but not soft enough to lose their shape. Cool and chill the peaches and serve from the dish with a bowl of raspberry sauce.

6 large ripe peaches
1 lemon, cut in half
6 tablespoons Chestnut Purée
5 tablespoons sherry
2 tablespoons rum
Raspberry Sauce (given below)

RASPBERRY SAUCE (in blender)

Thaw the berries until just soft and place them, with their juice, in the container of the blender. Cover and blend until smooth. Add cream and continue to blend until the sauce is light. Add rum, blend for a few seconds longer, and chill until needed.

1 package frozen raspberries
½ to ⅓ cup heavy cream
1 tablespoon rum, or to taste

POACHED PEACHES IN CUSTARD SAUCE

Scald the peaches in boiling water, draw off the skins, and cut them in half. Remove the stones and crack them with a nutcracker. Take out the almonds and draw off the brown skins. Boil sugar and water together in a deep saucepan until sugar is melted, add the peach halves and almonds, and simmer covered for 10 minutes. Add the kirsch and almond extract and simmer until tender, depending on the type of peach, this may take only a few minutes longer. Take from heat, and cool the peaches in the syrup. Take them out with a slotted spoon, and reduce the syrup by boiling uncovered for a few minutes longer, stir in the jam and cool. Place peaches in syrup-jam sauce and pass the custard sauce separately.

8 large ripe peaches
¾ cup sugar
¾ cup water
¼ cup kirsch
½ teaspoon almond extract
½ cup peach or apricot jam, strained
Custard Sauce (given below)

CUSTARD SAUCE

Beat yolks with sugar until very light and thick. Beat in the heated milk, in a thin stream, without stopping the beater. Transfer the mixture to the top of a double boiler *over* (not touching) simmering water and stir until the custard is thickened and coats the back of a spoon. Take from heat, add vanilla and rum, and cool. Before serving, fold in the whipped cream.

4 egg yolks
⅔ cup sugar
1 cup milk, heated but not boiling
1 teaspoon vanilla
1 tablespoon rum
½ cup heavy cream, whipped, optional

FRESH FRUIT DESSERTS

When peaches and pears are perfectly ripe, I use them in simple combinations, with commercial ice creams or ices, with easily made sauces, or bottled conserves. When they are not at the ripest moment, I poached them lightly in sugar or prepared syrup, or, better still, in a dry white wine with a little sugar and butter so that they are not oversweetened.

Peaches, whether they are ripe enough to eat raw, or whether they are going to be poached, should be scalded and skinned. Pears should be carefully peeled. Poaching fruit depends so entirely on its age that it varies with every poaching. But the time is usually very short—it can be less than 10 minutes. I would certainly watch summer fruit carefully and test it with a pointed knife blade, until it is soft but *not* until it is mushy or in any way loses its shape

The following combinations are for raw or poached fruit. When they are going to be served raw, they have to be peeled or skinned shortly before they are served.

PEACHES ON ICE CREAM

CARDINAL   Scalded peaches are halved and poached in a light sugar syrup to which a little vanilla has been added. They are cooled in the syrup, drained, and served on vanilla ice cream. Blend 1 pint hulled strawberries with 2 or 3 tablespoons heavy cream and powdered sugar to taste and pour over the peaches. Sprinkle with scalded shaved almonds.

CONDÉ   Scald and serve the peach halves as above. Dissolve apricot jam in the top of a double boiler over boiling water. Stir in a little kirsch to taste, or substitute apricot brandy, and serve the sauce with the peaches.

CHOCOLATE   Scald, halve, and poach peaches and serve them on butter pecan or any other nut ice cream. For the sauce, melt 2 regular candy bars of milk chocolate in the top of a double boiler over boiling water. Stir in enough heavy cream to make a flowing sauce. Serve the sauce ice cold.

CURRANT   Serve the scalded, poached, and halved peaches on vanilla ice cream. Beat curaçao into Bar-le-Duc red currant conserve (or melted currant jelly) and pour it over the peaches. Sprinkle heavily with chopped toasted nuts.

GREEK   Scald and serve the peach halves as for CARDINAL. For the sauce blend 1 cup drained whole figs (obtainable in No. 303 jars) with kirsch to taste and fold them into an equal quantity of whipped cream. Serve the sauce over the peaches and garnish with slivered almonds.

NINA   Reverse the arrangement as for CURRANT, place scalded, poached, and halved peaches on a mixture of crushed macaroons and curaçao (or any preferred liqueur) and serve under a sauce of softened and beaten vanilla ice cream. Set container of ice cream in refrigerator until it just feels soft, then beat ice cream in electric beater and serve.

PEARS ON ICE CREAM OR SHERBET

FELICITY   Place poached or ripe pear halves on vanilla ice cream and sprinkle heavily with crushed praline.

HELENA   This is a well-known dessert, but it can be improved by poaching the pears in a light sugar syrup flavored with kirsch. The chilled pear halves are served on a creamy vanilla ice cream with Swiss Chocolate Sauce.

MAXIMILIAN Center a dessert dish with a mound of raspberry sherbet, lay quartered poached pears against it, and grate a dark semisweet chocolate over the pears. These are served with *half-whipped* heavy cream.

SABAYON Place peeled and poached pear halves on vanilla ice cream and pour over Sabayon Sauce. If there is leftover homemade mousse, Biscuit Tortoni, or Maraschino Cream in the freezer, divide it into portions, set a half pear on each, and serve them with the sauce.

SPICED CHERRIES

Serve hot or cold with ice cream or whipped sour cream.

Drain cherries and cook cherry juice with red wine, jelly, and spices in the top of a double boiler over boiling water until thickened and reduced to 2 cups. Take out cinnamon and cloves, add cherries, and simmer for 15 minutes longer. Cool, add the brandy, and either chill the cherries or serve them hot over very cold vanilla ice cream. If preferred they may be served very cold in individual bowls with 1 container sour cream, whipped, and a muffineer filled with sugar mixed with cinnamon to taste.

1 No. 2 can pitted black cherries
1½ cups red wine
1 jar red currant jelly
1 cinnamon stick
4 cloves
1 jigger brandy, or to taste
1½ quarts vanilla ice cream, stored in
*   freezer and very cold*

BLACK CHERRIES WITH SOUR CREAM

Pit the cherries over a bowl to catch all the juice. Add half the kirsch and chill until needed. Whip the cream with sugar and cinnamon and pass it separately.

2 pounds large black cherries, pitted
1 large jigger kirsch, or to taste
1 cup sour cream
2 tablespoons sugar
1 teaspoon ground cinnamon

RIPE CHERRIES AND CREAM
(can also be made with strawberries)

Arrange the cherries in a dessert dish, sprinkle them with sugar, and chill. Shortly before serving, top them with the softly whipped cream. Sprinkle the chocolate generously over the cream and top with hazelnuts.

1 pound sweet black cherries, pitted
3 tablespoons powdered sugar, mixed with
* a pinch of ground cinnamon*
½ cup heavy cream, half whipped
Grated semisweet chocolate
2 tablespoons chopped toasted hazelnuts

CHAMPAGNE FRUIT

This takes wide, stemmed glasses, on the order of elegant fruit-cup glasses. Hull and chill the strawberries, scald and skin the peaches, drop them into acidulated water, and slice them just before serving. Arrange the fruit in the glasses, sprinkle brandy over it, and serve the glasses on dessert plates. Give each guest a fork and an iced split of champagne. Pass almond crescents separately.

1 quart strawberries
3 ripe peaches
Brandy to taste
6 splits of champagne
Almond Crescents

MARASCHINO CREAM WITH STEWED PEACHES

Beat yolks and sugar until very thick and almost white. Stir the gelatin into the maraschino and set it aside. Heat the milk to boiling, cool it slightly, and stir it into the yolks in a thin stream. Pour the mixture into the top of a double boiler, over boiling water, add the gelatin, and stir until it is dissolved. Take from heat and cool. When it is cold and beginning to thicken, fold in the stiff egg whites and whipped cream. Pour the cream into a crystal bowl or into a rinsed 1½-quart ring mold and chill for at least 2 hours. Unmold on a cold platter and fill the center with home-stewed peaches in syrup. If the cream was poured into a bowl, decorate the top with sliced peaches and sprinkle them with nuts.

4 egg yolks
½ cup sugar
2 envelopes gelatin
5 tablespoons maraschino liqueur
2 cups milk
2 egg whites, beaten stiff
1 cup heavy cream, whipped
Peaches in syrup
¼ cup chopped pistachio nuts

FROZEN SOUFFLÉ

All ingredients and utensils should be cold.

Set refrigerator gauge to coldest point. Beat egg yolks until light and creamy, gradually add sugar, and beat until very thick and palest cream color. Add the Grand Marnier, orange rind, and vanilla slowly and continue to beat until smooth. Whip cream until very stiff, fold into the yolk mixture, and fill into a bowl that will fit into the freezing compartment or freezer. Tie a wax paper cuff around a 4-cup soufflé dish and chill it. After 1 hour, take soufflé from freezer, beat it vigorously with a French wire whisk and pour it into the cuffed soufflé dish. Chill it for at least 6 hours, preferably until the following day. To serve, remove the cuff with the help of a knife blade dipped in hot water. Smooth the sides and sprinkle the top with cocoa powder and finely crushed macaroon crumbs.

6 egg yolks
¾ cup sugar
3 tablespoons Grand Marnier
1 tablespoon grated orange rind
½ teaspoon vanilla
2½ cups heavy cream, whipped
Cocoa powder
Macaroon crumbs

THICK CREAM

Place a wide, shallow, flat china dish in a warm place where it can remain undisturbed for 36 to 48 hours. Pour ½ pint heavy cream, preferably 3 or 4 days old, into the dish and leave it undisturbed until the cream has gathered into a thick coat across the surface. The wider the surface and the more cream that is exposed to the warm air, the better.

Draw the cream gently to one side with a spoon and pour off the whey. Beat the cream with a small whisk until it is smooth. Chill until ready to serve. Serve in a small bowl; thick cream is too thick to pour.

Thick cream may be served with a sprinkling of stale pumpernickel crumbs and sugar mixed with a little cinnamon.

for Winter and Cool Climates

MENUS

CHAPTER EIGHT

Menus, with Explanations, for All Meals.
Introducing New Cold Dishes to Serve with
One Hot Course for Year-Round Cookery
in Any Climate

THE BELIEF that the beginning is always the hardest holds good for most things in life but not for the cooking of dinner. *That* starts off like a breeze and usually ends in a tornado.

The initial preparations for a hot dinner are perfectly simple. We collect various ingredients, assemble the dishes, and put them on to simmer—or roast—or bake—as the case may be. We look at them now and then and do a little stirring or basting when necessary. Everything progresses peacefully until about half an hour before dinner . . . then suddenly all bedlam breaks loose. Vegetables have to be boiled, sauces have to be whipped, and plates have to be heated. We get into an absolute frenzy of draining, glazing, and garnishing. Skewers and strings have to be removed and butter has to be added. On top of all that *everything has to reach the table at the same time—and piping hot.*

After a few of these nightmare experiences we make menus that will ease the tension at the end. We omit the second vegetable and all garnishes, but the strain of getting even the simplest dinner to come out evenly—*and getting the plates hot too*—has driven most of us to casserole menus. It has driven me to cold cookery, irrespective of the seasons.

When we consider what makes entertaining difficult, it always boils down to whether we know the fine art of keeping food hot without overcooking it. Whether we know how to coast the roast and finish the hollandaise on the very instant the broccoli is at its greenest. We have to know how to gratinée the fish and time the soufflé to coincide with the removal of the previous course. All that is actually more difficult than the cooking.

Besides the knowledge and experience it takes to produce a good hot dinner, menu making depends on whether we have two ovens, a separate broiler, lots of stove-top burners, a deep-fat fryer, a plate warmer, a heated tray, and other heat-holding equipment. And I remember two disastrous dinner parties, after thunderstorms in Connecticut, when I discovered that hot dinners also depended heavily on whether or not we have electric current.

As a result of all this wear and tear we unconsciously make out menus with more thought for convenience and appliances than for the excellence of their combinations. We may love risi pisi with the roast chicken, but who wants to cook and drain rice and green peas to coincide with the ping of the oven timer? Who has the time to heat butter to bubbling and sprinkle Parmesan cheese just when the soup cups have to be collected and the gravy has to be made? And so we compose the menu around our beef casserole—over and over again—because the peas and carrots and potatoes are all right there in the same dish with the meat and the sauce. We forego our favorite menu combinations, and ultimately we forget there were lovely things like artichokes Cavour with the beef and eggplant fritters with the lamb and mint sauce.

I solved the problem long ago by overcoming the cold-food-in-winter prejudice. I serve cold artichoke salade Gambetta with hot beef and hot artichokes Cavour with cold filet of beef. I reverse the menu conventions to my heart's content, even when there is a foot of snow at the door. Needless to say there are exceptions; we do serve hot food during blizzards and to skiers returned from the slopes.

There should be a hot course on every winter menu, but the problem course—the one that takes four pairs of hands to complete—should be cold. One beautiful cold dish—not a summery salad but the sort of thing that made the cold-buffet tables famous—is worth an entire short-cut hot meal. No matter what the temperature is outside, our dining rooms verge on the tropical, and we do not actually need hot food. I am all for steaming soups, hot roasts or sizzling steaks, and flaming desserts . . . but not all at the same meal. Not if it means sacrificing good menu combinations just because there is only one oven.

We are presently serving cold courses at winter dinners with remarkable monotony. No one objects to starting out with a cold fruit or seafood cocktail and ending with ice cream, so long as the main course is hot. I am advocating new menus that are a change from our traditional menu-making conventions. Since they can be prepared in advance, they do not depend on the number of ovens available. And they save the housewife or working wife from that last agonizing half hour. They also intrigue the guests.

Warm dishes, suggested in the menus, are either of the type that "cook themselves" or they can be prepared at leisure and heated before serving. They are suggested only in a general way, and recipes for their preparation can be found in any basic cookbook.

Menus
[Hot dishes are in italics]
TURTLE SOUP

DECANTER OF SHERRY

MELBA BRIOCHE SLICES

DUCK CAVENDISH
sliced breasts of two roast duck glazed with aspic and arranged around one opened carcass filled with fruit salad

TART CHERRY SAUCE

HORSERADISH SAUCE

MI AMANTE
softened coffee ice cream blended with gin and served in stemmed glasses

LINZER TARTS
dry white wine

Prepare entire meal at leisure. Before serving: heat soup. Blend ice cream and gin just before serving

✺

PÂTÉ MAISON
with green grapes

FRIED AND DRIED TOAST

HAVANA LOBSTER
lobster slices on green asparagus spears covered with cucumber mayonnaise and sprinkled with dill

HOT POACHED PEACHES

RASPBERRY SAUCE

COFFEE
dry white wine

Prepare entire meal at leisure. Thirty minutes before serving: heat poached peaches, make coffee

✺

FOUR SEASONS SALAD
sliced tomatoes, cucumbers, radishes, and endive with lemon French dressing

HOT MULLIGATAWNY
large pieces of chicken in strong chicken and vegetable stock, flavored lightly with curry

OVEN-DRIED ITALIAN BREAD
sprinkled with Parmesan cheese

RICE JACKSON
rice flavored with grated lemon rind and bound with a white wine and orange Sabayon Sauce, garnished with orange sections

COFFEE
red wine

Prepare entire meal at leisure
Before serving: heat soup and make coffee

❀

SMALL MELONS FILLED WITH PORT WINE
BROILED STEAK OR INDIVIDUAL STEAKS

SLICED TOMATOES
with minced onions, parsley, and French dressing

POTATO SALAD
small new potatoes in herbed mayonnaise garnished with black olives

COFFEE CREAM
with a sauce of soft vanilla ice cream

COFFEE
red wine

Prepare entire meal at leisure
Before serving: broil meat, make coffee

❀

ITALIAN STUFFED MUSHROOMS
spinach-stuffed mushrooms glazed with aspic

OVEN-DRIED PARMESAN TOAST

LAMB KEBABS
marinated chunks of lamb strung on skewers with onions and tomatoes

CURRY SAUCE

HERBED RICE SALAD

NEW ORLEANS FRUIT WHIP

COFFEE
serve a vin rosé

Prepare entire meal at leisure
Before serving: broil kebabs and make coffee

❀

POLISH CAULIFLOWER
cooked cauliflower marinated in French dressing, covered with riced hard-cooked egg, slivered ham, and minced parsley

OVEN-DRIED TOAST

VITELLO TONNATO

MIXED GREEN SALAD

LEMON SOUFFLÉ

COFFEE
dry white wine

Prepare entire meal at leisure, prepare soufflé base
Before serving: bake soufflé (45 minutes), make coffee

❀

INDIVIDUAL CHEESE SOUFFLÉS

GARLIC MELBA TOAST

VEAL RICHMOND

roast veal glazed with Madeira aspic garnished with scallop shells of herbed vegetable salad and diced aspic

ESCOFFIER MAYONNAISE

ROQUEFORT PEAR

pears filled with creamed Roquefort cheese, sprinkled with paprika, masked with melted currant jelly sauce

COFFEE

dry white wine

Prepare soufflé base and entire meal at leisure
Before serving: bake soufflés for 25 minutes, make coffee

❁

QUICHE LORRAINE

SLICED BEEF

CUMBERLAND SAUCE

DIXIE SALAD

diced tomatoes and cut corn bound with mayonnaise thinned with French dressing, garnished with lettuce leaves

GLAZED BAKED APPLES

ENGLISH CHEDDAR CHEESE

COFFEE

red wine

Prepare entire meal at leisure
Before serving: bake quiche for 1 hour, make coffee

❁

ASPARAGUS VINAIGRETTE

with sliced Westphalian or prosciutto ham

TOAST

SALMON ADLON

poached and glazed slices arranged around a vegetable salad, garnished with lemon halves filled with green mayonnaise

RUSSIAN BANANAS

large bananas cut in half lengthwise, meat puréed with liqueur and cake crumbs, returned to shells and browned in oven

COFFEE

dry white wine

Prepare entire meal at leisure
Before serving: heat toast, brown bananas, make coffee

❁

RAKOWA

Russian shrimp soup garnished with dilled lemon slices

CHICKEN LAS PALMAS

Chicken breasts masked with tomato-tinted chaud-froid sauce, garnished with artichokes filled with rice, pimento, and stuffed-olive salad

HERBED BREAD

PINEAPPLE SAVOY

Fresh pineapple with crushed raspberry sauce

COFFEE

dry white wine

Prepare entire meal at leisure
Before serving: heat soup and bread and make coffee (for summer meals, chill soup)

❁

SMALL HORS D'OUVRE TRAY

sardines, olives, stuffed eggs, salami slices, pickled beets, celery, radishes, and bean salad

OVEN-DRIED FRENCH BREAD SLICES
SLICED FILET OF BEEF COQUELIN
SHOESTRING POTATOES
JELLIED MADEIRA SAUCE
ARTICHOKES CAVOUR

cooked artichoke bottoms drawn through melted butter, dredged with grated Parmesan cheese and browned in the oven. Remaining butter heated with anchovy paste and poured over finished artichokes. Hard-cooked egg riced over the top.

APPLES CONDÉ

poached apples under apricot sauce garnished with diced candied fruits

COFFEE

red wine

Prepare entire meal at leisure
Before serving: brown artichokes, heat butter, and make coffee

❋

GERMAN HERRINGS

mild herrings in sour cream under apple rings and hard-cooked egg slices

HOT BOILED POTATOES
BEEFSTEAK TARTARE

scraped raw beef with egg yolk, chopped onions, capers, mustard, paprika, caraway seeds, and seasonings

BLACK AND RYE BREADS

GORGONZOLA CHEESE

steins of beer

Prepare entire meal at leisure
Before serving: boil potatoes

❋

EGGS IN ASPIC
HOT GARLIC BREAD
VITELLO TONNATO

sliced veal under tuna fish-mayonnaise sauce garnished with capers

ITALIAN VEGETABLE SALAD
LEMON ICE
ESPRESSO

dry white wine

Prepare entire meal at leisure
Before serving: heat bread and make coffee

❋

JAMAICAN FRUIT

fruit with rum-flavored sherbet

BUTTERED PUMPERNICKEL
HAM ROLLS FILLED WITH HORSERADISH
ROAST BEEF ROLLS FILLED WITH HORSERADISH CREAM
POTATO SALAD STEPHAN

thin potato slices in white wine and pepper dressing

PANCAKES ASTOR

thin crêpes in a liqueur-flavored sauce

ICE COFFEE OR SANGRÍA

Prepare entire meal at leisure
Before serving: heat prepared pancakes in sauce

❋

JELLIED BOUILLON IN HALF CANTALOUPE SHELLS
ISTANBUL CHICKEN
strips of raw chicken meat fried for a few minutes at the table, served in a lightly flavored curry sauce
RICE WITH ALMONDS

CHIFFONADE SALAD
lettuce, endive, julienne of beets, French dressing, and riced hard-cooked eggs

COFFEE ICE
with powdered praline

Prepare entire meal at leisure
Before serving: cook rice, heat sauce, fry chicken at table

＊

ICED WATER CRESS AND POTATO SOUP BONVALET
TORN BREAD
chunks of bread dipped into garlic butter and dried until golden in a low oven
ROAST BEEF AU JUS
roasted without basting and served with its own juice
ARTICHOKE SALAD GAMBETTA
cooked artichoke bottoms marinated in sharp tarragon dressing, drained, diced, and bound with thin tarragon mayonnaise. Serve sprinkled with finely diced black olives
ITALIAN PEACHES
fresh sliced peaches macerated in kirsch under a sauce of blended figs in syrup. Garnished with crushed amaretti (Italian macaroons)
COFFEE

red wine

Prepare all but the beef at leisure. Roast beef at 18 minutes per pound in a 325° F. oven or according to taste.
Before serving: carve beef and make coffee

＊

GREEN SHRIMP
boiled shrimp under a sauce of minced water cress and lemon
SLICED FRENCH BREAD
FONDUE BOURGUIGNONNE
guests impale raw beef cubes on fondue forks and dip them into seething oil in a fondue pan; oil is lightly flavored with garlic

RÉMOULADE SAUCE

CATSUP-HORSERADISH SAUCE

MUSTARD SAUCE
SLICED TOMATOES WITH FRENCH DRESSING
serve tomatoes with the assorted French cheeses
FRENCH CHEESE TRAY

CRACKERS
COFFEE

red wine or beer

Prepare entire meal at leisure
Before serving: heat oil for fondue pan and make coffee

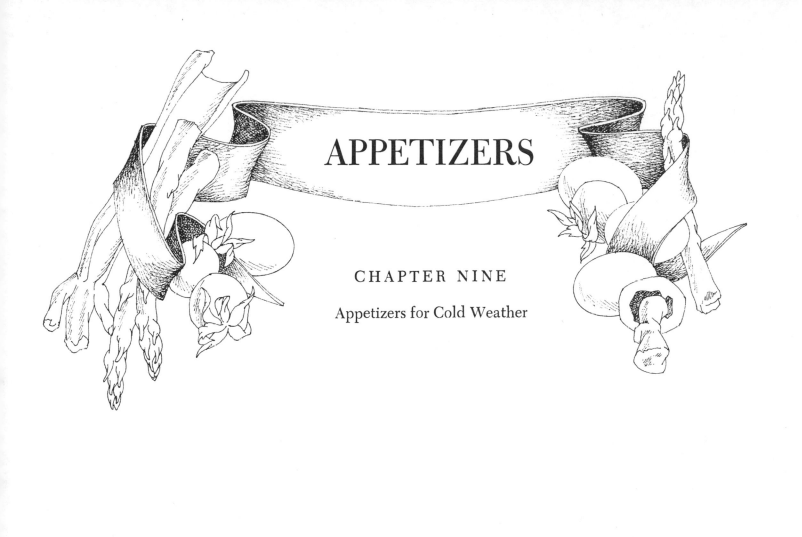

APPETIZERS

CHAPTER NINE

Appetizers for Cold Weather

THE cocktail hour is nothing new; it grew out of the old established French custom of stopping off at a bistro or café for an apéritif after work. It became the Apéro Hour, a meeting of kindred spirits—away from home—and any food that was consumed was done so unconsciously. Everything that suited a Frenchman had to be tried by all other Europeans, and the Apéro Hour, in one form or another, became universal in the West. In America, where many European customs go through surprising changes—and are later reintroduced to Europe as the NEWEST—the Apéro Hour moved into the home, included the ladies, stretched over several hours, and included FOOD. Appetizers and canapés increased until the hors d'oeuvre was lopped off dinner and eaten with cocktails in the living room.

At large cocktail parties it is easy to draw a line between an appetizer and a first course—if no fork is needed it's an appetizer—at small cocktail parties, forks, plates, and first courses often accompany cocktails. This seems as natural to us as it seems to some European hostesses to *raise* her guests from the table, after the main course, and give them dessert and coffee in the living room.

The following appetizers and first courses are listed together: the choice of *where* and with what beverage to eat them lies with the host and hostess, the selection of *what* to serve lies with the season of the year. In summer the effortless appetizers are more popular: seasonal vegetables and fruits, crisp, nonfilling, and refreshing, the less contrived the better. In cold weather the appetizers and first courses are still cold, but they take on a more fortifying, wintry character. The appetizers and first courses in Part I of this book are interchangeable with these in Part II. They are divided only because it is easier to buy a good melon in summer, while a Tuna or Kidney Bean Salad has rib-clinging, cold-weather quality.

The French have changed over their Apéro Hour, but they still take dinner very seriously and eating a great deal with cocktails is not acceptable. They rely on the mini-appetizers and call them *amuse-bouche*, or mouth amusers. They are miniature open-faced sandwiches that are by no means effortlessly made but they are rewardingly attractive.

It is a very nice feeling to butter a single slice of bread knowing it will make 8 or 9 appetizers.

Amuse-Bouche

All the amuse-bouche are based on bread slices cut into small rounds or diamond shapes. The largest of these can be cut to conform with the largest slice from the center of an egg, and the smallest should not have less than a ¾-inch diameter, lest it become too small to pick up. Use thinly sliced breads, at least 2 days old, as well as the very thinly sliced rye and dark breads that come in small packages. Some of the cheeses are enhanced by being spread on small home-baked cheese rounds, page 242.

BASE	COVER	GARNISH
1. White Bread Round	Herb butter, 1 hard-cooked egg slice	rolled anchovy fillet
2. White Bread Round	Horseradish butter, 1 round cut from outside of a peeled tomato with a cookie cutter, seeds removed and drained	tuft of freshly grated horseradish
3. White Bread Round	Horseradish butter, 1 round smoked salmon	minced capers
4. White Bread Round	Plain butter, *pâté de foie gras*	truffle slice
5. Whole-Wheat Bread Round	Mounded with anchovy butter dipped in minced egg white	center of riced egg yolk
6. Dark Bread Round	Mounded high with minced ham bound with mustard butter	gherkin slice
7. Rye Bread Round	Mound of butter and crushed canned salmon mixture	pickle relish
8. Rye Bread Round	Horseradish butter, 1 round smoked tongue	mustard
9. Cheese Round	Mounded with herbed Boursin cheese	stuffed olive slice
10. Cheese Round	Mounded with creamed Roquefort cheese	parsley tuft
11. Cheese Round	Minced red radishes mixed with cream cheese	1 large caper
12. Cheese Round	Piped rosette of salted cream cheese	small hollow filled with red caviar
13. Pumpernickel Round	Mustard butter, Emmental cheese	Triangle of pimento
14. Pumpernickel Round	Plain butter, 1 thin onion ring filled with sardine crushed with mayonnaise	grated lemon rind
15. Pumpernickel Round	Plain butter, ring of hollowed-out dill pickle filled with minced marinated herring	sprig of dill
16. Pumpernickel Round	Mounded butter and smoked trout paste	sliver of lemon peel

The Hors d'Oeuvre Tray

The hors d'oeuvre cart or tray is always popular in restaurants and should be served at home more often. It can be made up of a combination of salads, appetizers, and bought items—as sardines—and everyone helps themselves to a selection of their own choice. What is needed is a set of matched glass or porcelain dishes and a tray or table on which they can be aligned. The success of the hors d'oeuvre tray is its variety and the fact that everyone can choose their favorites. It is also a boon for the hostess who only has to prepare about one-third of the items. The hors d'oeuvre dishes are divided into four categories:

1. Homemade salads and pâtés that should be prepared well in advance and stored in jars in the refrigerator. Among these are:
   Spiced Button Mushrooms
   Sliced Pickled Mushrooms
   Pickled Beet Salad
   Lentil Salad
   Various Dried Bean Salads
   Cucumber Salad
   Chicken Liver or Other Pâté

2. Imperishable delicacies that are only available in cans or jars and are served more or less as they come:
   Sardines or Sprats
   Anchovies
   Olives, Ripe, Tree-Ripened, Green, or Stuffed
   Pimento, Plain or Roasted
   Pâté de Foie Gras
   Various Smoked Fishes, Trout, Mackerel, Haddock, Kippered Herrings, Eel
   Canned or Frozen Crab Meat
   Caviar
   Hearts of Palm
   White Asparagus
   Salmon
   Tuna Fish
   French Flageolet Beans
   White or Red Beans
   Artichoke Hearts or Artichoke Bottoms

3. Perishable meat and fish items that require little or no preparation are:
   Smoked Salmon
   Smoked Sturgeon
   Thinly Sliced Salami
   Thinly sliced Westphalian or Raw Smoked Hams

4. The home-prepared appetizers that can be started on the day before they will be served and require no last-minute preparation are:
   Stuffed Eggs
   Shrimp
   Stuffed or Sliced Tomatoes
   Fresh Vegetable, Chicken, or Meat Salads
   Fresh Fish or Lobster Appetizers
   Appetizers with Aspic
   Ham Rolls
   Smoked Salmon Rolls

The required accompaniments and garnishes for the hors d'oeuvre tray which can be prepared in advance are:
   Various Dressings and Sauces
   Various Mayonnaises
   Aspics

Crisp Lettuce, Parsley, Fresh Dill, and Chives
Gherkin fans and Pickle Slices
Thin Lemon Slices and Wedges
Hard-cooked Eggs
Crisp Hearts of Celery, Carrot Sticks, Radishes

Additional raw vegetables that can be cleaned and chilled and marinated shortly before serving are:

Cauliflower Roses in Curry Mayonnaise

Baby Zucchini or Young Cucumbers cut lengthwise into 4 or 6 parts and sprinkled with seasoning salt and freshly ground pepper

When planning for an hors d'oeuvre tray, do not forget to fill a plastic bag with shaved or crushed ice so that celery, carrots, radishes, zucchini, and cucumber slices can be served on a bed of ice.

The most convenient hors d'oeuvre tray for home entertaining should contain about eight dishes.

A TYPICAL HORS D'OEUVRE TRAY

1. Pickled fresh mushrooms under finely chopped onions and parsley
2. Large sardines garnished with lemon wedges
3. Tuna fish salad with pimento and Italian dressing
4. Stuffed Eggs with mustard-flavored filling
5. Liver pâté garnished with green grapes
6. Artichoke hearts vinaigrette
7. Shrimp with relish and chili mayonnaise
8. Celery, carrot sticks, radishes, cauliflower, fennel, zucchini, or cucumber wedges on crushed ice

The sardines, tuna fish, liver pâté and artichoke hearts require practically no preparation. The homemade pickled mushrooms, dressings, and mayonnaise can be made in advance. Eggs and shrimp should be boiled on the day before they will be served. The yolk mixture should be prepared at the same time. Raw vegetables can be cleaned and trimmed and left to crisp in the refrigerator. On the day that the hors d'oeuvre will be served, time has to be allowed for stuffing the eggs and arranging and garnishing the various dishes. The experienced hostess learns to select a combination of dishes that will not take time on the day of the party. If she is desperate, she can always arrange a dish of paper-thin salami slices, garnished with pickles, or olives enhanced with ice cubes.

PICKLED FRESH MUSHROOMS

Clean mushrooms with a soft damp cloth and trim stems even with heads. Combine garlic, onion, oil, vinegar, rind, and seasonings and pour them over the mushrooms in a bowl. Set them aside and stir them every 20 minutes until they are glossy and slightly darkened. Chill and serve sprinkled with parsley.

1 pound evenly sized button mushrooms, or medium mushrooms, thinly sliced
1 garlic clove, crushed
1 medium onion, finely chopped
½ cup salad oil
¼ cup tarragon vinegar
1 teaspoon grated lemon rind
½ teaspoon salt or to taste
Freshly ground pepper to taste
¼ cup chopped parsley

FRENCH HORS D'OEUVRE MEAT SALAD

Combine all ingredients and serve very cold as part of a first-course hors d'oeuvre.

1½ cups diced lean boiled beef
1½ cups diced boiled potatoes
¼ cup each chopped gherkins, shallots, and black olives
2 tablespoons each capers and chopped parsley
French Dressing to taste

FRENCH HORS D'OEUVRE BEAN SALAD

Marinate beans in vinegar overnight. Add the seasonings and herbs to the oil and shake well, pour it over the salad and chill. Arrange the salad in an hors d'oeuvre dish, cover with the onion rings and parsley and serve as part of a first-course hors d'oeuvre.

1 No. 303 can red kidney beans, well drained
½ cup tarragon vinegar
½ teaspoon salt
¼ teaspoon dry mustard
¼ teaspoon pepper
2 teaspoons finely chopped or dried chervil
½ teaspoon finely chopped or dried summer savory
¼ cup oil
2 small onions, thinly sliced and divided into rings
3 tablespoons finely chopped parsley

HEARTS OF ARTICHOKE FOR THE HORS D'OEUVRE TRAY

Combine artichokes, mushrooms, pimento, parsley, onion, and French dressing. Mix the salad gently, arrange it in an hors d'oeuvre dish, and cover it with egg slices. Serve as part of a first-course hors d'oeuvre.

1 package frozen hearts of artichoke prepared according to package directions and chilled
1 6¾-ounce can button mushrooms
1 pimento, diced
2 tablespoons chopped parsley
1 tablespoon chopped onion
French Dressing
2 hard-cooked eggs, sliced

MARINATED HERRING FOR THE HORS D'OEUVRE TRAY

Arrange the herring in a dish with a lid. Cover it with the other ingredients and let it marinate in the refrigerator overnight or until needed. Transfer all ingredients to an hors d'oeuvre dish and serve as part of a first-course hors d'oeuvre.

8 boned and watered herring fillets, cut into diagonal strips
1 onion, sliced and divided into rings
2 small pickled beets, sliced
1 small dill pickle, sliced
2 cups dry white wine
Juice of ½ lemon
2 tablespoons tarragon vinegar
2 bay leaves
1 pinch sugar
4 peppercorns
1 teaspoon pickling spices

SHRIMP SALAD FOR THE HORS D'OEUVRE TRAY

Combine the chilled shrimp and vegetables. Season them well and bind with mayonnaise. Arrange the salad in an hors d'oeuvre dish and sprinkle it with parsley. Serve as part of a first-course hors d'oeuvre.

1 pound large shrimp, peeled, deveined, and cooked
½ green pepper, seeded and diced
1 celery heart, diced
½ small cucumber, peeled and diced
2 teaspoons finely chopped onion
Salt and pepper to taste
½ recipe Chili Relish Mayonnaise
3 tablespoons chopped parsley

TUNA FISH SALAD FOR THE HORS D'OEUVRE TRAY

Drain tuna fish and set oil aside. Combine tuna with the remaining ingredients except dressing in an hors d'oeuvre dish and chill. Before serving, beat the dressing and pour it over the salad. Serve as part of a first-course hors d'oeuvre.

1 No. 1 can tuna fish in oil, about 1¾ cups
¾ cup diced cold boiled potatoes
3 solid tomatoes, peeled and sliced thin
1 onion, sliced thin and divided into rings
1 pimento, diced
¼ cup chopped Italian parsley
1 sprig fresh basil, coarse stem removed and chopped
2 teaspoons capers
Dressing (given below)

DRESSING

Depending on the amount of oil in the can, it may be necessary to add a little oil, but it should not exceed the amount of the vinegar. Blend all ingredients.

Oil drained from the can of tuna
¼ teaspoon salt
Freshly ground black pepper to taste
6 tablespoons red wine vinegar
Juice of ½ lemon
1 clove garlic, crushed

HERRINGS IN MUSTARD CREAM

Arrange the herring fillets under the sliced pickles, potatoes, and onions. Stir the cream with the remaining ingredients and pour it over the herring. Serve very cold as a first course with buttered pumpernickel triangles.

3 large watered and filleted herrings
2 small dill pickles, sliced
2 potatoes, peeled, cooked, and thinly sliced
2 onions, thinly sliced
2 cups 4-day-old heavy cream
Salt and a pinch of sugar to taste
2 to 3 teaspoons very mild brown mustard, or to taste
2 teaspoons wine vinegar

BIRD'S NEST

This is another one of those dishes that have to be *seen* before they are *tasted*. It also takes a remembrance of plane geometry, or how to bisect a circle. Given this ability and time, construct a circle of lovely chopped ingredients in pie-shaped wedges on a round platter and center it with an egg yolk. After all the guests have admired it—it is worth interrupting them for the purpose—mix it and serve it on plates as a first course or on bread rounds with cocktails. Depending on the diameter of your plate—it should not be bigger than 9 inches—chop:

Arrange the chopped and riced ingredients on the plate or platter in wedges, some larger than others. As the beets bleed, they should not adjoin the egg whites; put parsley lines next to them. Add the apple and place the raw yolk in the center shortly before serving. I always make 2 wedges of beets—opposite each other. It looks like a full day of chopping and it is all eaten in a few minutes.

1 cup drained marinated herring fillets
1 large dill pickle
2 large pickled beets (*pat dry after chopping*)
1 medium onion
½ cup parsley, loosely packed
2 hard-cooked eggs (*rice the yolks and chop the whites*)
1 large or 2 small tart apples, peeled and cored
1 large egg yolk

ANCHOIS

Drain the anchovies and spread them in a serving dish. Retain the oil from the can and add more oil, vinegar, and pepper. Spread the tomato slices over the anchovies and spread the onion rings and the egg white rings over them. Shake the dressing and correct its seasoning, bearing in mind that the anchovies are very salty. Pour the dressing over the onion and egg rings and rice the egg yolks over the dressing. Sprinkle with chervil or parsley and capers and chill. Serve with toast fingers or oven-dried French bread.

1 2-ounce can flat anchovies in oil
2 tablespoons oil
3 tablespoons tarragon vinegar
¼ teaspoon freshly ground pepper
3 tomatoes, peeled and sliced
1 onion, thinly sliced and divided into rings
2 hard-cooked eggs, sliced
¼ cup chopped chervil or parsley
2 tablespoons smallest capers

FINNAN HADDIE

Work the flaked fish with half the butter, egg, and onion into a thick paste. Shape it into 18 evenly sized balls and roll one side of them in parsley. Chill them for at least 2 hours. Stir the remaining butter with the anchovy paste and spread it on the bread rounds. Press a finnan haddie ball on each, parsley side up, and serve.

1 cup soaked, cooked, and flaked finnan haddie (smoked haddock)
1 cube or ½ cup soft butter
1 hard-cooked egg, riced
1 tablespoon finely chopped onion
2 tablespoons finely chopped parsley
1 teaspoon anchovy paste, or to taste
24 small bread rounds

STUFFED MUSHROOMS WITH ROQUEFORT

Parboil mushrooms for 2 minutes, drain them well, and break out the stems. Cut away the tough wooden part and chop the remaining stems fine. Beat cheese until smooth with the butter, add the stems, onion, mustard, and sherry, and season well. Fill the mixture into the mushroom caps and roll the tops, while they are soft, in the parsley or chives. Chill for at least 2 hours.

18 evenly sized small mushrooms
1 wedge Roquefort cheese, at room temperature
½ cube or 4 tablespoons soft butter
1 tablespoon finely chopped onion
½ teaspoon Dijon mustard
1 teaspoon dry sherry
Salt and freshly ground pepper to taste
1 tablespoon minced parsley or chives cut 1/16 inch long

STUFFED MUSHROOMS WITH CHICKEN LIVERS

Break stems out of mushrooms, trim ends, and chop them medium fine. Simmer the caps with 1 tablespoon of the butter in salted water to cover with lemon juice for 3 minutes, drain. Fry the onion in the remaining butter until puffed and transparent, add the chopped mushroom stems and stir for 1 minute longer. Add the chicken livers and fry until they are gray on the outside and pink on the inside. Take from heat and crush livers, mushroom stems and onions together. Season and cool. When the mixture is cold, twist it in double toweling to extract all the butter. Bind it with a very little mayonnaise and fill the caps with it. Sprinkle the tops with the chopped nuts and chill until ready to serve.

12 evenly sized medium mushrooms
5 tablespoons butter
1 tablespoon lemon juice
¼ cup chopped onion
1 8-ounce package frozen chicken livers, thawed
Salt and pepper to taste
1 to 2 tablespoons Herbed Mayonnaise to taste
3 tablespoons chopped salted pecans

SHRIMP COCKTAIL I with Madeira

Bring salted water to a rapid boil, drop in 5 or 6 shrimp so that the water will not stop boiling. Lift the shrimp out with a slotted spoon after exactly 4 minutes. Drop them in a colander or sieve. Continue in this way until all the shrimp are cooked and well drained. Transfer them to a bowl, sprinkle them with the vinegar, and chill. Divide the shrimp and asparagus over 6 lettuce-leaf-lined cocktail glasses. Beat or blend the mayonnaise, add the cream, chili sauce, orange juice, and Madeira, and beat until smooth. Pour about ¼ cup of the sauce over each shrimp cocktail and sprinkle with parsley. Chill until ready to serve.

1½ pounds fresh shrimp, shelled and deveined
2 tablespoons tarragon vinegar
12 spears cold cooked asparagus, sliced, optional
Lettuce leaves
1¼ cups mayonnaise
¼ cup heavy cream
1½ tablespoons chili sauce
1½ tablespoons orange juice
2 tablespoons old Madeira wine, or to taste
2 tablespoons finely chopped parsley

SHRIMP COCKTAIL II with chutney

Stir the butter into the curry powder until smooth. Add chutney and gradually stir in the mayonnaise, onion, and apricot jam. Season only if necessary. Stir in the cucumber and pour the sauce over the shrimp. Garnish with parsley. (Beat heavy cream into the mayonnaise if a thinner sauce is preferred.) Serve very cold.

1 tablespoon soft butter
1 to 2 teaspoons curry powder to taste
3 tablespoons chutney, minced
⅔ cup stiff mayonnaise
2 tablespoons finely chopped onion
1 tablespoon apricot jam
3-inch section cucumber, peeled, seeded, and diced
1½ to 2 pounds cooked shrimp
2 tablespoons minced parsley

SHRIMP COCKTAIL III with vodka

Drain freshly cooked shrimp and turn them in a bowl with the vodka. Stir several times until they are cold, add the next 4 ingredients, and season to taste. Serve sprinkled with fresh tarragon leaves or those obtainable in vinegar in jars.

1½ to 2 pounds cooked shrimp
½ cup vodka
½ cup Lemon Mayonnaise
½ cup whipped cream
2 tablespoons tomato catsup
1 splash Worcestershire sauce, or to taste
Salt and pepper
Chopped tarragon leaves

CHEESE MOUNTAIN

A cheese mountain is based on a large Camembert, not one that is divided into sections. The assortment of mixed cheeses that is added depends on their availability, but there has to be a soft creamy cheese to bind and a yellow cheese to blind—and to keep it from being a blue mountain.

Cut around the top of a COLD Camembert about ¼ inch in from the outside edge with a sharp pointed knife. Go about ½ inch down and lift out the top. Scoop out the cheese with a small spoon, leaving only the shell of its former self.

Let top crust and contents of the cheese come to room temperature and crush them with:

1 large cream cheese, at room temperature
1 wedge Roquefort, at room temperature
1 wedge yellow Cheddar, ground through
    the meat grinder
1 garlic clove, crushed
1 tablespoon minced herbs
2 tablespoons soft butter

The mixture should be absolutely smooth and can be pressed through a coarse sieve or put through the meat grinder. Beat the mixture until it is light and smooth with:

Dry sherry to taste
Salt and pepper to taste

Mound the cheese into the Camembert shell and chill it until about half an hour before it will be served. When it is lightly softened, sprinkle the top with ¼ cup walnuts that have been lightly toasted in the oven and chopped. Serve with buttered pumpernickel.

CAMEMBERT-APPLE APPETIZER

A lovely combination of flavors is achieved by serving a thick slice of peeled and cored sweet apple, covered with Camembert cheese that is cooled long enough so that it can be pressed through a sieve and mounded on the apple. Top each mound with a rolled fillet of anchovy and surround with buttered pumpernickel.

GARNISHED LIPTAUER CHEESE

Combine 3 soft cheeses, in equal quantities to form the Liptauer. Put the garnishes around it and mix them at table. This is often served on Sunday evenings with buttered black bread and cold beer.

12 ounces each Camembert, cream, and Liederkranz cheeses at room temperature

Scrape the rinds of the Camembert and Liederkranz and mash or sieve the 3 cheeses until smooth. Chill for at least 2 hours. To serve, mound the cheese neatly in the center of a platter or large wooden board, and surround it with small mounds of:

3 tablespoons minced onion
2 tablespoons finely cut chives
2 tablespoons finely chopped parsley
2 tablespoons finely chopped capers
2 tablespoons brown mustard
1 tablespoon paprika
1 tablespoon caraway seeds

Place on the board or accompany with:

1 salt cellar
1 pepper grinder
1 pyramid butter balls
Thinly sliced pumpernickel and rye breads
2 dill pickles, sliced

Anyone not wanting a certain ingredient asks to be given his or her portion before the ingredient is mixed into the whole. The exact amount of each ingredient used is a matter of taste. Some people mix paprika into the cheese from the beginning or sprinkle the mounded cheese with paprika before serving, to give it a pink color.

MAIN COURSES

CHAPTER TEN

Main Courses, Cold Meats, Poultry,
Game, and Seafood Suitable
for Winter Service

At THE turn of the century, when the cold buffet became incredibly elaborate, it was considered a separate branch of the culinary arts. Chefs had to study design and construction and made a specialty of building skillful edifices that were largely constructed of modeling fat or carved ice. Everything was raised onto a pedestal or socle, and the dish was often the smallest part of the structure.

All surfaces were glazed with aspic or ornamented with truffles, and the food was so heavily disguised that it wasn't always recognizable. It took a team of waiters to serve the guests with the edible parts of the cold buffet. When the classic Cold Kitchen disappeared with the Cold Chefs, the modest Home Cold Buffet became the acceptable meal for all such occasions when there were more guests than there were dining-room chairs. Buffets were always associated with cold food, whereas Sit-Down dinners were always supposed to be hot.

The hostess-cooks never attempted to copy the elaborate presentations of the great cold buffets, but there has always been an inclination to center them around some large, high object—namely a ham or a turkey. There are only a limited number of *big* food pieces, and every hostess—as well as her guests—would like to find something new. If we have to have hams and turkeys, they should be differently presented, and other cold meats, as roast beef, tongue, filet of beef, should be decorated and garnished in ways that make them look more important and attractive—without putting them on socles. The cold meat, poultry, and fish recipes in this chapter are interchangeable with those in Chapter Five of Part I, but they are more suitable for cold winter meals than for summer cookery. Cold beef, pheasant, and turkey can certainly be served in warm weather, but a cold winter dinner should not pivot around a crab ring or a chicken salad.

The ham is undeniably a year-round fixture, depending on how it is garnished, but no one wants to meet a cold roast goose on the dinner table in mid-July. Depending on the season and the occasion, select your main course carefully. Remember that in hot weather a chilled white wine or rosé is more welcome than an unchilled red wine, and remember that the white wines go with fish, chicken, and white meats, the hot weather dishes, while red wines go with the red meats and game, which are the cold weather dishes.

The Elaborate Cold Roasts

The elaborate cold roasts can be prepared in 3 steps over a period of 2 days. Roast the meat on the day before the dinner party or buffet, and make the aspic and sauce. On the morning of the following day, glaze and garnish the roast and chill it until late in the afternoon. Add diced aspic, water cress, or parsley, or any fruit that is needed to complete the platter. Whip the sauce, pour it into a sauceboat or bowl, and chill everything until it is served. The most suitable meats or poultry for this purpose are: Filet of Beef, Roast Beef, Saddle of Lamb, Saddle of Venison, Veal Roast, Roast Turkey, Roast Capon, Roast Duck, Roast Pheasant.

COLD TENDERLOIN OF BEEF

If a larded tenderloin is obtainable, lay it on strips of salt pork in a small roasting pan. If it is unlarded, use twice as much salt pork and bard it by laying strips over and under it. Roast in a 450° F. oven for about 25 to 30 minutes. Basting every 8 minutes with pan juices and butter. Transfer the filet to a sheet of foil, fold up the edges of the foil, and pour the pan juices over the meat. When it is cool, close the foil loosely and refrigerate the meat until the platter and garnishes are prepared and it is ready to serve. As the thickness of the filet plays a part in the roasting time and *cold beef has to be rarer than hot beef*, watch carefully. If necessary make a small incision. Take it out of the oven when it is still rare but not blue.

1 3-pound trimmed tenderloin or filet of beef, larded or barded
8 strips fat salt pork
½ cup melted butter or rendered beef suet

BRAISED TENDERLOIN OR FILET OF BEEF

Have your butcher prepare and lard beef. Spread diced larding pork and the prepared vegetables in the bottom of a casserole that will just hold the meat. Brown the meat well on all sides in the oil in a wide heavy skillet. Place it on the vegetables in the casserole, season it to taste, and add the braising liquid. Use ½ cup brandy or 1 cup red wine or Madeira. Cover the casserole tightly and braise the filet in a 350° F. oven for about 35 to 40 minutes. A larger filet will not require more time, it should be brown on the outside and very pink inside. Baste every 10 minutes with the accumulated liquids in the pan. Let the filet cool slowly in the casserole, then chill it until ready to garnish or prepare.

Strain the liquid from the casserole and discard the vegetables. Chill the liquid and lift off the fat, retain the remaining base in case it is needed for the preparation of the beef.

A roasted or braised filet of beef should be placed on a platter or on a MIRROR of aspic poured onto a platter or tray. Half the filet should be carved into slices and laid in front of the remaining uncarved meat in an overlapping line or fan. The uncarved section should be glazed or decorated. The various garnishes and accompaniments are then placed around the sides of the platter. A sauce is usually served separately.

1 small filet of beef, trimmed, larded, and tied
1 cup diced larding pork
2 carrots, scraped and diced
2 onions, sliced
¼ cup oil
Salt and freshly ground black pepper
½ to 1 cup braising liquid (brandy, red wine, or Madeira)

COLD TENDERLOIN OR FILET OF BEEF COQUELIN

Carve and arrange the beef as for Tenderloin Bouquetière. Pour a mirror of aspic onto the platter and use the rest to glaze the uncarved half of the filet. Place it on the platter at the end of the carved slices and surround the meat with alternating artichoke bottoms and tomato halves, emptied and drained. Stir mayonnaise with minced parsley and almonds. Chill it until very stiff and fill it into the tomatoes. Drain the beans, mix them with the tarragon, and fill them as high as possible into the artichoke bottoms. Garnish the platter with parsley and decorate the top of the uncarved meat with the bunch of grapes and parsley. Secure grapes with wooden picks.

1 roasted or braised filet
2 cups aspic, page 98
6 artichoke bottoms
3 tomatoes, peeled and cut in half
1 recipe Mayonnaise
1 tablespoon minced parsley
1 tablespoon finely chopped blanched almonds
1 14-ounce can French green flageolet beans
1 teaspoon minced tarragon
Parsley sprigs
1 very small bunch grapes, small enough to fit into 1 cup

COLD TENDERLOIN OR FILET OF BEEF BOUQUETIÈRE

Slice half the filet and glaze the uncarved part with a coat of aspic. Pour a ⅛-inch mirror of aspic onto the platter that will be used. Chill the platter until set, then arrange the slices on it, chill it until needed. Decorate the uncarved half of the filet with a flower made of red petals (8 to 10 oblong petals cut from the prepared tomatoes) and center the flower with the domed end of the hard-cooked egg. Secure the flower with wooden picks and brush it with several layers of aspic, chilling it between each application. Take out the picks when the flower is secure and push a sprig of very curly parsley under each side of it. Place the decorated half filet on the platter at the end of the carved slices and chill. The bouquets, from which the filet is named, should be attractively composed of the combined vegetables, placed around the meat and glazed with a brushing of aspic. Garnish bouquets with parsley; there should be as many as there are guests. Serve with rémoulade sauce.

1 roasted or braised filet of beef
1 quart aspic, page 98
2 firm tomatoes, peeled, cut in half, and emptied of all flesh, ribs, and seeds
1 hard-cooked egg white
Curly garnishing parsley
1 small cooked cauliflower divided into small rosettes
1 16-ounce jar tiny whole carrots
1 green pepper, seeded and cut into diamonds
12 very small cooked white onions
1 6-ounce can whole button mushrooms
1 recipe Rémoulade Sauce

COLD ROAST BEEF

Roast the beef in an empty pan in a 325° F. oven for 15 to 20 minutes per pound for rare, or when a meat thermometer registers an internal temperature of 140° F. Always serve cold roast beef rare. Pour a mirror of melted aspic on a large platter. Trim the cold beef to expose a layer of creamy fat and either cut the roast from the ribs or mask the ribs with parsley. Carve part of the roast beef and arrange the overlapping slices in front of the uncarved meat. Decorate the top of it with a pyramid of cherry tomatoes, on wooden picks, interspersed with parsley sprigs. Arrange the glazed asparagus bunches, at least 1 for each guest, around the meat, garnish with parsley, and serve the 2 sauces in separate sauceboats.

1 3- or 4-rib roast, bearing in mind that cold beef carves rather thickly
2 cups aspic, page 98
Parsley sprigs
1 basket cherry tomatoes
1 recipe Glazed Asparagus Spears
1 recipe Horseradish or Mustard Mayonnaise
1 recipe Trianon Sauce

ROAST BEEF with GRAPEFRUIT SECTIONS

Roast the beef according to directions on page 204. If leftover cold beef is being used, carve it into 6 thick slices and trim them carefully. Peel ½ grapefruit with a potato peeler and set the peel aside. Cut peel from remaining grapefruit with a very sharp knife going down to the fruit. Cut out the sections carefully, freeing them of all white membranes and pits. Do this over a bowl to catch the juice. Chill grapefruit sections and make the sauce.

To serve the beef, arrange the 6 slices on 6 chilled plates. Arrange an overlapping row of grapefruit sections next to the beef and sprinkle the grapefruit with chopped herbs and pistachio nuts. Pass the sauce separately.

1 3-rib roast of beef or 6 thick slices of rare, leftover cold roast beef
3 large grapefruit (reserve the rind of ½ grapefruit)
Red Currant Sauce (given below)
3 tablespoons finely chopped parsley or mint
½ cup chopped pistachio nuts

RED CURRANT SAUCE

Melt the currant jelly in the top of a double boiler. Add the orange juice after removing the outside peel with the potato peeler. Cut the peels into long very thin slivers with kitchen scissors and boil them in the sherry for 1 minute. Add sherry, slivered peels, horseradish, and mustard to the sauce and let mixture cook, uncovered, for another 20 minutes, over boiling water. Cool and chill the sauce.

1 jar red currant jelly
1 orange, juice and rind
½ cup sherry
¼ cup grated horseradish
2 tablespoons mild brown mustard

COLD SPENCER STEAKS

Have your butcher cut the eye from the ribs and give you 2 thick slices. They will weigh about 2¼ pounds each. Broil in the infrared broiler for about 15 minutes on each side, or according to taste, but always keep beef *rare* for cold service. Cool and chill the meat.

2 3½-inch-thick slices of the eye of the rib or Delmonico steaks
1 recipe Stuffed Onions
1 recipe Cold Béarnaise Sauce

Carve one of the steaks, on an angle, into medium-thin slices and arrange them on a steak board. Place the unsliced steak next to them and garnish the steak board with the onions and accompany it with a bowl of the béarnaise sauce.

SADDLE OF LAMB SUÉDOISE (Directions for preparation follow the 4 lists of ingredients)

1 saddle of lamb, about 8 pounds before trimming
3 lemons, juice and grated rind
½ cup chopped aromatic herbs in any available proportion (parsley, chives, rosemary, chervil, basil, or orégano)
1 garlic clove, crushed
Salt and freshly ground black pepper to taste
¼ cup melted butter

APPLE HORSERADISH SAUCE

6 large cooking apples, quartered
2 cups dry white wine
2 to 4 tablespoons sugar, to taste
½ cup freshly grated horseradish
¼ cup homemade mayonnaise, optional

MAYONNAISE SAUCE

¾ cup homemade mayonnaise
The remaining marinade

STUFFED TOMATO GARNISH

Have the butcher trim the saddle of lamb, fold under the 2 sides, and tie it. (Ascertain the accurate trimmed weight from him.) Marinate the saddle for 1 hour in a small pan with the lemon juice, herbs, and garlic. Place it in the marinade with the meat side down and tilt it in both directions so that the sides are marinated. Season it to taste and roast it on a rack in a 325° F. oven for 14 minutes to the pound. A

6 evenly sized, small, round tomatoes
2 cups cooked green peas
¼ cup homemade mayonnaise

meat thermometer should register 140°. Cold lamb should always be *pink*. Brush it with a little melted butter every 15 minutes. Take it from the oven and let it cool. When it is cold, wrap it loosely in foil, and refrigerate it until needed.

Cook the quartered apples in the wine, with very little sugar, until tender. Drain them well and blend them into a thick purée. Cool and chill the sauce and fold in the grated horseradish shortly before serving. Add a little sugar if necessary. The addition of the mayonnaise is optional; try a teaspoon stirred into a little of the applesauce before adding all of it.

For the sauce, use ¾ cup mayonnaise and beat in the chopped herbs from the remaining marinade. Add as much of the lemon juice as needed to make a smooth sauce. Blend it for a few seconds if the herbs are only roughly chopped.

For the tomato garnish, dip them in boiling water for a few seconds and draw off the skins. Cut lids from the top and scoop out the pulp with a small spoon. Drain the tomatoes well and fill them with the peas, lightly bound with mayonnaise.

Place the saddle of lamb on a silver platter or on a carving board. Surround it with the tomatoes, and, if the board is large, fresh water cress. Carve the lamb in long horizontal slices, running the length of the saddle. Turn the saddle and cut out the 2 very small filets, cut these across in ½-inch slices, and add them to each portion. Serve each guest with a tomato and pass the apple horseradish sauce separately.

This reads like a long recipe, but the meat will roast in less than 1½ hours. Apples may be cooked at any time, and only the horseradish is a late addition, although it will not turn black after it is stirred into the applesauce.

COLD LOIN OF VEAL RICHMOND

Have your butcher trim the bones and take them to make the stock. Put them in cold water and boil while the meat is roasting. Lay roast on slices of larding pork in an open roasting pan. Season it well, spread it with the soft butter, and add the onion and carrot to the pan. Roast meat in a 325° F. oven, basting it frequently, until the meat is lightly browned, about 45 minutes. Add the boiling stock, made from the veal bones, sprinkle the meat generously with paprika, and continue roasting and basting until the meat is brown and done, about another 1½ to 2 hours, or until a meat thermometer registers 170° F. Let the meat cool in the pan, then refrigerate it until needed. To serve, arrange it on a platter with a half circle of cauliflower roses with vinaigrette topping. Serve with a bowl of Escoffier mayonnaise. If preferred the veal can be boned. Use the kidney for another purpose, or buy the loin without the kidney.

1 loin of veal
4 to 6 slices larding pork, enough to cover the pan under the meat
1 tablespoon seasoning salt
⅓ cup soft butter
1 onion, sliced
1 carrot, sliced
2 cups boiling stock
Paprika
2 cold cooked cauliflowers, divided into roses
1 recipe Vinaigrette Sauce
1 recipe Escoffier Mayonnaise

VITELLO TONNATO

In a deep kettle, combine the veal with the vegetables, herbs, anchovy fillets, tuna fish, pickle, garlic, olive oil, and the juice and thinly cut rind of 1 of the lemons. Add the wine and simmer covered for about 2 hours, or until the meat is tender. Take from heat, season to taste, and cool the meat in the kettle. When it is cold, take it out and slice it. Arrange the slices on a deep platter and strain the contents of the pan. Crush or blend the fish and vegetables into a smooth purée, adding as much of the cooking liquid as necessary. Chill the purée and fold mayonnaise into it to make a thick sauce. Pour the sauce over the sliced meat and sprinkle it with some of the capers. Serve the remaining capers with gherkins and 2 lemons, sliced, separately.

Vitello tonnato may be prepared in advance and left in the kettle until the following day.

Serve an Italian white wine.

3½ pounds lean leg of veal in 1 piece
2 medium onions, sliced
3 celery stalks
2 carrots, quartered
3 sprigs each thyme and parsley
1 2-ounce can flat fillets of anchovies
2 13-ounce cans tuna fish in oil
1 dill pickle, sliced
2 garlic cloves, crushed
¼ cup olive oil
3 lemons
1 bottle dry white wine
Salt and freshly ground pepper to taste
2 cups mayonnaise, or to taste
½ cup smallest capers
½ cup sliced gherkins

BRAISED TURKEY BREAST WITH APPLES

Put wing tip with chicken bouillon cubes in 2 cups water and simmer for 1 hour. Secure the skin to the turkey breast by tying it across with trussing string. Season the breast inside and out and brown it slowly in butter, about 25 minutes, in a heavy casserole. Turn it frequently to brown both sides. Take out the breast, spread the onion, carrot, and apple in the casserole, put turkey breast on top, and add 1 cup strained stock. Cover the casserole closely and simmer over low heat for about 2 hours, or when a skewer, inserted for a moment in the wing end, produces a colorless liquid and the breast feels soft. Take from heat, cool, and chill the turkey. Carefully remove the cold turkey breast from any remaining carcass. Arrange it on a platter or steak board with the apples. Serve with Cranberry Relish and a vegetable salad. Slice the breast across into strips to serve.

1 4½- to 5-pound turkey breast (can be purchased with wing attached and represents the front quarter of the turkey)
2 chicken bouillon cubes
Salt and freshly ground pepper to taste
½ cube or ¼ cup butter
2 onions, thinly sliced
1 carrot, thinly sliced
1 apple, cored, peeled, and diced
1 cup stock from wing tip
6 cold baked apples

STUFFED BONED HALF TURKEY

Have your butcher bone the turkey or do it yourself. Starting at the backbone and using a sharp pointed knife, cut the skin and meat away from the carcass. When the hip and wing joints are reached, cut the leg and wing from the carcass and continue until the meat is freed from the top of the breastbone. Make stock out of bones and wing tip. Scrape the meat down the leg and wing bones and pull the leg and wing meat inside the half turkey; add the bones to the stock. Make the stuffing by frying the onions and sage in the butter for about 6 minutes without browning it. Add the mushrooms and cook gently for 6 minutes longer. Add olives, ham, and bread crumbs and beat in the egg yolk and enough Marsala to bind. Season to taste, place the stuffing on the inside of the half turkey. Roll it up and tie it securely at several points. Rub the roll with seasonings and butter and roast it on a rack in a 325° F. oven, basting it frequently with stock and pan juices until it is golden and tender, about 2½ hours. Cool and chill the roll and serve it half sliced and garnished with parsley and half oranges filled with thick Cumberland Sauce or cranberry sauce.

1 6- to 7-pound ready-to-cook half turkey
2 onions, chopped
6 sage leaves or ½ tablespoon dried sage
½ cup butter, reserve 3 tablespoons for rubbing into rolled turkey
6 medium mushrooms, sliced
6 pitted black olives, chopped
¼ cup small ham dice
3 cups stale bread crumbs
1 egg yolk
½ cup Marsala wine
Salt and freshly ground pepper to taste

GALANTINE OF TURKEY

A galantine can also be made of chicken, duck, salmon, pheasant, or a boned and stuffed leg of lamb.

Put the wing tips, giblets, and neck of the turkey in 12 cups cold water with the vegetables and herbs, hold the liver aside. Add the peppercorns and salt, cover, and simmer while preparing the bird. Turn the bird onto its breast and slit the skin down the length of the back. Peel the meat away from the bones on both sides with a sharp knife, severing the wing and leg bones from the carcass. Do not cut through the skin. Put the carcass and scraps into the simmering stock and spread the boned turkey out on a table. Gently loosen and draw out the leg and wing bones and add them to the stock. Pull the wings and legs into the turkey—like turning a jacket inside out. Take the drumstick meat to lay along the center where the meat is thinnest. Grind scrapple, veal, and liver sausage together. Stir in the yolks, spices and herbs. Season the mixture and spread a layer of it over the turkey. Arrange ½-inch thick fingers cut from the tongue, bologna, and ham over the mixture and sprinkle with a few pistachios. Continue in this way, adding pieces of the turkey liver until the ingredients are used up. Roll up the turkey and sew up the skin securely to form a thick roll. Wrap and tie the roll in sheets of fresh pork fat if they are obtainable; otherwise wrap it in wax paper and roll it into a kitchen towel. Tie up the 2 ends and place it in a small kettle. Strain the simmering stock over it and add enough boiling water to just cover. Cover the kettle and simmer very gently for 3 hours. Let the galantine cool in the stock. Take it out and place it on a platter, put a small cheese board or any even flat weight on the galantine, and put something on it so that the total weight will be about 1 pound. Place the galantine and its weight in the refrigerator overnight. Remove towel and wax paper. If it was wrapped in pork fat, leave it intact but remove the tying strings.

TO SERVE GALANTINE: Either slice it and serve the slices with Cumberland Sauce or present it on a platter. If the galantine has a

1 6-pound baby turkey
5 carrots, quartered
5 onions, quartered and stuck with 5 cloves
Bouquet of parsley, thyme, and 1 bay leaf
4 peppercorns
Salt to taste and freshly ground pepper
1 cup scrapple
1½ pounds ground lean veal
1 3-inch slice liver sausage
2 egg yolks
½ teaspoon each ground cinnamon, cloves, and ginger
1 teaspoon each minced parsley, chervil, and chives
2 ½-inch thick slices of tongue
2 ½-inch thick slices of bologna sausage
1 ½-inch thick slice of ham
¼ cup shelled pistachio nuts
Sheets of fresh pork fat if obtainable

cover of white pork fat, slice half of it and glaze the unsliced half with aspic made of gelatin and clear consommé, page 98. If the galantine is not covered with fat, glaze the unsliced portion with White Chaud-Froid Sauce, and glaze it with aspic after the chaud-froid has set. Garnish the platter with orange and grapefruit sections and serve with Cumberland Sauce. If preferred, the Cumberland Sauce may be put into emptied half orange shells and used to garnish the platter. Serve toasted brioche slices with the galantine.

PHEASANT WITH ORANGES

Simmer giblets in 3 cups salted water. Season the pheasant inside and out. Truss and bard them with slices of larding pork tied over their breasts. Brown them slowly in the butter in a Dutch oven, turning them from side to side to brown evenly. This has to be done patiently and will take about 15 minutes. Turn the birds, breast side down, add the juniper, pepper, and 1 cup stock. Close the Dutch oven tightly and simmer, basting and turning frequently, until the pheasants are tender, about 40 more minutes. Peel outside rind from oranges with a potato peeler and cut it into long julienne slivers with kitchen scissors. Cut all white pulp from oranges and cut out the sections free of all membrane and pits. Remove the larding pork, drain off the liquid, and set it aside. Add the remaining stock, the orange sections and rind, the grapes, wine, and jelly to the Dutch oven and roast uncovered in a 375° F. oven, basting frequently, for 15 minutes. Cool the pheasants in the Dutch oven and chill them in the fruit sauce until ready to serve. Chill liquids drained from the pan and lift off the fat; add the remaining juices to the fruit sauce. Correct seasoning and transfer the birds and sauce to a shallow casserole. Carve them at the table and serve with crisp water cress, any green vegetable salad, and a small bowl of finely chopped toasted filberts or pecans. Use salted parched nuts if they are available.

2 fat pheasants
Salt to taste
4 slices larding pork
1 cup or 2 cubes butter
4 each juniper berries and peppercorns
2 cups stock from giblets
2 large oranges
2 cups seeded red grapes
½ cup red Malaga wine
½ cup melted red currant jelly

COLD ROAST OF VENISON

The saddle, loin, and rack of venison do not need marination. If the meat is old and dry, it is better to use it for a venison stew. Have your butcher lard the venison or lard it in 2 rows on each side, starting about ½ inch from the backbone, with lardoons of fat pork or bacon rolled in powdered juniper berries, salt and pepper before being inserted in the larding needle. If the butcher larded the roast, rub it with ½ tablespoon powdered juniper berries. Rub the venison well with soft butter and insert a thin metal rod, if available, in the spinal column to prevent the back from curling upward at each end while roasting. Roast it in an open pan for 15 minutes per pound. Start it at 550° F. and roast for 5 minutes, reduce heat to 450° F. and roast it about 15 minutes longer. Reduce heat to 350° F. and roast for the remaining time. Baste every 5 or 6 minutes with pan juices and, if it seems dry, with more butter. Since much depends on the age of the venison, the exact roasting time cannot be specified. When the roast is brown, make a small incision at the edge of the backbone, the meat should be *rare*, but not blue. Cool the venison and chill it before carving and glazing.

Cut the 2 larded filets from the backbone and ribs in 1 piece each. Slice them diagonally in even slices and replace them on the rib bones. Prepare an aspic with gelatin, sherry, and clear bouillon and glaze the whole roast according to one of the following ways.

1 double rack of venison
¼ pound fat larding pork, or bacon, chilled and cut into lardoons
2 tablespoons powdered juniper berries
Salt and freshly ground pepper
1 cube soft butter, or more if needed

WITH GREEN GRAPES

Stir the gelatin into the sherry or port and set it aside for 15 minutes. Bring the bouillon to a boil, with the onion, take it from heat, stir in the gelatin until dissolved, and take out the onion before it starts to thicken. Brush the chilled venison roast with the glaze and chill it again. After applying the second coat, apply a line of half grapes, cut side down, along the backbone. If any of them show an inclination to slide, secure them with wooden picks on the 2 sides until set. Con-

2 envelopes gelatin
½ cup sherry or port wine
2 cups clear bouillon
1 slice onion
1 cold venison roast, carved and replaced on the carcass
Seedless green grapes
8 apples, peeled, cored, and cut in half
½ bottle dry white wine
1 cup Purée de Marrons

tinue to glaze the venison until the aspic is used. Place the roast on a large platter and garnish it with half apples, gently stewed for 10 minutes in white wine. Fill the apples with 1 tablespoon French purée de marrons, obtainable in jars and cans. Serve Cumberland Sauce separately. The traditional salad is sliced cooked or canned celery root in French Dressing.

WITH WALNUTS OR BLANCHED ALMONDS

Prepare and glaze as above, substituting a row of walnut halves or almonds for the grapes and continue to glaze until the aspic is used up. Surround the cold roast with halved poached apples and fill them with apricot jam mixed with chopped walnuts or almonds and a splash of apricot brandy.

GAME SAUCES

CUMBERLAND SAUCE: With equal quantities of orange and lemon rind and reduced to a thicker sauce than is usually served.

APPLE HORSERADISH: Combine very thick applesauce with grated orange rind and freshly grated horseradish. Add a little orange juice to taste.

ROSE HIP: Prepare as Cumberland Sauce, using thick rose-hip jam in place of the red currant jelly and increasing the amount of brown mustard.

Cold Ham

A plain cold cooked ham, with or without potato salad, is so closely associated with buffets and suppers that it is difficult to lift it out of its present role and make it into a gala entree for a cold dinner party. There are, however, only a limited number of meats for the *big* entrees, and the ham is far too good and too beautiful to be neglected only because we have met it so often. For years I started planning party menus saying, *"I cannot give them ham,"* and broke my head for replacements that were as easily prepared, as economical, or as adaptable.

Now I simply serve cold ham in new combinations and with new garnishes (even with potato salad) that transform it into something new. Select a fully cooked ham, a cook-before-eating ham, a country ham, a half ham, or a canned ham. The fully cooked hams are better for a little extra cooking and the cook-before-eating hams are benefited by a little more soaking and/or cooking than the wrapper directions call for.

Follow your own method of preparation that is best for the hams your market stocks, or use any of the following suggestions. Always remember that, whether you baked or cooked your ham, the leftover cold ham tasted good, so that either method of preparing it will give you a good cold ham, but some methods will give you a better-looking cold ham. Count 2 servings per pound of ham with bone and 3 servings per pound of boned ham.

COOK-BEFORE-EATING HAM

If there is time enough to prepare and cook this type of ham, it will give you an opportunity to add flavors in the cooking that cannot be given to a fully cooked or ready-to-eat ham. A cook-before-eating ham is differently cured and smoked than an old-fashioned or country ham. These hams do not need to be soaked or parboiled, and they require a shorter cooking time. However, a little soaking or parboiling or a little longer cooking time can enhance these mild hams even further.

FULLY COOKED HAMS

If there is not enough time to prepare and cook a cook-before-eating ham, select a fully cooked or ready-to-eat ham and bake or simmer it as the recipe suggests for additional flavor and tenderness.

BONED HAM

A rolled boned ham has the advantage that it can be easily carved and there is no waste. It is ideal for some of the presentations and may be substituted for any of the regular bone-in ham recipes.

OLD-FASHIONED OR COUNTRY HAM

These hams are usually saltier than the commercially processed hams, and the surface may be dark and moldy. They need a good scrubbing and they have to be soaked from 12 to 24 hours—as all hams used to be—before they are boiled. Country hams from certain areas are famous for their special flavor and quality, as Smithfield or Virginia. Follow cooking directions on wrapper.

FULL HALF HAM

If a half ham is all that is needed and a whole ham presents too much leftover cold ham, buy a full butt half or shank half of ham. The definition *full* means that you are buying one half of a ham—either half—without the choice center slices having been cut from either end. The shank half is the one with the projecting bone, the butt half is the one with the rounded end.

BUTT OR SHANK END

These cuts are equally as good as the full half hams, but the best center slices have been cut off and the remaining end serves only 2 for every pound of weight. A boned shank or butt will serve 3 per pound.

CANNED HAM

There are Danish, Dutch, and Polish canned hams. The Danish ones are flavored with sherry, scotch, champagne, or white wine, and they come in 1½-pound tins. Others come in 1- to 3-pound tins, and whole boned hams come in 5- to 10-pound tins. They can be opened, garnished, and served, or they can be baked long enough for flavors to be added and the surface to be glazed.

COOKING AND BASTING LIQUIDS FOR HAM
(some are also used for soaking)

Water	Beer for basting only
Cider or water and cider	Ginger ale
Dry white wine or water and wine	Vegetable stock
Red wine or port wine	Pineapple juice or orange juice
Madeira or sherry	

GLAZES FOR HAM

Apricot nectar or honey or corn syrup
Jellies or marmalades
Cranberry sauce or crushed pineapple
Orange juice or champagne

HAM GARNISHES

Most of these are described with each recipe, but the garnishes that are suitable for all hams are the following:

ALGERIAN With tomatoes and artichoke bottoms, either in a salad or stuffed with vegetable salad. Mayonnaise mixed with diced pimento.

ARGENTEUIL Is always with cooked asparagus and one of the egg sauces, as Gribiche.

BEANS Garnish with water cress and artichoke bottoms filled with a salad of white beans and serve Herbed Mayonnaise separately.

CAULIFLOWER Place 2 small cooked cauliflowers at either end of the platter, pour Dill Mayonnaise over them, and surround with cucumber salad.

GLAZED ONIONS Arrange small glazed onions in large scooped-out tomato halves, serve with Spiced Ham Sauce.

GREEN PEPPERS Thick green pepper rings filled with one of the cold rice salad combinations.

HELVETIAN Tomato halves filled with chopped steamed onions and tomato dice bound with mayonnaise. Serve with Raisin Sauce.

ORANGE Orange halves filled with fruits bound with Cumberland Sauce.

VERT-PRÉ Garnish with crisp water cress and surround the ham with bouquets of Green Beans and Asparagus Vinaigrette.

VICTOR HUGO Tomato halves filled with Cold Sauce Béarnaise mixed with freshly grated horseradish to taste.

THAI HAM

Place the ham in a large kettle, add the wine and enough water to cover, and set aside for 3 hours. Place over heat, bring to a boil, and reduce heat to simmer. Depending on the quality of the ham, simmer for 1 to 2½ hours until the small bone is loose and the ham is tender. Cool in the liquid. When cold, cut rind away from about ⅔ of the ham and trim the surface of the fat to expose a layer of white. Store the ham in a cool place until needed.

Cut pineapple in half lengthwise, through the leaves, and cut out the meat, leaving 2 half shells. Discard the core, dice the meat, and set juice aside for the sauce. Combine pineapple dice with the broken marrons and the onions and fill the mixture back into the 2 half-pineapple shells. If pineapple chunks were used, drain and combine them with the broken marrons and onions and serve in a bowl.

Serve the ham on a rack and accompany with the chilled pineapple, Portuguese potatoes, and lime marmalade sauce.

1 10-pound fully cooked ham
1 bottle white Bordeaux wine
1 medium fresh pineapple or 1 No. 2 can
*   pineapple chunks*
6 whole Marrons Glacés, or 1 7-ounce can
1 recipe Cold Glazed Onions (given below)
1 recipe Portuguese Potatoes (given below)
Lime Marmalade Sauce (given below)

COLD GLAZED ONIONS

Put onions in a saucepan with boiling water, add salt, and cook until the onions are just tender, not until the centers boil out. Drain them well, add butter, honey, and thyme, and shake the saucepan over low heat until onions are coated with a glaze, continue glazing until lightly gilded. Cool and chill the onions.

1 pound smallest obtainable white onions,
*   trimmed and peeled under water*
1 teaspoon salt
3 tablespoons butter, melted
3 tablespoons honey
1 teaspoon chopped fresh thyme

PORTUGUESE POTATOES

Peel and boil the potatoes in salted water until barely soft, depending on their size. This can take 10 minutes; watch carefully, they should not be soft. Drain them well and let them cool. Before they are cold, sprinkle them with ¼ cup of the dressing. When they are cold or shortly before serving, combine potatoes, tomato dice, olives, capers, and dill. Crush the garlic into the remaining dressing and pour it over the potatoes. Serve very cold.

2½ pounds smallest potatoes, or 3 pounds
*   large potatoes, halved and trimmed*
*   into ovals*
¾ cup Lemon French Dressing
3 tomatoes, peeled, seeded, and diced
8 stuffed olives, sliced
1 tablespoon smallest capers
3 tablespoons finely cut dill
¼ or ½ garlic clove

LIME MARMALADE SAUCE

Melt marmalade with the juice and lemon rind in the top of a double boiler over boiling water, stir and cook for 20 minutes, uncovered. Cool and serve in a chilled bowl, covered with very thin slices of lime.
 Serve a white Bordeaux with this.

1 16-ounce jar lime marmalade
Pineapple juice or drained juice from
 pineapple chunks
Slivered rind of 1 lemon
1 lime, thinly sliced

COLD STUFFED ONIONS

Boil onions in salted water for about 20 minutes until tender but not soft enough to lose their shape. As soon as they are cool enough to handle, remove the centers, leaving a ⅓-inch-thick shell. Chop the centers and add them to the remaining ingredients. Stuff the onions and chill them until needed. Arrange them in a serving dish, with sprigs of water cress between the onions, and serve French dressing separately.

6 round medium-large onions, peeled under
 water
1 teaspoon salt
6 tablespoons chopped salted walnuts
6 stuffed olives, diced
½ cup chopped celery
2 tablespoons finely diced green pepper
½ bunch water cress
French Dressing II

COUNTRY HAM

Red wine, cider, champagne, grapefruit, orange, or tomato juice may be substituted for the white wine.
 Scrub the ham with a stiff brush to remove mold. Soak it in a large kettle in cold water to cover for 24 hours. The water can be changed 3 or 4 times. Take out the ham, pour off the water, scrub the ham once more, and replace it in the kettle. Cover it again with cold water. Set it on high heat and, when it comes to a boil, reduce the heat to simmer and cook the ham covered for 15 minutes per pound. Drain off the water again, add wine and vegetables and enough water to come at least halfway up on the ham. Cover the kettle very tightly and steam the ham for another 15 minutes per pound, or until the small bone next to the shank bone can be moved from side to side or even pulled out. Let the ham cool in the liquid. When it is cold, take it out and trim off the rind. Lay it, fat side up,

1 16- to 18-pound country cured ham
1 bottle dry white wine
3 onions, stuck with 6 cloves
3 carrots, scraped and quartered
1 cup dark brown sugar
2 tablespoons cloves

in an open roasting pan. Score the fat diagonally into diamond shapes and cover it generously with dark brown sugar. The diamonds may be studded with cloves. Bake the ham in a 400° F. oven until the sugar has melted and browned, about 30 minutes. Cool the ham and serve it cold with any of the suggested ham sauces.

READY OR FULLY COOKED HAM

Place ham, fat side up, on a rack in an open roasting pan and roast in a 325° F. oven for 2 hours. Take from oven, remove fat from pan, and cut rind from ham. Score the fat with a sharp knife, going about ⅛ inch deep and cutting the diagonal lines about 1 inch apart. Stud the intersecting lines with cloves and return the ham to the pan and the oven. Pour over the burgundy (if the pan is very large, use more wine). Increase the oven temperature to 450° F. and bake the ham, basting every few minutes, for another 30 to 40 minutes. Remove the rack and let it cool in the pan, continuing to brush it with the burgundy.

1 8- to 10-pound bone in, ready-to-eat ham
3 tablespoons whole cloves
½ bottle burgundy
1 small cluster red grapes
1 recipe Cumberland Fruit

Serve it cold on a ham rack with a cluster of red grapes fastened to the high bulge, opposite the shank end of the ham, with wooden picks or an attelet. Serve with a bowl of cumberland fruit, cold stuffed onions, and a vegetable salad.

COLD ROAST HALF HAM

Select a ready-to-eat half ham, shank or butt end, and bake it in a 325° F. oven for 2 hours. A meat thermometer should register 130° F. Turn oven up to 450° F., pour maple syrup or melted red currant or apple jelly over the half ham, and glaze for 20 minutes, basting every 5 minutes. Cool and chill.

CANNED HAM

Heat the ham on a rack in an open pan in a 325° F. oven for 15 minutes to the pound, or for 2½ hours. Melt marmalade and honey together. Increase oven temperature to 450° F. and pour the glaze over the ham. Bake for 15 minutes longer. Pour the glaze remaining in the pan over the ham and cool it slowly. When it is cold, decorate it with orange sections, free of membrane and pits, and halved seedless green grapes. Arrange it on a platter with baked apples filled with cranberry sauce and serve with chilled melon balls, mustard mayonnaise, and a dried bean or potato salad.

1 10-pound boneless whole canned ham
½ jar orange marmalade
½ cup honey
1 large orange
1 small cluster green seedless grapes
6 baked apples
1 cup cranberry sauce
2 cups melon balls
1 recipe Mustard Mayonnaise

GARNISHING HAM PLATTERS

Arrange ham on a rack on a large platter, or half carve it and place the ham at one end of a large platter and overlap the carved slices in front of it. Surround the ham or the ham slices with any of the following:

1. Scooped-out orange halves containing apple salad bound with mayonnaise, or Cumberland Sauce or lingonberry or cranberry sauce.
2. Scooped-out half tomatoes containing a green salad, as peas or cut beans, bound with French Dressing, or fill tomatoes with stiff mayonnaise sauce.
3. Artichoke bottoms filled with a piquant salad or with a piped rosette of Lemon Mayonnaise, sprinkled with cut chives.
4. Orange slices covered with round slices of canned cranberry jelly.
5. Large mushrooms filled with a well-seasoned egg and celery salad.
6. Two small Cauliflowers Vinaigrette.
7. Small individual portions of potato salad in lettuce leaves, the salad heavily sprinkled with chives and capers.
8. Baked apples filled with nuts and raisins or with lingonberry or cranberry sauce.

HAM SAUCES

Also suitable for other cold meats. See salad chapter for additional sauces and accompaniments for ham.

SPICED CRANBERRY SAUCE

Stir spices with vinegar until smooth. Melt cranberry sauce in top of double boiler, stir in the vinegar mixture, and cook uncovered for 15 minutes.

½ teaspoon ground cinnamon
½ teaspoon ground cloves
2 teaspoons English mustard
¼ cup red wine vinegar
1 16-ounce can strained cranberry sauce

SPICED CURRANT JELLY SAUCE

Prepare the sauce as Spiced Cranberry Sauce (above).

1 teaspoon English mustard
¼ teaspoon each ground cinnamon, cloves, and ginger
2 tablespoons tarragon vinegar
1 12-ounce jar red currant jelly

SPICED SOUR CHERRY SAUCE

Drain juice from cherries and set them aside. Cook the juice with orange juice, vinegar, and brown sugar until sugar is completely dissolved. Stir granulated sugar with cinnamon, cornstarch and mustard and stir into the juice mixture. Continue cooking and stirring until the sauce is thickened and clear, about 15 minutes. Take sauce from heat and stir in the cherries, orange rind, and almonds. Correct sweetening if the sauce is still too sour. Cool and chill the sauce and stir in sherry before serving.

1 No. 2 can sour red cherries
⅓ cup orange juice
2 tablespoons vinegar
½ cup brown sugar, tightly packed
½ cup sugar
½ teaspoon cinnamon
1½ tablespoons cornstarch
1 teaspoon English mustard
Grated rind of 1 orange
¼ cup slivered almonds
¼ cup sherry

WHIPPED CREAM MUSTARD SAUCE

Whip mayonnaise with the mustard and add sugar to taste, chill. Whip the cream and fold it into the sauce, not earlier than 2 hours before serving. Chill and serve.

1 cup Herbed Mayonnaise
⅓ cup hot prepared mustard
1 pinch sugar, or to taste
½ cup heavy cream, whipped

NORWEGIAN SAUCE

Stir vinegar, mustard, salt, and sugar into egg yolks until smooth. Stir in the oil drop by drop as for mayonnaise until the sauce is smooth and thick, then add it in a thin stream. Add gherkins and dill and chill until needed.

2 tablespoons dill-flavored vinegar, or plain vinegar
2 tablespoons brown mustard
¼ teaspoon salt, or to taste
1 pinch sugar
3 hard-cooked egg yolks, riced
1 cup oil
1 tablespoon finely chopped gherkins
1 tablespoon finely cut dill

RAISIN SAUCE

Wash raisins and simmer them gently for 15 minutes with the cloves and 1 cup water. Stir cornstarch into sugar with salt and allspice and stir a little cold water into the mixture, add it to the water and raisins. Place over low heat and continue to stir until the sauce is a few minutes longer. Add sugar if necessary and serve cold. Add thickened. Add the port wine and orange juice and rind and cook for almonds with the port wine if wanted.

1 cup raisins
6 cloves
1 tablespoon cornstarch
½ cup brown sugar, packed, or to taste
1 pinch each salt and allspice
⅔ cup port wine
⅓ cup orange juice
2 teaspoons grated orange rind
½ cup slivered almonds, optional

SPICED CURRANT SAUCE FOR HAM

Combine all ingredients in the top of a double boiler over boiling water and cook, uncovered, until slightly thickened, about 30 minutes. Put a tablespoonful of the sauce into a cup and stir in the mustard until smooth. Return it to the sauce, stir well, and serve cold with ham, tongue, or game.

1 jar red currant jelly
The slivered outside rind of 1 orange
2 tablespoons tarragon vinegar
½ teaspoon powdered cinnamon
¼ teaspoon powdered cloves
1 pinch powdered ginger
1 teaspoon dry English mustard

JELLIED MADEIRA SAUCE

Madeira sauce is brown sauce mixed with Madeira wine. For a jellied Madeira sauce stir the gelatin into the wine.

Stir the gelatin into the wine and set it aside. Cook the brown sauce, uncovered, in the top of a double boiler over boiling water until reduced to about 1½ cups. Take from heat and stir in the gelatin until it is dissolved. If a thinner sauce is preferred, stir in a little more Madeira wine *after* the sauce is taken from heat.

2 envelopes gelatin
½ cup Madeira wine
2½ cups Brown Sauce (given below)

BROWN SAUCE

Melt the drippings or butter in a heavy saucepan, add the carrot and onion, and stir until lightly browned. Stir in the flour, little by little, and continue to stir until it is browned. Add the brown stock, a cup at a time, and stir until it is thickened before adding the next cup. When the stock has been added, stir in the tomato purée, reduce heat to lowest simmer, and cook, stirring occasionally, until the sauce is reduced to about 2½ cups. Strain and cool. Skim the surface and use.

¼ cup beef drippings or butter
½ carrot, chopped
½ onion, chopped
¼ cup flour
4 cups rich brown stock
2 tablespoons tomato purée

COLD BEEF TONGUE

For a large party use a 4- to 5-pound tongue and follow the recipe directions. For a small party, buy one of the small precooked beef tongues, which should be prepared according to its package directions. Two of the small tongues may be preferable to one large when time is short. The larger tongue requires 2 to 3 hours' cooking, whereas the prepared precooked tongues have to be cooked for only a few minutes and can then be cooled. The smoked beef tongue is considered a great delicacy in cold cookery and should not be neglected because hot tongue may be unpopular. It combines beautifully with various cold sauces and garnishes, it can be prepared one—or even two—days in advance, and it is economical.

TO COOK A WHOLE TONGUE

Wash the tongue in cold water, place it in a heavy kettle with all other ingredients, add water to cover, and bring it to a fast boil. Skim off all foam, reduce heat, and simmer until tender. A skewer will easily pierce the tongue when it is tender. Test it from the underside at the thickest part. Boiling will take between 2 to 3 hours. A very salty tongue may be improved by being soaked in water overnight, but ask your butcher whether this is necessary. Cool and chill the tongue in its own liquor. Skin the tongue by running a sharp knife under the side of it, or start with a sharp cut at the center top and draw off the rough outside skin. Trim off the heavy base and slice part of it before arranging it on the platter. If two small tongues are used, one may be arranged in the center of the platter, while the second one may be sliced and the slices arranged fanwise on the platter. There are several combinations of Cold Beef Tongue and Cold Chicken among the main course dishes.

1 large 4- to 5-pound smoked beef tongue
2 celery stalks
2 carrots, sliced
1 medium onion stuck with 6 cloves
2 bay leaves
¾ cup sweet apple cider
2 tablespoons honey

COLD BEEF TONGUE PALERMO

Boil the tongue with celery, carrots, onion, bay leaf and water to cover for 1½ hours. Take it out, strain the liquor, discard the vegetables, and return the liquor to the kettle with the wine. Add the tongue, cover the kettle tightly, and continue boiling until tender, about 1 more hour. Let the tongue cool in the liquor. Take it out and reduce the liquor to 4 cups. Strain it into a bowl, cool, and chill. Lift off any fat and thicken the sauce by cooking the ginger crumbs in it until they are soft. Add raisins and almonds and the grated rind of 2 of the oranges and of the lemons. Season with pepper and lemon juice, and if the tongue is very mild, add salt as needed. Chill the sauce. Cut the skin from the oranges with a very sharp knife and add the sections, free of white membrane, to the fruit salad. Arrange the tongue in the center of a platter and half slice it. Place Boston lettuce leaves at either end to simulate small heads of lettuce and fill them with fruit salad. Pass the sauce separately. Serve red wine.

1 4- to 5-pound beef tongue
2 stalks celery
2 carrots, sliced
1 onion, stuck with 4 cloves
1 bay leaf
½ bottle light dry white wine
1½ cups stale ginger cookie crumbs or 1 cup
*   stale gingerbread crumbs*
½ cup raisins
½ cup slivered almonds
4 oranges
2 lemons
Pepper
Salt
1 recipe Fruit Salad (given below)

FRUIT SALAD (for Cold Beef Tongue Palermo, omit the oranges)

Unfortunately the salad cannot be prepared too long in advance, but oranges can be sectioned, peaches can be scalded, grapes cut, berries picked over, and cantaloupe balls prepared. Add apples and pears as late as possible. Sprinkle them with lemon juice and pour over the dressing.

3 oranges, peeled and cut into sections without white membranes
2 eating apples, peeled, cored, and sliced
2 pears, peeled, cored, and sliced
2 bananas, sliced
3 peaches, scalded, peeled, and sliced
1 small bunch grapes, cut in half and seeded
1 pint berries if available
1 cantaloupe, cut into small melon balls or large dice
1 lemon, juiced
1 recipe Italian Dressing

SLICED TONGUE IN ASPIC

Stir the gelatin into ½ cup of the cold stock and set it aside for 15 minutes. Bring the remaining stock and consommé to a boil, take it from heat, and stir in the gelatin until it is dissolved. Add the port and let the aspic cool slowly. Steam the apples with sugar and wine or cider in a covered kettle until they are just tender; do not let them fall apart. The length of time needed depends entirely on the quality of the apples, so watch them carefully. Transfer them to a bowl and chill them. Carve the tongue and arrange overlapping slices around the apples. Pour the aspic over the tongue and chill it until set. Serve with horseradish mayonnaise.

2 envelopes gelatin
1 cup stock from boiling the tongue
1 cup clear consommé
1 cup white port wine
8 large cooking apples, peeled, cored, and quartered
⅓ to ½ cup sugar, to taste
1 cup dry white wine or apple cider
1 small tongue, boiled
1 recipe Horseradish Mayonnaise (given below)

HORSERADISH MAYONNAISE (for cold fish, beef, tongue, or tomatoes)

Fold cream and mayonnaise together and stir in horseradish and salt just before serving.

½ cup heavy cream, whipped
¾ cup thick Lemon Mayonnaise
¼ cup freshly grated horseradish or well-drained bottled horseradish
Salt to taste

HORSERADISH CREAM (for cold tongue, smoked salmon, trout, or mackerel or fresh salmon or trout)

Fold horseradish into chilled whipped cream. Add salt, cover with a bowl, and chill for a short time. Horseradish turns black if exposed too long to light and air.

¾ cup freshly grated horseradish
¾ cup heavy cream, whipped
Salt to taste

DESSERTS

CHAPTER ELEVEN

Desserts and Dessert Sauces, Including Heavier
Chocolate, Chestnut, and Other Cold Desserts
That Are Not Light Enough for Summer Service

DESSERTS do not have to be hot to be suitable for cold winter weather. We have made ice creams and frozen desserts such an important part of our year-round menus that we can no longer designate them as being typical of a cold summer or a cold winter dinner. The best guide for choosing the right dessert is the season. When berries and fruits are *in season*, that is the time when they are most tempting. The heat that ripens them makes us hungry for them, and nothing tastes better than a fresh fruit dessert in midsummer.

An icy fruit sherbet is clearly made for a hot August evening, while a rather rib-lining rum mousse is just as clearly made for cold December weather. The whole thing is more a matter of suggestion than of actual suitability. The foods that have always been associated with autumn and winter, whether we serve them hot or cold, are still the ones we prefer between October and April. We have an appetite for rum, chocolate, nuts, dried fruits, and chestnuts because they remind us of winter holidays, while a red raspberry dessert will always look like summer.

All desserts that look as though they had taken *long hot hours of cooking or baking*, even though they are served cold, are more suitable for winter, while the light and effortless fruit desserts look like summer. Whether we want to think about the work that is involved or not— or whether we analyze the reason—the cold rice pudding (for which the oven was turned on for an hour) will always feel more like a winter dessert than the bowl of cold fruit for which the oven was not turned on at all.

Any cold dessert may be served in winter; it is the course that has swung over to cold cookery long ago. Cakes, ice creams, jellies, and creams far outnumber the steamed pudding, hot soufflés, and pancakes on American menus today. The desserts in this chapter are perhaps a little more suitable for winter, but they are interchangeable with the desserts in Chapter Seven. All of them can be made ahead, and many of them can be made way ahead.

BELGIAN STEWED PRUNES I

Depending on the size of the prunes, count from 4 to 6 per portion. Try for giant dried prunes if obtainable. For packaged quick-cooking prunes, do not soak overnight, and follow changes in cooking time as noted at end of recipe.

Soak the well-washed prunes in cold water overnight. In the morning simmer them gently in the wine and 1 additional cup of water. Add the spices and cook uncovered for about 15 minutes. Add the sugar and continue to cook until prunes are tender and liquid has been reduced to half. If the prunes are done before the liquid is sufficiently reduced, take them out with a slotted spoon and return them to the liquid only after it is reduced and cooled. Divide prunes and their liquid over 6 dessert dishes and serve very cold with the softly whipped cream.

    Boil the quick-cooking prunes as above for 20 minutes, add sugar to taste depending on the sweetness of the prunes, and boil until they are puffed and tender. Take them out and reduce the liquid.

1 pound dried prunes, not quick-cooking
2 cups light red wine
1 to 2 pinches each ground cinnamon and cloves, or to taste
1 cup sugar, or to taste
1 cup heavy cream, whipped until thick but not until stiff

BELGIAN STEWED PRUNES II

Soak the well-washed prunes in water overnight. Simmer them in 2 cups water with curaçao and sugar until they are puffed and tender. Take them out with a slotted spoon and add the almonds. Cook until liquid is reduced to 1½ cups. Cool and pour over the prunes. Sprinkle with peel before serving.

1 pound dried prunes, not quick-cooking
1 cup curaçao
½ cup sugar, or to taste
½ cup large blanched almonds
3 tablespoons chopped candied orange peel

STEWED PRUNES IN RUM

Soak the prunes in the water overnight. Next morning cook them in the same water until tender and plump. When nearly tender add sugar to taste and simmer for a few minutes longer. Strain off the liquid and cool the prunes. Return the liquid to the saucepan and boil it rapidly until it is slightly reduced, put in the lemon slices, and cook for 5 minutes longer. Add rum to taste. When cold, pour the syrup over the prunes and serve topped with whipped cream. Grate the cold chocolate heavily over the cream.

1 pound large dried prunes
4 cups water
⅓ to ⅔ cup sugar to taste
1 lemon, very thinly sliced
2 tablespoons rum, or to taste
1 cup heavy cream, whipped
1 chocolate bar, with orange flavor, chilled

WINTER COMPOTE

Use the full containers of dried and canned fruits and store leftover compote in a jar in the refrigerator until needed.

Cook the prunes and apricots according to the package directions. Take them out when they are tender and reduce the water in which they boiled with the cinnamon and cloves by boiling uncovered over high heat. Add the syrups drained from figs, peaches, and kumquats, and apricots (if whole apricots were used) and reduce them by about one-fourth. Take from heat, strain through a fine sieve, and add rum to taste. Arrange the fruit in a deep crystal bowl, pour over the rum-flavored syrup, garnish with lemon slices, and serve with whipped cream.

1 15-ounce tub package jumbo dried prunes
1 14-ounce container jumbo dried apricots, or
  1 30-ounce can whole apricots in heavy
  syrup
1 stick cinnamon
6 cloves
1 15-ounce jar figs in heavy syrup
1 15-ounce can white nectar peaches in heavy
  syrup
1 30-ounce can pitted Bing cherries, drained
1 20-ounce jar kumquats in heavy syrup,
  optional
Heavy rum to taste
1 lemon, thinly sliced
1 cup heavy cream, softly whipped with sugar

WHOLE ORANGES IN SYRUP

Peel the thinnest outside rind from the oranges with a potato peeler, and set it aside. Peel long, wide strips from the body of the oranges. With a very sharp knife, slice off all the white pulp down to the flesh, leaving the oranges intact. Set them in a shallow dessert dish. Boil the sugar and water for about 10 minutes, add the orange peel and simmer for 5 minutes longer. Add one of the orange liqueurs to taste. Spoon the syrup over the oranges and sliver the orange rind into long thin shreds with a kitchen scissors. Sliver enough of the rind to make a generous topping of shreds on each orange. Chill in the coldest part of the refrigerator; the oranges must be served very cold. Each guest, should have a small knife and fork.

6 to 8 sweet oranges
Sugar syrup of 1 cup water, 2 cups sugar
Grand Marnier, curaçao, Cointreau, or Triple Sec

COLD BAKED APPLES

Core the apples without going all the way through. Stir the next 4 ingredients together and fill ⅔ of the mixture into the apples. Place them in a shallow pan with ¼ inch water and bake them in a 350° F. oven until tender but not soft. Depending on the type of apple, about 20 minutes. Five minutes before they are ready to take from the oven, add the remaining filling to the tops of the apples and push them under a hot broiler with the oven door open. Watch them and take them out when the tops are browned. Serve cold with half-whipped cream or whipped sour cream.

6 large baking apples, peeled
¼ pound, 1 cube, butter at room temperature
½ cup dark brown sugar
2 tablespoons brandy
2 tablespoons Grand Marnier, or all brandy
1 cup heavy cream or 1 cup sour cream

GLAZED BAKED APPLES

Peel apples halfway down from the stem end. Core them carefully to just below the pips, but do not cut them through. Hollow them out slightly with a small spoon. Place apples in a shallow baking pan and divide jam, honey, butter, and almonds over the cavities, in that order. Fill the cavities with apricot brandy and pour ½ inch of cold water into the pan. Place the pan in a 400° F. oven and bake for 20

6 large Golden Delicious or other eating apples
2 tablespoons raspberry or apricot jam
2 tablespoons honey
2 tablespoons butter
¼ cup chopped toasted almonds
¼ cup apricot brandy
¼ cup granulated sugar
½ pint heavy cream or 1 recipe Thick Cream

minutes. Sprinkle the apples generously and evenly with granulated sugar and bake for 10 minutes longer. Sprinkle them again and bake until they are tender and caramelized. An average apple should bake for about 40 minutes. Depending on the type of apple used, it may be necessary to sprinkle them only once with sugar; in that case, be very generous with the sugar to insure a deep brown caramel. Serve cold with heavy cream or with thick cream.

BAKED BANANAS

Peel the bananas, cut them in half lengthwise, and arrange them in a well-buttered baking dish from which they can be served. Sprinkle them with the spices mixed with the brown sugar and grated orange rind and pour over the orange juice and rum. Dot with butter and bake in a 350° F. oven, basting frequently, for about 25 minutes, or until bananas are lightly browned. Let them cool in the pan and serve with a pitcher of heavy cream.

8 large bananas
3 tablespoons soft butter for the dish and for
dotting
1 teaspoon ground cinnamon
¼ teaspoon ground cloves
⅓ cup brown sugar
2 oranges, grated rind and juice
½ cup heavy rum
1 cup heavy cream

Frozen Desserts

The records of cold cookery wind through the long history of food and crop up in the most unexpected places . . . always associated with luxury and good living. Alexander the Great commanded the digging of deep holes, to which ice and snow were dragged from distant mountains, so that he could enjoy his chilled desserts when he was on campaign. Nero's wines were cooled in snow in midsummer and teen-ager Catherine de Médicis sailed to her marriage, endowed with a *Gelatiere* and brought frozen delights to France. Furst Püchler is better known today for having combined frozen cream with crushed macaroons than for his conquests.

Precious ice and snow were used to freeze sweets, cool fruits and salads, and chill wines centuries ago. We accept and even expect icy desserts on the coldest winter days, and there has never been the slightest resistance to beginning and ending our dinners with a chill. Our frozen desserts are as self-understood in July as in December. They are *year round,* and the hostess need not steam a pudding just because it is snowing outside.

Planning a dinner menu is much easier when a Coffee Mousse or a lovely Bombe Coppélia are ready in the freezer. They can be home frozen or they can be compositions of various ice creams from the market. A few basic recipes for creams and their many flavor variations follow, but for the rest, the entire array of magnificent frozen desserts is rather a description of how to *use* ice cream than how to *make* it.

Learn to make the nonchurned frozen desserts with cold egg yolks, sugar, and cream, or with custard, gelatin, or egg whites. Parfaits, mousses, frozen soufflés, biscuit tortoni, and their many variations are all much easier to prepare in the freezer, or in the freezing compartment of your refrigerator, than they sound. Furthermore they can be as velvety and creamy as the most beautiful French parfait. The granular ice-tray ice creams, which discouraged most of us from further experiments long ago, were either made of the wrong ingredients or by the wrong method. All that are needed are heavy cream, cold itensils, and *the knack.*

We shy away from the homemade nonchurned ice creams only because our first attempts to make them were unsuccessful and because commercial ice creams are so easily come by. Many of them are undeniably very good, but there is a long distance between a scoop of bought ice cream and a proper dessert for a dinner party. We may have the best-prepared foods in the world at our disposal, but by common consent we do not feel that they are worthy of guests until we *do* something to them.

Among the most attractive things we can *do* to commercial ice creams is to fill them into bombe molds. The more varied the combinations of color and taste the better. We can further enhance them with additions of powdered praline, nuts, *marrons,* candied fruits, and flavorings. We can fill them into individual molds or parfait glasses and combine them with fruits, nuts, and/ or sauces. If there are interesting ice cream molds available, a good quality ice cream can be *packed* into them and *unpacked* before serving. I remember a mold for making one great big beautiful strawberry (out of strawberry ice cream), which was then crowned with bright green leaves and absolutely buried in spun sugar.

As long as there is a deep freeze, a freezer section in the refrigerator, or a large ice-tray compartment, frozen desserts can be produced from homemade mixtures or from commercial ice creams. If the ice cream is packaged, it has to be solid; the airy, porous kinds do not adapt themselves to shaping and refreezing. The related desserts, which rely on gelatin to hold their shape, are *set* in the refrigerator in 2 to 4 hours and do not require the low temperature of a freezer.

The hostess and housewife who has a cache of frozen bombes, soufflé dishes filled with mousse, or molds full of parfait in her freezer is way ahead. When she plans for a dinner party or when she has unexpected guests, she can devote herself to the main course without giving the dessert another thought. For some reason it is the dessert that usually presents the problem, and when it is right there, ready to be unmolded and make a gala ending to the meal, the rest seems easy.

If a dish or mold is needed for another purpose and cannot be spared to wait in the freezer, the mousse or parfait can be unmolded in the usual way—a dip into hot water—and immediately wrapped in foil or a plastic bag and put back into the freezer. The surface may not be quite as immaculate as when it comes straight out of the mold, but surfaces can be disguised or smoothed. I have an individual mold that makes an ornate, rather baroque saucer. When I need several little vanilla ice cream saucers to fill with velvety raspberries, I make one after the other and wrap them in soft film. They go into a retired cracker can and I hardly miss the other eleven molds.

All this molding and modeling of the same substance that fills thousands of ice cream cones on a hot summer day may seen unnecessary . . . but just try a *dish of ice cream* as against a glamorous Bombe Camargo, made of exactly the same ice cream. When a bombe comes to the table, it invariably produces a hush, and when you slice it to reveal its dissimilar heart, there is an audible sigh.

The knack for making smooth frozen desserts without a churn ice cream freezer depends on the following rules:

1. Chill heavy cream in refrigerator for at least 24 hours before using.
2. All utensils should be cold. Most important, do not fill the completed ice cream or mousse mixture into a room temperature mold or dish. *Everything* should be chilled before you start.
3. All ingredients, as marrons or fruit, must be in small pieces. Large pieces of fruit can deter smooth freezing.
4. Turn the refrigerator temperature control to the lowest point 3 or 4 hours *before* making ice cream.

5. The final knack is the second whipping. Recipes usually suggest that ice-tray ice creams be stirred after the crystals start to form around the edge. Actually there should not be any visible crystals, but the cream "thickens" around the edge and the contents of the tray or dish should be thoroughly *whipped*. The best utensil for this purpose is a French wire whisk. The whipping can be repeated if the cream does not seem to be freezing smoothly.
6. The proportions of the ingredients are important. Adding or subtracting can wreck the whole thing. Too much sugar, too many yolks, too fat cream can prevent proper freezing.
7. After the ice cream, or parfait, has been put into the freezer or freezing compartment, the door should not be opened. If absolutely necessary, open it for as short a time as possible. The ice cream will be frozen after 2 to 4 hours, depending on whether the door had to be opened or not.
8. When filling a bombe mold with a combination of commercial ice creams, put the mold into the freezer before you go to market, and fill the mold immediately upon your return. The commercial ice cream will have softened slightly in transport, and it is better to fill it into the mold at once, then chill it and then re soften it in order to line the mold.

PARFAIT AU MOCA

Stir sieved instant coffee with vanilla and 2 teaspoons boiling water into a thick, smooth paste. Beat yolks with ⅓ cup of the sugar until they are lighter and thicker than you ever thought they could be. Beat in the cold coffee paste. Try a smudge on the end of your finger and be sure you feel no granulation from sugar or coffee. Scrape the mixture into a cold bowl and chill it while you whip the cream. Rinse beaters and bowl and set the bowl in a pan of ice cubes. Ideally, the cream should be whipped over ice. If a hand electric beater is being used, there is no problem. If a stand beater, which does not detach from the stand, is being used, chill the bowl and work quickly. Whip the cream until it thickens, gradually add the remaining sugar, and continue to beat until very stiff. Fold the cream into the yolks and fill the mixture into a chilled soufflé dish or into individual ramekins or dishes. The cream should not completely fill the dish, or dishes, since it will be whipped at least once more. Look at the parfait after about 40 minutes; if the edges have begun to harden, whip it vigorously with a French wire whisk (very small whisks are available), scraping the hardened edges into the cream. Either repeat the whipping, when the edges of the cream harden again, or top with the crumbs, cover the cream with foil, and freeze for 2 to 3 hours longer, or until needed.

3 tablespoons instant coffee
1 teaspoon vanilla or coffee extract
3 egg yolks
1 scant cup superfine sugar
3 cups heavy cream, chilled
1 cup macaroon or cookie crumbs

APRICOT BAVARIAN CREAM

This should not be made more than 24 hours before it will be served.

Drain the apricots well, remove pits, and blend them into a smooth purée. Stir the gelatin into ¼ cup of the syrup from the can of apricots and set it aside for 10 minutes. Heat half a cup of the remaining syrup to boiling, take it from the heat, and stir in the softened gelatin until it dissolves. Cool the mixture and stir in the apricot purée and almond extract. Whip the cream until half stiff. Note, if the apricot syrup is very sweet, the sugar should be reduced to taste. Fold the cream into the apricot purée and pour it into a rinsed 1½-quart mold or ring mold and chill the cream for at least 3 hours. Serve with Apricot Brandy Sauce (given below).

1 No. 2½ can skinless apricots, chilled
2 envelopes plain gelatin
½ teaspoon almond extract
2 cups heavy cream, chilled
½ cup superfine sugar

APRICOT BRANDY SAUCE

Heat all ingredients in the top of a double boiler over boiling water and serve.

1 jar thick apricot jam
⅓ cup apricot brandy
⅓ cup blanched and skinned almonds
Any remaining syrup from the can of apricots

BISCUIT TORTONI

Dry the macaroons in a 200° F. oven for 30 minutes and crush them with a rolling pin. Divide the sugar in half and gradually beat half into the egg whites, after they have been beaten half stiff. Continue to beat until they are very stiff. Transfer them to a bowl and whip the cream until it is half stiff. Gradually add the remaining sugar to the cream and continue to whip until it is stiff. Fold the egg whites and cream together gently with the sherry and half the crushed macaroons. Mound the mixture into paper cases or ramekins and cover tops with the remaining crumbs. Freeze them for at least 2 hours in deep freeze, freezing section of refrigerator, or in the ice-tray compartment.

12 macaroons (if the small Italian amaretti
 are available, use 24)
¾ cup powdered sugar
3 egg whites
3 cups heavy cream
¼ cup sherry

KIRSCH MOUSSE

Beat the yolks with half the sugar until unbelievably light and creamy and chill. Whip the cream until half stiff and gradually add the remaining sugar. Continue to beat until stiff. Stir the kirsch into the yolks and fold in the whipped cream. Pour the cream into a soufflé dish and freeze for about 40 minutes. Whip it with a French wire whisk and put it back into the freezer for at least 4 more hours or until needed. Serve the kirsch mousse with Black Cherry Sauce (given below).

3 egg yolks
14 tablespoons superfine sugar
3 cups heavy cream
¼ cup kirsch

BLACK CHERRY SAUCE

Drain cherries and reduce their juice to ⅓ by boiling it, uncovered, over high heat. Melt the red currant jelly in the top of a double boiler over boiling water and add the reduced cherry juice. Cool the sauce, stir in the kirsch and brandy, and return the cherries to the sauce. Serve it warm or cold.

Cold foods can include these touches of warmth that do not really mean a cooking effort, but rather an accent to the cold mousse.

1 No. 2 can pitted black cherries
1 jar red currant jelly
2 tablespoons kirsch
1 tablespoon brandy

PRINCE PÜCHLER'S PUDDING

Whip cream until almost stiff, then gradually add the sugar and continue whipping until very stiff. Fold in 1¼ cups of the macaroon crumbs and pour the mixture into a rinsed spring form. Place the mold in the freezer for about 45 minutes. Take it out and whip the pudding very thoroughly with a French wire whisk. Return the pudding to the freezer and repeat the whipping as soon as it starts to thicken and set around the edges. Sprinkle top with the remaining crumbs, cover with foil, and chill for at least 3 to 4 hours. Remove the spring form and serve the pudding, cut in wedges like a regular cake, with sabayon sauce.

3 cups heavy cream, whipped
½ cup superfine sugar
2 cups crushed dry macaroon crumbs
½ teaspoon almond extract, optional
1 recipe Sabayon Sauce

CHOCOLATE CHIPOLATA

Melt the chocolate in the top of a double boiler over, not touching, boiling water, whisk it until smooth, and whisk in the egg yolks, one by one, and last of all the rum. Take from heat and beat until cold. Stir in the fruit and nuts. Beat the egg whites until very stiff and fold them gently into the mixture. Pour the chipolata into a dessert bowl and chill for at least 6 hours before serving. Serve the dessert plain or with a bowl of sweetened whipped cream.

6 squares, or 6 ounces, semisweet chocolate
  (the imported Dutch bittersweet
  chocolate is perfect for the purpose)
6 eggs, separated
2 tablespoons rum, or to taste
½ cup quartered candied cherries
¼ cup diced candied orange peel
¼ cup diced citron
½ cup broken marrons glacés
¼ cup chopped walnuts
1 cup heavy cream, whipped, optional
1 tablespoon powdered sugar

CHOCOLATE MOUSSE I Frozen

Beat yolks and sugar with a hand electric beater or French wire whisk in the top of a double boiler over—not touching—barely simmering water. Beat until light and until it *ribbons* from the beater when you lift it. Take from heat and continue to beat until cold (this can be speeded by substituting ice or ice water for the simmering water in the double boiler). Beat in the vanilla and chocolate, melted over hot water. Fold in the stiffly whipped cream. Pour the mixture into a rinsed 8-cup mold, cover it with foil, and place in freezer or freezing compartment for at least 4 hours. Whip it thoroughly after 40 minutes with a French wire whisk.

6 large egg yolks
½ cup confectioner's sugar
½ teaspoon vanilla
4 squares, or 4 ounces, semisweet chocolate
3 cups heavy cream, whipped

CHOCOLATE MOUSSE II Chilled

Beat yolks and sugar as for Chocolate Mousse I (given above) and flavor with rum or Grand Marnier and beat until cold. Melt chocolate over hot water. When it is cold, beat in the butter and combine the mixture with the yolks. Beat the egg whites until very stiff and fold them lightly into the yolk mixture. Pour into a crystal dessert bowl and chill for at least 6 hours, preferably longer. Sprinkle the top with any preferred garnish—chopped pistachio nuts, roughly ground praline, chopped walnuts, or diced candied orange rind. Serve with softly whipped cream since there is none in the mousse.

5 large eggs, separated
¾ cup confectioner's sugar
2 tablespoons rum or Grand Marnier
5 squares, or 5 ounces, sweet cooking chocolate
1 tablespoon soft butter
1 cup heavy cream, softly whipped

RUM MOUSSE

Boil sugar and water until sugar is dissolved, boil 5 minutes longer. Cool the mixture and place it in the top of a double boiler over simmering water, add the yolks and rum, and stir constantly until the mixture coats the back of a spoon. Take from heat and beat until cold. If time is short, beat over a bowl of ice. Beat in the orange juice and rind and fold in the stiffly whipped cream. Pour into a rinsed mold and freeze in deep freeze or freezer compartment for at least 4 hours. Serve with Swiss Chocolate Sauce (given below).

¾ cup sugar
½ cup water
6 egg yolks
½ cup rum
1 tablespoon orange juice
Grated rind of 1 orange
2 cups heavy cream, whipped

SWISS CHOCOLATE SAUCE

Melt chocolate in top of double boiler over boiling water, beat in the cream until the sauce is light and creamy, flavor with rum, and serve.

2 triangular bars Toblerone Chocolate
⅓ to ½ cup heavy cream, to taste
1 tablespoon rum

MACAROON COFFEE BISCUIT

Crush the macaroons with a rolling pin and toast them in a 300° F. oven for about 15 minutes, set them aside. Heat the cream, take it from heat, and stir in the instant coffee until it is dissolved. Add 1 cup of the macaroon crumbs, sugar, rum, and vanilla. Chill the mixture for 1 hour. Whip the heavy cream and fold it into the macaroon mixture. Fill the mixture into 6 paper cases, muffin cups, or ramekins and place in freezer for 20 minutes. Sprinkle tops with remaining macaroon crumbs and freeze until a few minutes before serving. Transfer the cases or cups to the refrigerator to soften slightly. Depending on temperature of refrigerator, about 10 minutes should be enough. Serve when just beginning to soften.

½ pound or 12 macaroons, or 1½ cups
*   crushed macaroons*
¾ cup light cream
2 tablespoons instant coffee
3 tablespoons sugar
1 teaspoon rum
1 teaspoon vanilla
1 cup heavy cream, whipped

COFFEE MOUSSE

Beat the egg yolks with a hand electric beater or a French wire whisk in the top of a double boiler *over*—not touching—simmering water. When they are creamy, add the sugar and the instant coffee, dissolved in ¼ cup boiling water and cooled, and the vanilla. Beat the mixture until it no longer increases in volume and is light and smooth. Take it from heat and continue to beat until cold. Fold in the stiffly beaten egg whites and the whipped cream. Pour the mousse into a dessert bowl and chill it in the coldest part of the refrigerator for at least 6 hours. Serve plain or with softly whipped cream.

6 egg yolks
¾ cup sugar
3 tablespoons instant coffee
½ teaspoon vanilla
3 egg whites, beaten stiff
2½ cups heavy cream, whipped

RICE PUDDING

Cook the rice with the milk and salt in the top of a double boiler over boiling water until the rice is just tender and the milk is absorbed, about 25 minutes. Beat the egg yolks with the sugar and gradually beat in the cream, add the well-drained rice and raisins. Pour the mixture into 6 buttered individual baking dishes and bake in a 350° F. oven until the top is brown, about 15 to 20 minutes. Serve cold with a pitcher of heavy cream.

1⅓ cups long-grained rice
2⅔ cups milk
1 teaspoon salt
4 egg yolks
¼ cup sugar
½ cup cream
½ cup raisins

TOURINOISE

Melt the chocolate with the rum over hot water. Cool and beat in the chestnut purée and soft butter. Depending on whether the chestnuts were sweetened, add sugar to taste and flavor with vanilla. Pour the mixture into a rinsed mold, or into a buttered wax-paper-lined loaf pan, and chill in coldest part of refrigerator for at least 6 hours. Unmold and serve with sweetened whipped cream or, if it was made in a loaf pan, slice it and serve with Sabayon Sauce. If fresh chestnuts are used, boil them in water for 20 minutes, then in milk for about another 20 minutes or until they are soft enough to drain and mash.

8 squares, or 8 ounces, bitter chocolate
2 tablespoons rum
2 17-ounce cans chestnut purée or 2 pounds shelled chestnuts
2 cups milk, if fresh chestnuts are used
6 tablespoons soft butter, whipped
Powdered sugar to taste
½ teaspoon vanilla

BAKING FOR COLD COOKERY

There is actually very little baking needed in cold cookery, and the entire purpose of serving cold food as a means of simplification and liberation would be defeated if long hours were spent over baking breads or cakes or rolling puff pastry. The only baked pieces that are suggested on the menus are cheese sticks or wafers to serve with cocktails, soup, or salad, and small cookies to serve with fruit desserts, and one biscuit so that there can be a yule log at Christmas. The following pastes are basic, and small variations in shape and topping can make them suit many purposes.

BAKING DIRECTIONS

The moment when a piece of baking is *done* is hard to determine. While oven temperatures are usually accurate, there are circumstances that play an important part. The size of the oven in relation to the size of the baking sheet, the weight of the baking sheet or pan, and even altitude plays a part. The best way of judging when baking is done is to look at it and try to move it with a spatula or pancake turner. Baking *is not done* when the pieces are pale and have a raw look and when they stick to the sheet. Baking *is done* when the pieces are faintly golden and move easily. Take them from the baking sheet at once with the pancake turner, as they continue to brown on the hot sheet even after they leave the oven. Cheese wafers turn bitter when they are too brown.

CHEESE PASTE FOR COCKTAIL ROUNDS AND BASES FOR CANAPÉS AND AMUSE-BOUCHE

The dough can be prepared in any quantity as long as the ingredients are used in equal *weight*. Bring cheese and butter to room temperature and put the cheese through the medium blade of the meat grinder. Work the butter, flour, and salt into it to make a smooth paste. Chill until needed. (Recipe continued below.)

8 ounces sharp Cheddar cheese
½ pound or 2 cubes butter
2 cups sifted flour
1 pinch salt
1 egg, beaten with 1 tablespoon water
¼ cup shaved scalded almonds
Salt to taste

CHEESE ROUNDS AND SQUARES

Roll the cheese paste out on a *very* lightly floured pastry canvas with a stockinet-covered rolling pin to ⅛-inch thickness and cut it into rounds or squares with a plain or fluted cookie cutter. Brush with the beaten egg, sprinkle with almonds and salt to taste, and bake on an unbuttered baking sheet in a 375° F. oven until golden and until they are loose from the baking sheet, about 15 minutes. Take them out with a spatula and serve with cocktails, cold soups, or salads.

CHEESE STICKS: Cut the paste into 5-inch-long sticks with a pastry wheel, brush them with egg, and sprinkle with caraway, poppy, or sesame seeds. Bake as Cheese Rounds (above) and serve with cocktails. The same seeds may be sprinkled on cheese rounds instead of the almonds.

CHEESE BASES

Substitute a mild imported Cheddar for the sharp Cheddar, which can be found packaged in all supermarkets. The imported Cheddar is light in color and can be found in cheese shops and departments in specialty shops.

Roll the paste out a little thicker than for Cheese Rounds and cut it into 1½- to 2-inch rounds, suitable for canapé bases. Bake them as Cheese Rounds, about 18 minutes, until they are dry and golden; they should not be browned.

1 12-ounce wedge imported light Cheddar cheese
¾ pound or 3 cubes butter
3 cups sifted flour
Salt to taste

CHEESE DOUBLES

Roll the paste out as for Cheese Rounds and cut it into small rounds with a 1- to 1⅛-inch-diameter fluted cookie cutter. Bake them as Cheese Rounds and let them cool on a strip of wax paper. Turn half the little rounds over and top them with a dab of the herbed Boursin cheese. Sandwich a second round on top of it and spread the filling by pressing the top round down lightly. Store in a cool place or refrigerate until shortly before they are to be served. Serve with cocktails.

1 recipe Cheese Paste
1 Herbed Boursin Cheese

BASIC PASTE FOR SMALL TURNOVERS TO SERVE WITH COCKTAILS, COLD SOUPS, OR FOR DESSERT

Bring butter and cheese to room temperature and work quickly into a soft paste with the flour. Add up to ¼ cup more flour, if necessary, to make the paste easier to handle. Roll it out on a very lightly floured pastry canvas with a stockinet-covered rolling pin. Cut, fill, and shape the pieces as suggested in the following recipes and bake them on an unbuttered baking sheet in a 325° F. oven for 20 to 30 minutes, or until puffed and golden.

2 cubes or ½ pound butter
1 8-ounce package cream cheese
2 cups flour

HAM CRESCENTS

Divide the paste and roll it into 2 even, thin rounds, measuring about 10 inches across. Stir ham, relish, mustard, and seasonings into a smooth filling. Cut each round into 8 even pie-shaped wedges and put a spoon of the ham filling on the wide end of each wedge. Roll up the paste toward the pointed end and turn to catch the tip on the underside. Bend the 2 ends toward the center to form a crescent. Bake the crescents on an unbuttered baking sheet as directed above. Serve with cocktails or with cold soup.

1 recipe Basic Paste for Small Turnovers
1 cup ground ham
2 tablespoons sweet pickle relish, drained
½ tablespoon brown mustard, or to taste
Salt and pepper to taste

JAM TURNOVERS

Roll the paste out thin on a lightly floured pastry canvas with a stockinet-covered rolling pin. Cut it into 2½- to 3-inch squares with a fluted pastry wheel or sharp knife and place a half teaspoon of strawberry jam on the center of each square. Fold up the 4 corners to the center and pinch them together tightly. Pinch the 4 little seams together and bake the turnovers on an unbuttered baking sheet in a 350° F. oven for about 25 minutes. They will open slightly, which doesn't matter, and if a little jam runs out it will only serve to caramelize the corner. Sprinkle with powdered sugar and serve with ice cream, iced tea, or sherbets.

1 recipe Basic Paste for Small Turnovers
½ cup thick strawberry jam
Powdered sugar

YIELD: 55 turnovers at 2½ × 2½ inch squares with ⅓ teaspoon jam on each or about ⅓ cup.

40 turnovers at 3×3 inch squares with ½ teaspoon jam on each or about ½ cup.

SHORT PASTE FOR LINZER TARTS OR FILBERT OR PECAN HALF-MOONS

Beat the yolks and sugar until light and thick. Beat in the lemon rind and work the mixture into the butter, which should be creamed in a second bowl. Last of all work in the flour and chill the dough for at least 4 hours, preferably overnight.

2 egg yolks
½ cup sugar
Grated rind of 1 lemon
1 cup less 2 tablespoons butter, creamed
2⅔ cups sifted flour

LINZER TARTS

Roll the paste out thin on a lightly floured pastry canvas and cut it into 3½-inch rounds. Cut the center out of half the rounds with a 1¼-inch-diameter cookie cutter. Place all the solid rounds on a lightly buttered baking sheet and bake them in a 375° F. oven for about 20 minutes, or until the rounds are pale golden and are loose from the baking sheet. Cool the sheet and butter it lightly. Put the cut-out rounds on it and bake them for 1 minute or until they stick to the sheet. Take them out, cool them, and then brush the rings with beaten egg. Spread the almonds on the rings and tilt the sheet to tap off the shaved almonds that fell on the sheet. Continue baking in the usual way. Spread the even underside of the solid rounds thinly with jam and sandwich a cut-out round on each. When they are all done, fill a little more jam into the hollows. Serve with fruit or cream desserts or with iced tea in the afternoon. Small *Linzer* cutters can be found in most kitchenware shops, and when they are used the top is left plain and the tarts are sugared before they are served.

1 recipe Short Paste (above)
1 egg beaten with 1 tablespoon water
Shaved blanched almonds
Seedless raspberry or apricot jam

FILBERT OR PECAN HALF-MOONS

(If possible use the parched nuts that are packed in jars. Wash them to remove all salt and let them dry well before chopping them.) Roll out the paste as for Linzer Tarts (above), cut it with a half-moon cutter—or any other shape that is available—and brush the surface with beaten egg. Sprinkle it heavily with chopped nuts and bake in a 375° F. oven for about 18 minutes, or until golden and loose from the baking sheet.

The same paste may be used for Linzer Strips or as a base for Fruit tarts (both given below).

½ recipe Short Paste (given above)
1 egg beaten with 1 tablespoon water
½ cup toasted filberts or pecans

LINZER STRIP

Roll the Short Paste into a thin 6-inch-wide strip and brush the 2 long edges with beaten egg white. Fold the 2 edges back on themselves and press them down well. Brush the surfaces of the 2 borders with egg and sprinkle them with shaved almonds. Bake the strip, or strips, in a 375° F. oven until barely golden. Fill it carefully with apricot or raspberry jam and return it to the oven for a few minutes to *set* the jam. Let the strip cool on the baking sheet. Cut it into diagonal slices and serve them as dessert or with a light cream dessert.

FRUIT TARTS

Roll the Short Paste to as large a round as possible and place it in a straight-edged tart pan, or use it to line a flan ring set on a very lightly buttered baking sheet. Press the paste into the pan or ring with the fingers and trim the edge. Pinch it into an attractive border and fill the shell with cherry pits or dried beans. Bake it *blind* in a 375° F. oven until golden and let it cool in the pan. Fill it with a layer of apricot jam and arrange fresh fruit closely on it in an attractive design. Use whole strawberries, standing upward, half strawberries on their sides, or overlapping peach or plum wedges. Glaze the fruit with melted red currant jelly and chill until ready to serve. The tart may be sprinkled with chopped pistachio nuts, or it can be served with sweetened whipped cream.

SPRITZ TONGUES

In electric beater, cream butter, gradually add the sugar, and beat until it no longer feels granular. Add the egg yolk and vanilla and beat in the flour. It is important that the paste be smooth and soft; at the same time it should not be beaten until it separates. Fill the paste into a cookie press fitted with a ridged slit disk, so that the paste can be pressed onto an unbuttered pastry sheet in long ridged strips about ½ inch apart. The above amount will fill 2 pastry sheets. Cut the strips into 1½-inch lengths with a knife and push the lengths apart with the knife. Bake in a 375° F. oven for about 10 minutes. The size of the cookie sheet in relation to the size of the oven makes a great difference in baking thin cookies; watch carefully. Each sheet will yield about 48 cookies. This method saves rolling out and handling the paste, which means that less flour is rolled into it and the tongues are very tender.

½ pound cold butter, sliced
½ cup confectioner's sugar
1 egg yolk
1 teaspoon vanilla
2 cups flour

ALMOND HORSESHOES

Cream the butter, beat in the sugar until very light, add vanilla. Gradually work in the flour and almonds until the dough is smooth and light. Chill the dough for a few minutes and then break off pieces as large as a golf ball and work with 1 piece at a time. Roll about half the piece into a thin sausage with palms of both hands on a very lightly floured pastry canvas. Each small roll should be about ½ inch in diameter. Cut it into 2½-inch lengths and curve each short length around your first finger to make a horseshoe. Place them on a lightly buttered baking sheet. A 14×17 inch baking sheet will just take the 80 little horseshoes that the dough will yield. Bake in a 350° F. oven until deep cream colored and dry enough to lift with a pancake turner, about 18 to 22 minutes. Shake a thin layer of vanilla sugar onto a wide platter through a fine sieve. Transfer the horseshoes from the baking sheet onto the sugar with a pancake turner and shake the rest of the vanilla sugar over them while they are warm. Resugar them before serving.

12 tablespoons butter at room temperature
⅔ cup granulated sugar, lightly packed
1 teaspoon vanilla
1⅔ cups twice-sifted flour
1 cup ground blanched almonds, loosely
    packed
1 cup vanilla sugar

VANILLA SUGAR   *Store a fresh vanilla bean in a canister of sifted powdered sugar.*

BISCUIT ROLL or Yule Log

Butter a jelly-roll pan well, line the bottom with brown paper, and butter the paper well. Turn oven to 375° F.

Beat egg yolks with half the sugar until very light and very thick, beat in the vanilla. Whip the egg whites half stiff, then gradually add the remaining sugar and continue to beat until they are stiff and will not move when you invert the bowl. Fold the egg whites quickly into the yolks, while sprinkling in the flour. Pour the batter into the prepared pan and spread it evenly into the corners with a spatula. Bake it for about 12 minutes until it is golden and springs back when lightly pressed with a finger. Invert the biscuit sheet onto a piece of waxed paper and spread it at once with mocha butter cream filling. Cut off the brittle edges with a knife before rolling. Roll up evenly, stripping off the paper as you roll, and secure by rolling the biscuit into waxed paper and twisting the ends to hold it firmly. Refrigerate for at least 2 hours until filling is set. Pipe outside of roll with rows of chocolate butter cream. Chill for a short time and serve whole or sliced. At Christmas time make the roll into a yule log. Cut a 4-inch piece, diagonally, from one end of the roll before it is piped with chocolate butter cream. Attach it to the side of the roll to simulate a branch and make a few swirls in the icing to represent the bark of the yule log. Decorate with holly and chill until served.

4 large eggs, separated
7½ tablespoons sugar
1 teaspoon vanilla
⅔ cup flour, sifted
1 recipe Mocha Butter Cream Filling
1 recipe Chocolate Butter Cream

MOCHA BUTTER CREAM FILLING

Cook the sugar with ½ cup water over low heat, stirring constantly, until it is dissolved. Cover and cook for 5 minutes longer, uncover, increase heat to boil, and place a candy thermometer in the syrup. As soon as it reaches 238°, take the saucepan from heat. Beat the yolks until light and creamy in an electric beater. Without turning off the motor, add the sugar syrup in a thin stream, and the coffee, dissolved in the boiling water. Add vanilla and continue to beat at low speed until the mixture is cold. Fold it into the soft butter. Chill the filling, if necessary, until it reaches a soft, spreadable consistency.

1⅔ cups sugar
4 egg yolks
1½ tablespoons instant coffee
1 tablespoon boiling water
1 teaspoon vanilla
½ pound butter at room temperature

CHOCOLATE BUTTER CREAM

Melt the chocolate over hot water. Cream the butter in an electric beater and gradually add the sugar, alternating with the cream. With motor running at low speed, add the chocolate and vanilla, and beat until creamy and spreadable. If too thick, beat in a little more cream; if too thin, beat in a little more sifted sugar.

2 ounces, or 2 squares, semisweet chocolate
¼ cup butter
3 cups confectioner's sugar, sifted
6 tablespoons heavy cream
1 teaspoon vanilla

PUMPKIN BREAD

Sift the flour twice with the dry ingredients and set it aside. Cream the shortening, add the sugar, and beat until light. Beat in the eggs, one after the other, until the mixture is fluffy. Carefully stir in the dry ingredients. Add the pumpkin, vanilla, water, and nuts and pour the batter into 2 buttered 9×5×3 inch loaf pans. Bake them in a 350° F. oven for 45 minutes, or until a straw tests done. Cool the loaves, wrap, and store them until the next day, when it will be possible to slice the bread thin.

2⅔ cups sifted flour
2 teaspoons baking soda
½ teaspoon baking powder
2 teaspoons salt
1 teaspoon each ground cinnamon and ground cloves
⅔ cup vegetable shortening
2⅔ cups granulated sugar
4 eggs
2 cups crushed and strained pumpkin
1 teaspoon vanilla
⅔ cup water or milk
1⅓ cups chopped walnuts or pecans

ORANCE NUT BREAD

Sift flour with baking powder and salt into a large bowl. Stir in the nuts. Beat the sugar, marmalade, butter, rum, milk, and egg together and add them to the dry ingredients in the bowl. Stir only until dry ingredients are incorporated, and set aside. Butter 1 standard loaf pan or 3 miniature loaf pans and turn oven to 350° F. After about 15 minutes, pour the batter into the prepared pan or pans and bake the large loaf for about 60 minutes, or until a straw tests done; test the miniature loaves after about 35 minutes.

2½ cups flour
1 tablespoon baking powder
¼ teaspoon salt
1 cup roughly chopped walnuts
⅔ cup light brown sugar
⅓ cup thick orange marmalade
¼ cup butter, melted
1 tablespoon rum
14 tablespoons milk
1 large egg

A HOT BEVERAGE BEFORE A COLD MEAL

In the middle of the winter, especially in the country, when guests have come through snow and cold, they are ready for something hot. What we usually give them, instead, is an ice cold cocktail. This has its warming effects, and a cold meal is actually more welcome than a warm and heavy one. But some of the hot beverages are a nice way to start a cold meal. In Scandinavia, where winters are cold and long, guests are often greeted with glögg. In England there are hot grogs, toddies, and mulled wines. In Scandinavia the meal always begins— and very often ends—with cold smorgasbord, smoked fishes, and meat, and no one ever thinks about the fact that it is all cold because they were greeted—before they came in the door—with a punch cup of hot glögg.

GLÖGG

Tie cloves, cardamom, cinnamon, and orange peel in a cheesecloth bag. Put it in a bowl with the raisins and almonds. Add brandy to cover and set aside at room temperature for 24 hours. Transfer the cheesecloth bag to a large kettle, pour over the claret and port. Heat to just below the boiling point for 15 minutes. Discard the cheesecloth and add the raisins and almonds, with what remains of the brandy, to the wine in the kettle. Place a fine wire mesh or grille over the kettle, about 3 inches over the hot wine. Put the sugar on it, pour over the warmed brandy, and flame. The saturated sugar will burn and melt into the glögg. When the flames die down, ladle it into punch cups with raisins and almonds.

24 cloves
24 cardamom seeds
6 cinnamon sticks
Dried orange peel of 2 oranges
1 pound raisins
1 pound scalded almonds
1 bottle brandy
2 bottles claret
2 bottles port wine
1 pound lump sugar

Index

Abjy l'Amid Soup, 58
African Mayonnaise, 126
Allemande Salad, 149
Almond(s): Horseshoes, 247
  Roast Venison with, 213
Ambassadrice Soup, 58
Amuse-Bouche, 187
Anchois, 194
Anchovy(ies): Eggs with, 83
  Hors d'Oeuvre, 194
  Mayonnaise, 125
Andalusian Salad, 149–50
Appetizers, 29–54, 185–97
  Amuse-Bouche, 187
  Anchovies (Anchois), 194
  Apple, Camembert-, 197
  Artichoke(s): Bottoms, Shrimp on, 52
    Hearts, 192
    Frankfort, 53
    Italian, 54
  Asparagus Spears, Glazed, 38–39
  Avocado, Iced, 44–45
  Bean Salad, French, 191
  Beef: with Caviar, Roast, 47
    Salad, French, 191
  Beefsteak Tartare, The Best, 46
  Bird's Nest, 194
  Carrot Sticks with Onion Cream, 37
  Cauliflower with Curried Mayonnaise, Raw, 37
  Caviar: Hearts of Leek with, 51
    Hearts of Palm with, 50
    Roast Beef with, 47
    Rounds, Red, 44
    in Tomato Slices, 46

Celery: Gorgonzola-Stuffed, 38
  with Roquefort Sauce, 37
Cheese: Camembert-Apple, 197
  Garnished Liptauer, 198
  Mountain, 197
Chicken Liver Pâté, 44
Cucumber(s): Cups, Filled, 39–40
  Smoked Salmon in, 53
Eggs, 32–35
  Boulognaise, 34
  Christopher Columbus, 35
  Cleopatra, 34
  Oeufs des Bons Viveurs, 35
  Romanoff "Hard-Cooked," 36
  Stuffed, 32–34
    with Anchovy Flavor, 33
    Basic, 32
    with Curry Flavor, 33
    with Garlic Flavor, 33
    with Mustard Flavor, 33
    with Salmon, 34
    with Sardines, 33
Endive Taylor Terrace, Stuffed, 37
Finnan Haddie, 195
Fish, Fruit with, 42
Fruit, 40–45
Grapefruit: Cocktail, 45
  with Shrimp, 42
Ham: with Fruits, 41
  with Melon, 41
Herring, 42, 51–52
  Bird's Nest with, 194
  French, 52
  Italian, 51–52
  Marinated, 192

in Mustard Cream, 193
  Smoked Salmon in Cucumbers with, 53
  with Sour Cream, 52
Hors d'Oeuvre Tray, 188–89
Leek, Hearts of, 51
Liver Pâté, Chicken, 44
Lobster: Cocktail, 49
  in Mustard Sauce, 49
  Meat, Fruit with, 40, 41
  Salad, 191
Melon: Filled with Mustard Fruits, 43
  Filled with Shrimp and Fruit, 43
  with Ham, 41
  Shrimp with Fruit, 42
  with Smoked Tongue, 43
Mushrooms: Pickled Fresh, 191
  Stuffed: with Chicken Livers, 195
    Italian, 38
    with Roquefort, 195
Palm, Hearts of, with Caviar, 50
  with Smoked Salmon, 50
Salmon: in Cucumbers, Smoked, 53
  Hearts of Palm with Smoked, 50
  Stuffed Eggs with, 34
Sardines, Stuffed Eggs with, 34
Shrimp: on Artichoke Bottoms, 52
  Cocktail, 196
  with Fruit, 42
  Salad, 192
Tomatoes, Filled Cherry, 36
Tongue, Melon with Smoked, 43
Trout in Aspic, 48
Tuna Fish Salad, 193
Vegetable, 36–40

Apple(s): Baked, 232–33
   Camembert and, Appetizer, 197
   Chutney, 135
   Ham Garnish, 219
   Herring with (First Course), 42
   Horseradish Sauce, 206, 213
   Jelly, Minted, 133
   Meat with (Appetizers, First Courses), 41
   Relish, Lime and, 134
   Salad: Dutch, 155
      Merry Widow I, 150
   Soup, 58
   Turkey Breast, Braised, with, 208
Apricot: Bavarian Cream, 236
   Brandy Sauce, 237
Arabella's Green Pea Soup, 61
Arabian Chicken Salad, 113
Artichoke Bottoms: Ham Garnish, 219
   Shrimp on, 52
Artichoke Hearts, Hors d'Oeuvre, 192
Artichokes: Frankfort, 53
   Italian, 54
   Vinaigrette, 142
Asparagus: Glazed Spears, 38–39
   Ham Mousse with, 107
   and Ham Salad, 154
   with Ham Sauce, 161
   Poached Eggs Vinaigrette with, 86
   Steamed, Cold, 161
   Vinaigrette, 141–42
Aspic, 98
   Eggs in, 86–90
   Mayonnaise, Lemon (Mayonnaise Collée), 140
   for Salmon, 103–4
   Tongue, Sliced, in, 224
   Trout in, 48
Aurora Soup, 58–59
Avocado: Iced, 44–45
   Salad, 132
   Soup, 57, 59

Bacon: Dressing, 130
   and Rice Salad, Italian Artichokes with, 54
Bananas, Baked, 233
   Ham Appetizers with, 41
Barszcz, Ukrainian, 69
Bavarian Cream, Apricot, 236

Bean(s): as Ham Garnish, 215
   Salad, French Hors d'Oeuvre, 191
   Soup, Black, 59, 75
   Vinaigrette, Green, 142–43
Béarnaise Sauce, Cold, 135
Beef, 202–6
   Boiled, Cold, 116
   Bouquetière, Tenderloin or Filet, 204
   Braised, Tenderloin or Filet, 202–3
   Coquelin, Tenderloin, 203
   Pear with (First Course), 41
   Roast, Cold, 204
      with Caviar, 47
      with Grapefruit Sections, 205
      Tenderloin of, 202
   Salad, French Hors d'Oeuvre, 191
   Soup, Okroschka, 74
      Ukrainian Barszcz, 69
   Spencer Steaks, Cold, 205–6
   Tongue. See Tongue
   Vinaigrette, 117
Beefsteak Tartare, 115–16
   The Best, 46
   Beet Soup, Polish Cherry and, 72
   See also Barszcz; Borsch; Kolodnik
Belgian Stewed Prunes, 230
Bird's Nest, 194
Biscuit: Roll, 248–49
   Tortoni, 237
Black: Bean Soup, 59, 75
   Cherries. See Cherries
Bombay Eggs. See under Eggs
Bon Valet Soup, 58
Borsch, Clear, 57
Botwinja Soup, 58
Bouillon: Celery, 74
   Court, 103, 104
Box Lunch Menus, 16
Brandy Sauce, Apricot, 237
Bread: Orange Nut, 249
   Pumpkin, 249
Broccoli: Curried Eggs Baroda, 93–94
   Soup, 58
Brown Sauce, 222
Brunch Menus, 14–15
Buffet Menus, 17, 18
Butter, Filbert Orange, 136

Butter Cream: Chocolate, 249
   Mocha Filling, 248

Cabbage Salad. See Coleslaw
Caesar Salad, 150
Cantaloupe. See Melon
Carrot Sticks with Onion Cream, 37
Casanova Salad, 151
Catsup, Mustard, and Horseradish Sauce, Hot, 138
Cauliflower: Curried Eggs Baroda, 93–94
   Mayonnaise, Raw, 37
   for Ham Garnish, 215, 219
   Salad, German, 152
   Soup, Chilled Cream of, 62
   Vinaigrette, 142, 143
Caviar: Hearts of Leek with, 51
   Hearts of Palm with, 50
   Roast Beef with, 47
   Rounds, Red, 44
   in Tomato Slices, 46
Cebolla Española, 75
Celery: Bouillon, 74
   Gorgonzola-Stuffed, with Grapes and To-kay Wine, 38
   with Roquefort Sauce, 37
   Soup, Cream of, 63
Ceviche, 58, 66–67
   Ecuadorian Shrimp, 67
   Lobster, 66
Champagne Fruit, 173
Chantilly Soup, 58
Chatelaine Soup, 59
Chaud-Froid: Brown, 111
   with Egg Yolks, 112
   White, 108–9
Cheese: Apple Appetizers, Camembert, 197
   Bases, 242
   Carrot Sticks with Onion Cream, 37
   Celery: with Roquefort Sauce, 37
      Stuffed with Gorgonzola, 38
   Crust, Golden, 115
   Doubles, 243
   Dressing, Roquefort, 132
   Endive Taylor Terrace Stuffed with Roquefort, 37
   Liptauer, Garnished, 198
   Mountain, 197

Mushrooms Stuffed with Roquefort, 195
Pastry, 115, 242–43
Rounds and Squares, 242
Sauce, Roquefort, Celery with, 37
Sticks, 243
Tomatoes, Cherry, Filled with, 36
Cherbah, Turkish, 76
Cherry(ies): and Cream, 173
Sauce, Black, 238
Spiced Sour, 220
Soup, 73
Polish Beet and, 72
with Sour Cream, 172
Spiced, 172
Chestnut Tourinoise, 241
Chicken, 107–15
Chaud-Froid: Brown, 111
White, 108–9
with Rice Salad, 111
Consommé, Chilled Oyster and, 69
Fricassee, Cold, 112
Liver(s): Mushrooms Stuffed with, 195
Pâté, 44
Purée, Eggs in Ramekins with, 88
Mousse, 107
Pie, Cold, 114
Salad: Arabian, 113
Bagration, 113
Green, 115
Opera, 114
Rice and, 146
Soup: Consommé, Oyster and, 69
Cream of, Agnès Sorel, 65–66
Dolgoruki with, 70
Maryland, 70
Mulligatawny, 60
Mulligatawny, Clear, 50
Okroschka, 74
Sénégalaise, 71
See also Soups: Canned, Enhanced
Chiffonade Salads, 146–47
Chipolata, Chocolate, 238
Chive Mayonnaise, Water Cress and, 123
Chocolate: Butter Cream, 249
Chipolata, 238
Mousse, 239

Sauce, with Peaches on Ice Cream, 171
Swiss, 240
Tourinoise, 247
Chutney, Apple, 135
Cinnamon Toast Fingers, 73
Clermont Soup, 58
Cocktail Party Menus, 13
Coffee: Biscuit, Macaroon, 240
Mousse, 240
Parfait (au Moca), 236
Coleslaw: Danish, 150
German, 154
Compote, Winter, 231
Consommé, Chilled Oyster and Chicken, 69
Cookies: Almond Horseshoes, 247
Spritz Tongues, 247
Court Bouillon, 103
to Clarify, 104
Crab Meat: Cucumber Cups Filled with, 40
Eggs Boulognaise with, 34
with, Frankonian, 82
Purée Mongole with, 72
Ring, 99
Cranberry: Relish, 134
Sauce, Spiced, 220
Cream, Cherries and, 173
Horseradish, 225
Maraschino, with Stewed Peaches, 173
Mustard: Herrings in, 193
Sauce, Whipped, 221
Thick, 174
See also Sour Cream
Cream Cheese. See Cheese
Cream Mayonnaise, 125
Herb, 47
Cream Sauce. See Sauces; specific flavors
Crécy Soup, 58
Cressonière Soup, 58
Croutons, Garlic, 151
Cucumber: Cups, Filled, 39–40
Salad, 155
Smoked Salmon in, 53
Soup, Cream of, 64
Cumberland: Fruit, 136
Salad, 151
Sauce, 136, 213
Currant Sauce: Peaches on Ice Cream with,
171

Red, 205
Spiced, 220, 221
Curried: Eggs Baroda, 93–94
Fruit Soup, Cold, 73
Mayonnaise, Raw Cauliflower with, 37
Curry: Cold Shrimp, 100
Mayonnaise, 122
Custard Sauce, 170

Danish Coleslaw, 150
Desserts, 163–74
Almond Horseshoes, 247
Apples, Baked, 232–33
Apricot Bavarian Cream, 236
Bananas, Baked, 233
Bavarian Cream, Apricot, 236
Biscuit: Roll, 248–49
Tortoni, 237
Champagne Fruit, 173
Cherries: and Cream, 173
with Sour Cream, 172
Spiced, 172
Chestnut, Tourinoise, 241
Chocolate: Chipolata, 238
Mousse, 239
Coffee Biscuit, Macaroon, 240
Mousse, 240
Parfait au Moca, 236
Cold Weather, 227–50
Compote, Winter, 231
Frozen, 234–35ff.
Fruit: Compote, Winter, 231
Tarts, 246
Jam Turnovers, 244
Kirsch Mousse, 237
Linzer: Strip, 246
Tarts, 245
Macaroon Coffee Biscuit, 240
Maraschino Cream with Stewed Peaches,
173
Orange(s): Nut Bread, 249
Parfait, Rum, 168
Sabayon, 168
in Syrup, 232
Parfait: Rum Orange, 168
au Moca, 236

Peaches: Champagne Fruit, 173
    Filled with Chestnut Purée and Raspberry Sauce, 169
    Fruit Tarts, 246
    on Ice Cream, 171
    Maraschino Cream with Stewed, 173
    Poached, in Custard Sauce, 170
Pears on Ice Cream or Sherbet, 171–72
Plums, Fruit Tarts with, 246
Prince Püchler's Pudding, 238
Prunes: Stewed, Belgian, 230
    Stewed, in Rum, 231
Pumpkin Bread, 249
Raspberries: Ripe, 167
    under Sabayon Sauce, 167
Rice Pudding, 241
Rum: Cream, 169
    Mousse, 239
    Mousse with Strawberries or Raspberries, 166
    Orange Parfait, 168
Sabayon: à la Créole, 168
    Orange, 168
    Raspberries under, 167
    Sauce, 167
Soufflé, Frozen, 174
Spritz Tongues, 247
Strawberries: Champagne Fruit, 173
    and Cream (Substitute), 173
    Fruit Tarts, 246
    Mélange, 166
    Thick Cream, 174
    Tourinoise, 241
    Yule Log, 248–49
Dilled New Potato Salad, 144
Dill Mayonnaise, 162
    Lemon, 124
Dinner Menus, 7–10, 15–16, 19–27. See also
    Menus: Cold Weather
Dolgoruki, 70
Duck, Okroschka with, 74
Dutch Apple Salad, 155

Ecuadorian Shrimp Ceviche, 67
Eel, Egg Sandwich Copenhagen with, 92
Eggs, 77–94
    with Anchovy(ies): Flavor, Stuffed, 33
        Stuffed, 83

Appetizers, 32–35
Arizona, 80
in Aspic, 87–90
Baroda, Curried, 93–94
Bernadot, 80
Bombay, 80, 83
Boulognaise, 34
Budapest, 80
Byron, 78
Cebolla Española with, 75
Christopher Columbus, 35
Cleopatra, 34
Curried, Baroda, 93–94
with Curry Flavor, Stuffed, 33
Dubois, 91
Frankonian, 82
French, 80
with Garlic Flavor, Stuffed, 33
Genoa, 78
Hamburg, 80
Hard-Cooked, 79, 80. See also Eggs: Stuffed; specific recipes
Imperial Salad, 85
Julienne, 81
Lexington, 86
Limousine, 83–84
Lucullus, 78
Marie, Molded in Aspic, 90
Mollets, Six-Minute, 80. See also specific recipes
Monaco, 78
Montpellier, 82
with Mustard Flavor, Stuffed, 32
Niçoise, 80
Normandy, 85
Norwegian, 80
Oeufs des Bons Viveurs, 35
Paysanne, 85
Poached, 80, 84–87. See also specific recipes
in Ramekins, Tyrol, 88–89
Red Caviar Rounds with, 44
Rhode Island, 80
Romanoff, 80
    "Hard-Cooked," 36
Russian, in Tomatoes, 93
with Salmon, Stuffed, 34

Sandwiches, Open, 92
    Bergen, 92
    Bornholm, 92
    Copenhagen, 92
    Margot, 92
with Sardines, Stuffed, 33
Scrambled, 91–92
    Bergen Sandwich, 92
    Copenhagen Sandwich, 92
    Dubois, 91
    Sultan, 91
Seville, 78
Stuffed, 81–84
    Appetizers, 32–34
Sultan, 91
Tarragon, 89
with Tongue, Poached, 86
Totally Stuffed: French, 82
    Indian, 81
Tourangelle, 86
Valencia, 84
Vinaigrette, 86, 142
Zurich, 84
Endive: Salad, Grapefruit and, 156
    Taylor Terrace, Stuffed, 37
Escoffier Mayonnaise, 124

Figs, Ham with, 41
Filbert: Half-Moons, 246
    Mayonnaise, 51
    Orange Butter, 136
Finnan Haddie, 195
First Courses. See Appetizers
Fish: Buffet Menu, 18
    Ceviche, 58, 67
    Fruit with, 42
    See also specific kinds
Frankfort Artichokes, 53
Frankfurters, Russian Salad with, 159
Frankonian Eggs, 82
French Dressing, 126–30
    Herb, 128
    Lemon, 128
    Mustard, 128
    Paprika, 129
    Potato Salad with, 144
    Provincial, 129

Sour Cream, 129
Tarragon, 130
French: Eggs, 80
 Herrings, 52
 Hors d'Oeuvre: Bean Salad, 191
  Meat Salad, 191
  Wine Dressing, 50
Fruit: Appetizers, 40–45
 Champagne, 173
 Compote, Winter, 231
 Cumberland, 136
 Salad, 224
 Salad Dressing, 130
 Soup, Cold Curried, 73
 Tarts, 246
 See also specific kinds

Galantine of Turkey, 210–11
Garlic Croutons, 151
Gazpacho Andaluz, 67–68
German: Salad, 149
 Cauliflower, 152
 Coleslaw, 154
Glögg, 250
Gloucester Sauce, 140
Grapefruit: and Beef, Roast, 205
 Cocktail, 45
 Dressing, 156
 and Endive Salad, 156
 Shrimp with, 42
Grapes: Melon with Fruit and Shrimp, 43
 with Pâté, Appetizer, 41
 Roast of Venison with, 212–13
Green: Beans Vinaigrette, 142–43
 Chicken Salad, 115
 Mayonnaise, 123
 Peas. *See* Pea Soup
 Peppers, as Ham Garnish, 215

Ham, 214–21
 Algerian, 215
 Argenteuil, 215
 with Bean Garnish, 215
 Boned, 214
 Butt or Shank End, 215
 Canned, 215, 219
 with Cauliflower Garnish, 215, 219
 Cook-Before-Eating, 214

Cooking and Basting Liquids, 215
Country (Old-fashioned), 214, 216–17
Crescents, 244
Eggs with, Limousine, 83–84
 Molded in Aspic, Marie, 90
 in Ramekins (Variation), 88
 Zurich, 84
with Fruits, 41
Full Half, 215, 217
Fully Cooked or Ready Cooked, 214, 218
Garnishes, 215, 219
Glazes, 215
with Green Pepper Garnish, 215
Helvetian, 215
with Melon, 41
Mousse, 106
 with Asparagus, 107
with Onion Garnish, 215
with Orange Garnish, 215, 219
Roast Half, 217
Salads with: Asparagus, 154
 Russian, 159
 Substitute, 160
 Vegetable and, Frankfort Artichokes
  with, 53
Sauce, Asparagus with, 161
Sauces for, 220–22
Soup with, Okroschka, 74
Thai, 216
Three Menus Using, 16
Vert-Pré, 215
Victor Hugo, 215
Hazelnuts. *See* Filbert
Herb: French Dressing, 128
 Mayonnaise (Herbed Mayonnaise), 123
  Cream, 47
 Sauce, 137
Herring, 51–52
 Allemande or German Salad with, 149
 with Apples (First Course), 42
 Bird's Nest with, 194
 Egg Sandwich Bornholm with, 92
 French, 52
 Italian, 51–52
 Marinated, Hors d'Oeuvre, 192
 in Mustard Cream, 193
 Smoked Salmon in Cucumbers with, 53
 in Sour Cream, 52

Hollandaise Salad, 156
Hors d'Oeuvre Tray, 188–89
Horseradish: Cream, 225
 Mayonnaise, 224
 Sauce, 137
  Apple, 206, 213
  for Appreciators, 138
  Catsup, Mustard, and, 138
Hortense Soup, 58

Ice Cream, 232ff.
 Peaches on, 171
 Pears on, 171–72
 See also Desserts
Imperial Salad, 85
Italian: Artichokes, 54
 Dressing, 131
 Herrings, 51–52
 Salad, 152
 Stuffed Mushrooms, 38

Jam Turnovers, 244
Jelly, Minted Apple, 133
 See also Aspic

Kirsch Mousse, 237
Kolodnik, 57, 59

Lamb: Okroschka with, 74
 Saddle of, Suédoise, 206–7
Leek: Hearts of, 51
 Soup. *See* Vichyssoise
 Vinaigrette, 142
Lemon: Cream Dressing, 131
 French Dressing, 128
 Mayonnaise, 124
  Collée, 140
  Dill, 124
Lillienne Soup, 59
Lime: and Apple Relish, 134
 Marmalade Sauce, 217
Linzer: Strip, 246
 Tarts, 245
Liver(s): Mushrooms Stuffed with Chicken,
  195
 Pâté, Chicken, 44
 Purée, Eggs in Ramekins with (Variation),
  88

Lobster: Bisque, 59
    Ceviche, 66
    Cocktail, 49
    Flamenco, 101
    in Mustard Sauce, 49, 101
    Oeufs des Bons Viveurs with, 35
    Salads with,
        Lorette, 152
        Monte Cristo, 157
        Russian, 159
    Victoria, 100
Lorette Salad, 152
Luncheon Menus, 10–14, 16–17
    See also Menus
Lunch Menus, Box, 16

Macaroon Coffee Biscuit, 240
Mackerel, Eggs in Ramekins, Tyrol, with, 88
Madeira: Sauce, Jellied, 222
    Soup, 58
Madrilène Soup, 59
Maraschino Cream with Stewed Peaches,
    173
Marinade, White Wine, 48
Maryland Chicken Soup, 70
Mayonnaise, 122–26
    African, 126
    Anchovy, 125
    Chive, Water Cress and, 123
    Cream, 125
    Cream Herb, 47
    Curried, Raw Cauliflower and, 37
    Curry, 122
    Dill, 162
        Lemon, 124
    Escoffier, 124
    Filbert, 51
    Green, 123
    Herb, Cream, 47
    Herbed, 123
    Horseradish, 224
    Lemon, 124
        Collée, 140
    Montpellier, 35
    Mustard, 126
    Pink, 35
    Sauce, 206
    Swedish, 126

Tarragon, 122
    in Blender, 125
    Water Cress and Chive, 123
Meat: in Aspic Vinaigrette, 142
    with Fruit Appetizers, 40, 41
    Okroschka with, 74
    Salad, Hors d'Oeuvre, 191
    See also specific kinds
Melon: with Ham, 41
    with Mustard Fruits, 43
    Shrimp with, 42
    with Shrimp and Fruit, 43
    with Smoked Tongue, 43
    Sturgeon with Cantaloupe (First Course),
        42
Menus, 3–27, 177–84
Merry Widow Salad, 153
    Apple, 150
Minted Apple Jelly, 133
Mocha Butter Cream Filling, 248
Monte Cristo Salad, 157
Montpellier Mayonnaise, 35
Mousse: Chicken, 107
    Chocolate, 239
    Coffee, 240
    Ham, 106
        with Asparagus, 107
    Kirsch, 237
    Rum, 239
        with Strawberries or Raspberries, 166
    Salmon, Parisienne, 106
Mulligatawny, 50, 60
Murillo Soup, 59
Mushrooms: Chicken Liver-Stuffed, 195
    Ham Garnish, 219
    Italian Stuffed, 38
    Pickled Fresh, 191
    Roquefort-Stuffed, 195
Mustard: Cream, Herrings in, 193
    Cream Sauce, 141
    French Dressing, 128
    Mayonnaise, 126
    Sauce: Catsup, Horseradish, and, 138
        Cream, 141
        Lobster in, 49, 101
        Whipped Cream, 221

Norwegian: Eggs, 80
    Sauce, 221

Oeufs des Bons Viveurs, 35
Okroschka, 74
Onion(s): Cream, Carrot Sticks with, 37
    Glazed, with Ham, 215
    Sauce, White Wine, 47
    Soup: Cebolla Española, 75
        Iced Cream of, Soubise, 63
    Stuffed, Cold, 217
Opera Salade, 114
Orange(s): Butter, Filbert, 136
    Ham Garnish, 215, 219
    with Meat as First Course, 41
    Nut Bread, 249
    Parfait, Rum, 168
    Pheasant with, 211
    Sabayon, Cold, 168
    in Syrup, Whole, 232
Orégano Dressing, 131
Oyster and Chicken Consommé, Chilled, 69

Palm, Hearts of: with Caviar, 50
    with Smoked Salmon, 50
Paprika French Dressing, 129
Parfait: au Moca, 236
    Rum Orange, 168
Pastry, 240–48
    Cheese, 115, 242–43
    Short Paste, 245
    Turnover, 244–45
Pâté: Chicken Liver, 44
    Fruit Appetizers with, 41
Peaches: Champagne Fruit, 173
    Cumberland Fruit, 136
    Filled with Chestnut Purée and Raspberry
        Sauce, 169
    Fruit Tarts with, 246
    Ham with, 41
    on Ice Cream, 171
        Cardinal, 171
        Chocolate, 171
        Condé, 171
        Currant, 171
        Greek, 171
        Nina, 171

Maraschino Cream with Stewed, 173
Poached, in Custard Sauce, 170
Pears: with Beef (First Course), 41
on Ice Cream or Sherbet, 171–72
Felicity, 171
Helena, 171–72
Maximilian, 172
Sabayon, 172
Pea Soup: Cream of Green, 61
Arabella's, 61
Gaspé, 62
Italian, 61
Potage Navarin, 62
with Shrimp, 61–62
Pecan Half-Moons, 246
Peppers, Green, as Ham Garnish, 215
Pheasant with Oranges, 211
Picnic Menus, 15
Pie: Chicken, Cold, 114
Crust, Cheese, 115
Pineapple, Ham Appetizer with, 41
Pink Mayonnaise, 35
Plums, Fruit Tarts with, 246
Polish Cherry and Beet Soup, 72
Pork with Apple (First Course), 41
Portuguese Potatoes, 216
Potage Navarin, 62
Potato: Salad, 153
Allemande or German, 149
Dilled New, 144
with French Dressing, 144
Ham Garnish, 219
Hollandaise, 156
Monte Cristo, 157
Portuguese (Portuguese Potatoes), 216
Stefan (White Wine Potato Salad), 145
Soup. See Vichyssoise
Prince Püchler's Pudding, 238
Provincial: French Dressing, 129
Salad, 158
Prunes, Stewed: Belgian, 230
in Rum, 231
Pudding: Prince Püchler's, 238
Rice, 241
Pumpkin Bread, 249
Purée Mongole, 72

Raisin Sauce, 221

Rakova, 76
Raspberry(ies): Ripe, 167
Rum Mousse with, 166
under Sabayon Sauce, 167
Sauce, 169
Red: Caviar Rounds, 44
Currant Sauce, 205
Wine Vinegar Dressing, 132
Relish: Cranberry, 134
Lime and Apple, 134
Rice: Pudding, 241
Salad, 145
Andalusian, 149
Bacon and, Italian Artichokes with, 54
Chicken and, 146
Rose Hip Sauce, 213
Rum: Cream, 169
Mousse, 239
with Strawberries or Raspberries, 166
Orange Parfait, 168
Russian: Egg in Tomatoes, 93
Salad, 159

Sabayon: Cold Orange, 168
à la Créole, 168
Sauce, 167
St. Regis Dressing, 132
Salad Dressings, 122–33
African Mayonnaise, 126
Anchovy Mayonnaise, 125
Bacon, 130
Chiffonade, 147
Chive Mayonnaise, Water Cress and, 123
Curry Mayonnaise, 122
Dill Mayonnaise, 162
Lemon, 124
Escoffier Mayonnaise, 124
French, 126–30
Potato Salad with, 144
Wine, 50
Fruit Salad, 130
Grapefruit, 156
Green Mayonnaise, 123
Herbed Mayonnaise, 123
Herb French, 128
Italian, 131
Lemon Cream, 131
Lemon French, 128

Lemon Mayonnaise, 124
Mayonnaise, 122–26. See also specific flavors
Mustard: French, 128
Mayonnaise, 126
Oregano, 131
Paprika French, 129
Provincial French, 129
Red Wine Vinegar, 132
Roquefort, 132
St. Regis, 132
Sour Cream French, 129
Swedish Mayonnaise, 126
Tarragon: French, 130
Mayonnaise, 122
Blender, 125
Vinegar, 126
Vegetable Salads, 133
Vinaigrette Sauce, 141
Water Cress and Chive Mayonnaise, 123
Wine: French, 50
Vinegar, 132
Zucchini Salads, 133
See also Salads
Salads, 141–62
Allemande, 149
Andalusian, 149–50
Apple: Dutch, 155
Merry Widow, 150
Artichoke Vinaigrette, 142
Avocado, 133
Asparagus: Cold Steamed, 161
and Ham, 154
with Ham Sauce, 161
Vinaigrette, 141–42
Bean(s): French Hors d'Oeuvre, 191
Vinaigrette, Green, 142–43
Beaucaire, 155
Beef, French Hors d'Oeuvre, 191
Cabbage. See Salads: Coleslaw
Caesar, 150
Casanova, 151
Cauliflower: German, 152
Vinaigrette, 142, 143
Chicken: Arabian, 113
Bagration, 113
Green, 115

Opera, 114
  Rice and, 146
Chiffonade, 146–47
Coleslaw: Danish, 150
  German, 154
Cucumber, 155
Cumberland, 151
Eggs Vinaigrette, 142
Endive, Grapefruit and, 156
Fruit, 224
German, 149
  Cauliflower, 152
  Coleslaw, 154
Grapefruit and Endive, 156
Green Beans Vinaigrette, 142–43
Ham: Asparagus and, 154
  Substitute, 160
Herring, Allemande, 149
Hollandaise, 156
Imperial, 85
Italian, 152
Leek Vinaigrette, 142
Lobster in: Lorette, 152
  Monte Cristo, 157
  Russian, 159
Lorette, 152
Meat in Aspic Vinaigrette, 142
Merry Widow, 153
  Apple, 150
Mixed and Combined, 148–62
Monte Cristo, 157
Niçoise, 157–58
Potato, 153
  Allemande or German, 149
  Dilled New, 144
  with French Dressing, 144
  Ham Garnish, 219
  Hollandaise, 156
  Monte Cristo, 157
  Portuguese (Portuguese Potatoes), 216
  Stefan (White Wine Potato Salad), 145
Provincial, 158
Rice, 145
  Andalusian, 149
  Chicken and, 146
Russian, 159
Shrimp: in Dill Mayonnaise, 161
  Hors d'Oeuvre, 192

Spanish, 159
Stroganoff, 160
Sunday, 110
Tongue, 160
Tourangelle, 161
Tuna: Hors d'Oeuvre, 193
  Niçoise, 157, 158
Vegetable, 133
Vinaigrette, 141–43
Water Cress, 153
Zucchini, 133
See also Appetizers; Salad Dressings
Salmon, 101–5
in Cucumber Cups, 39
in Cucumbers, 53
Egg(s): in Ramekins with (Variation), 88
  Sandwich Bergen with, 92
  Stuffed with, 34
Green Pea Soup Gaspé, Cream of, with, 62
Mousse Parisienne, 106
Palm Hearts with Smoked, 50
to Poach Whole, 102–3
Ring, 99
  with Green Pea Salad, Cold, 104–5
Steaks, 105
Sandwiches, Open Egg, 92
Sardines: Cold Poached Eggs Normandy
  with, 85
  Stuffed Eggs with, 33
Sauces, 135–41
Alexandra, 134
Apple Horseradish, 206, 213
Apricot Brandy, 237
Béarnaise, Cold, 135
Brown, 222
Catsup, Mustard, and Horseradish, 138
Chaud-Froid: Brown, 111
  with Egg Yolks, 112
  White, 108–9
Cherry: Black, 238
  Spiced Sour, 220
Chocolate: Peaches on Ice Cream with,
  171
  Swiss, 240
Cranberry, Spiced, 220
Cumberland, 136, 213
Currant: Peaches on Ice Cream with,
  171

Red, 205
Spiced, 220, 221
Custard, 170
Game, 213
Gloucester, 140
Gribiche, 137
for Ham, 220–22
Ham, Asparagus with, 161
Horseradish, 137
  Apple, 206, 213
  for Appreciators, 138
  Catsup, Mustard, and, 138
Lemon Mayonnaise Collée, 140
Lime Marmalade, 217
Madeira, Jellied, 222
Mayonnaise, 206. See also Mayonnaise
Mustard: Catsup, Horseradish, and, 138
  Cream, 141
  Lobster in, 49, 101
  Whipped Cream, 221
Norwegian, 221
Onion, White Wine, 47
Raisin, 221
Raspberry, 169
Ravigote, 138–39
Rémoulade, 139
Roquefort, Celery with, 37
Rose Hip, 213
Sabayon, 167
Tartar, 39
Tomato, 87
Trianon, 140
Tyrolean, 40
Vinaigrette, 141
White Wine Onion, 47
Scallop(s): Eggs Cleopatra with, 34
Soup, Cream of, 65
Substitute for Shrimp Ceviche, 67
Sénégalaise: with Chicken, 71
with Shrimp, 71
Shrimp: on Artichoke Bottoms, 52
Ceviche, 58, 67
Cocktail, 196
Curry, Cold, 100
in Dill Mayonnaise, 162
Eggs: Boulognaise with, 34
  in Ramekins with (Variation), 88

with Fruit, 42
  Melon with, 43
with Lobster in Mustard Sauce, 49
Salad, Hors d'Oeuvre, 192
Soups with,
  Cream of Green Pea, 61
  Kolodnik, 59
  Potage Navarin, 62
  Rakova, 76
  Sénégalaise, 171
Spring, 99
Soufflé, Frozen, 174
Soups, 55–76
  Abjy l'Amid, 58
  Ambassadrice, 58
  Apple, 58
  Aurora, 58–59
  Avocado, 57, 59
  Barszcz, Ukrainian, 69
  Bean, Black, 59, 75
  Beef: Barszcz, 69
    Okroschka, 74
  Beet. See also Barszcz; Borsch; Kolodnik;
    Polish Cherry and, 72
  Bon Valet, 58
  Borsch, Clear, 57
  Botwinja, 58
  Broccoli, 58
  Canned, Enhanced, 58–59
  Cauliflower, Chilled Cream of, 62
  Cebolla Española, 75
  Celery: Bouillon, 74
    Cream of, 63
  Ceviche, 58
    Ecuadorian Shrimp, 67
    Lobster, 66
  Chantilly, 58
  Chatelaine, 59
  Cherbah, Turkish, 76
  Cherry, 73
    Polish Beet and, 72
  Chicken: Consommé, Oyster and, 69
    Cream of, Agnès Sorel, 65–66
    Dolgoruki with, 70
    Maryland, 70
    Mulligatawny, 60
      Clear, 50
    Okroschka, 74

Sénégalaise, 71
  See also Soups: Canned, Enhanced
Clear, 56–57
Clermont, 58
Cream, 58, 61–66
Crécy, 58
Cressonière, 58
Cucumber, Cream of, 64
Curried Fruit, 73
Dolgoruki, 70
Duck, Okroschka, 74
Fish, Ceviche, 58, 67
Fruit, Cold Curried, 73
Gazpacho, 67–68
Ham, Okroschka, 74
Hortense, 58
Kolodnik, 57, 59
Lamb, Okroschka, 74
Lilienne, 59
Lobster: Bisque, 59
  Ceviche, 66
Madeira, 58
Madrilène, 59
Meat, Okroschka, 74
Murillo, 59
Okroschka, 74
Onion: Cebolla Española, 75
  Iced Cream of, Soubise, 63
Oyster and Chicken Consommé, 69
Pea: Cream of, 61–62
  Arabella's, 61
  Gaspé, 62
  Italian, 61
  Potage Navarin, 62
  with Shrimp, 61–62
Purée Mongole, 72
Rakova, 76
Scallop: Ceviche (Substitute), 67
  Cream of, 65
Sénégalaise: with Chicken, 71
  with Shrimp, 71
Shrimp: Ceviche, 58
  Ecuadorian, 67
  Kolodnik, 59
  Rakova, 76
  Sénégalaise, 71
Spinach, Cream of, 64
Tomato, Cream of, 59

Uncooked, 58. See also specific kinds
Vichyssoise, 59, 66
Water Cress, Cream of, 63–64
Sour Cream: Black Cherries with, 172
  French Dressing, 129
  Herrings in, 52
Spanish Salad, 159
Spinach Soup, Cream of, 64
Spring Shrimp, 99
Spritz Tongues, 247
Strawberries: Champagne Fruit, 173
  and Cream (Substitute), 173
  Cumberland Fruit, 136
  Fruit Tarts, 246
  Mélange, 166
  Rum Mousse, with, 166
Stroganoff Salad, 160
Sturgeon: with Cantaloupe (First Course),
    42
  Kolodnik with, 59
Sunday Salad, 110
Supper Menus, 10–11, 17, 18. See also
    Menus
Swedish Mayonnaise, 126
Swiss Chocolate Sauce, 240

Tarragon: Eggs, 88
  French Dressing, 130
  Mayonnaise, 122
    in Blender, 125
  Vinegar, 126
Tartar Sauce, 39
Tarts: Fruit, 246
  Linzer, 245
Tea Menus, 13
Thai Ham, 216
Tomato(es): Caviar in Slices, 46
  Filled Cherry, 36
  Garnish: for Ham, 219
    for Lamb, 206
    for Lobster Victoria, 100
  Pink Mayonnaise with, 35
  Russian Egg in, 93
  Sauce, 87
  Soup, Cream of, 59
Tongue, 222–24
  Cold Poached Eggs with, 86

Melon with Smoked, 43
Palermo, 223
Salad with, 160
  Opera, 114
  Russian, 159
Tourinoise, 241
Trianon Sauce, 140
Trout: in Aspic, 48
  Eggs in Ramekins, Tyrol, with, 88
  Salad: Hors d'Oeuvre, 193
    Niçoise, 157, 158
  Vitello Tonnato, 208
Turkey, 208–10
  Breast with Apples, Braised, 208
  Galantine of, 210–11
  Pâté, Eggs in Ramekins with (Variation), 89
  Stuffed Boned Half, 208
Turkish Cherbah, 76

Tyrolean Sauce, 40

Ukrainian Barszcz, 69

Vanilla Sugar, 247
Veal: Loin of, Richmond, 208
  Vitello Tonnato, 208
Vegetable: Appetizers, 36–40
  Salads. See also Salads
    Dressing for, 133
Venison, Cold Roast of, 212–13
  Apple Horseradish Sauce for, 213
  Cumberland Sauce for, 213
  with Green Grapes, 212–13
  Rose Hip Sauce for, 213
  with Walnuts or Blanched Almonds, 213
Vichyssoise, 59, 66
Vinaigrette: Salads, 141–43
  Sauce, 141

Vinegar, Tarragon, 126
Vitello Tonnato, 208

Walnut(s): Bread, Orange, 249
  Roast Venison with, 213
Water Cress: and Chive Mayonnaise, 123
  Salad, 153
  Soup, Cream of, 63–64
Wine: Dressing, French, 50
  Marinade, White, 48
  Onion Sauce, White, 47
  Potato Salad, White, 145
  Vinegar Dressing, 132
  See also specific kinds

Yule Log, 248–49

Zucchini, Salad Dressing for, 133
Zurich Eggs, 84

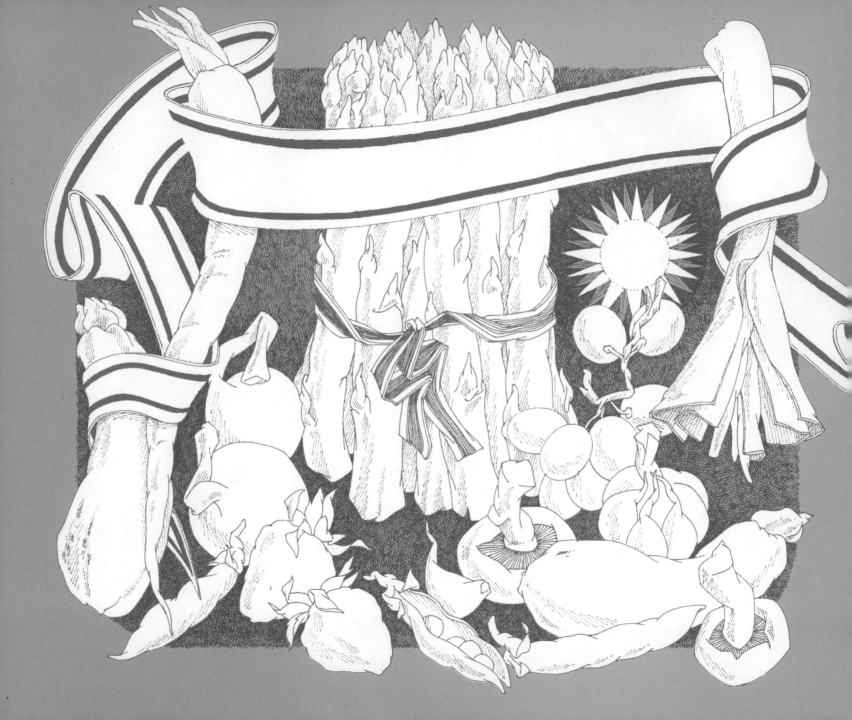